The Corporation

Arguably, the most important economic development of the twentieth century was the evolution of the large corporations, with some growing to become more powerful than entire nations.

This book is a comprehensive study into these firms. Looking at the life of a firm and its growth into a corporation, Dennis C. Mueller turns his expert eye to such themes as:

- the goals of managers
- corporate governance structures
- investment in capital
- mergers and acquisitions.

Accessibly written and giving equal weight to theoretical and empirical developments in the field, *The Corporation* will be an excellent guide for students and academics involved in the theory of the firm, corporate governance and also for the interested business reader.

Dennis C. Mueller is Professor of Economics at the University of Vienna, Austria.

Routledge studies in business organizations and networks

The Corporation
Investment, mergers, and growth

Dennis C. Mueller

LONDON AND NEW YORK

First published 2003
by Routledge
2 Park Square, Milton Park, Abingdon, Oxon, OX14 4RN

Simultaneously published in the USA and Canada
by Routledge
270 Madison Ave, New York NY 10016

Routledge is an imprint of the Taylor & Francis Group

Transferred to Digital Printing 2006

© 2003 Dennis C. Mueller

Typeset in Times New Roman by
Newgen Imaging Systems (P) Ltd, Chennai, India

British Library Cataloguing in Publication Data
A catalogue record for this book is available from the British Library

Library of Congress Cataloging in Publication Data
Mueller, Dennis C.
    The corporation: investment, mergers, and growth / Dennis C. Mueller.
      p.cm. – (Routledge studies in business organizations and networks; 25)
    Includes bibliographical references and index.
    1. Corporations. 2. Corporations – Growth. 3. Corporations – Finance. 4. Consolidation
and merger of corporations. I. Title. II. Routledge studies in business organization and
networks; 25.

    HD2731 .M754 2003
    338.7′4–dc21
                                        2002033315

ISBN10: 0–415–27135–5 (hbk)
ISBN10: 0–415–77111–0 (pbk)

ISBN13: 978–0–415–27135–6 (hbk)
ISBN13: 978–0–415–77111–5 (pbk)

To Judith for her continuing patience

Contents

Acknowledgments

This started out as a revision of my previous survey of the literature on the corporation (Mueller, 1987). So much new material has been added, however, that it is hard to recognize much of a relationship between the current work and its predecessor. The book continues to have a survey format, particularly in the chapters on mergers, but I have also tried to present the material in a way that would be accessible to students of industrial organization or business.

I would like to thank Steven Klepper and Kenneth Simons for allowing me to reproduce some of their figures in Chapter 4. Thanks are also extended to B. Burcin Yurtoglu for compiling some of the information included in several tables. A particular note of thanks goes to Heide Wurm for putting the manuscript into a form suitable for the publisher. Last of all, I would like to thank my wife Judith for her continued support and patience down through the years. In recognition of the importance of her contributions to my work, I am dedicating this book to her.

1 Introduction

Adam Smith's famous discussion of the organization of production in a pin factory articulated the advantages of the division of labor, and the economic gains from specialization and large production. But Smith expressed considerable skepticism concerning the relative efficiency of that particular form of business organization we now name the corporation, in which ownership and control are separated (1937, p. 700). Yet, it has been this organizational form that has come to dominate the business landscape in both Smith's own homeland and in most other Anglo-Saxon countries – a development that the Scottish sage could scarcely have imagined.

Large corporations exist, of course, in all of the highly developed countries of the world and in many of the developing ones. Outside of the Anglo-Saxon countries, however, control and ownership are usually combined. We shall devote considerable space in this book to discussing these differences across countries and examining their consequences for corporate performance (see, in particular, Chapters 6 and 7).

The extent of the development of the corporate form in the United States is revealed in Table 1.1. In 1998, there were 4,849,000 corporations in the United States – roughly one for every 60 Americans. Moreover, as a group they accounted for nearly 90 percent of business receipts in 1998, a fraction that is up from 2/3rds in 1945.[1] Table 1.1 also reveals how the nature of economic activity in the United States evolved over the last century. While the number of corporations in the manufacturing sector in 1998 was a little more than three times the figure in 1920, the number of corporations in the service sector increased hundred fold over the same period.

Not only do corporations as a group account for a large fraction of economic activity, but the largest of these also take on a scale that makes the word "firm" seem a misnomer. In the year 2000, Wal-Mart had 1,244,000 employees, which made it roughly the same size as the Salt Lake City/Ogden Utah metropolitan area (see Table 1.2). Exxon, the largest company in the world, had sales of more than $200 billion.

The twentieth century might well be called "the century of the automobile," given both the economic importance of the automobile industry and the impact of its spread on other industries, on the way people organize their lives, on the environment, and so on. Table 1.2 reveals that the economic importance of this

Table 1.1 Number of US corporations, by industrial division: 1920–98 (thousands)

	1920	1930	1940	1950	1960	1970	1980	1990	1998
Total active corps.	346[a]	463	473	629	1,141	1,665	2,711	3,717	4,849
Agriculture, forestry, and fishing	9	10	8	8	17	37	81	126	135
Mining	18	12	10	9	13	15	26	40	31
Construction	10	19	16	28	72	139	272	407	552
Manufacturing	78	92	86	116	166	198	243	302	310
Transportation and public utilities	21	22	22	26	44	67	111[c]	160	168
Wholesale and retail trade	79[b]	109	123	194	335	516	800	1,023	957
Finance, insurance, and real estate	79	137	143	172	334	406	493	609	740
Services	18	38	41	55	121	281	671	1,029	1,837

Sources: *Historical Statistics, Colonial Times to 1970*, Part II, p. 914. Table titled "Number of Corporations, by Industrial Division: 1916 to 1970." *Statistical Abstract of the United States*, 1984, 1995, 2001, tables 890, 854, and 719, respectively.

Notes
a Includes inactive corporations.
b Includes nonallocable corporations (about 25).
c Includes private utilities.

industry remains significant at the close of the twentieth century. Eight of the ten largest corporations in the world in the year 2000 were either manufacturers of automobiles or refiners of petroleum. Wal-Mart, the giant variety store chain, and General Electric were the only two corporations in the top ten that were neither in, nor heavily dependent upon, the automobile industry.[2]

Of the 100 largest corporations of the world, 37 have their corporate headquarters in the United States. Although this is a larger figure than for any other country, it clearly indicates that large corporations are to be found all around the globe. For this reason, we shall devote considerably more space in this volume to the characteristics of corporations and corporate governance institutions outside of the United States than was the case in its predecessor (Mueller, 1987).

As the title of this book suggests, its focus is upon the activities of large corporations. Virtually all corporations start out as small firms, however, and so before examining the characteristics and activities of large corporations, we shall focus upon the characteristics and origins of small firms. Essentially, two different accounts exist in the literature for why firms come into existence. One sees them as institutions for minimizing transaction costs, the other as a vehicle for bringing innovations into existence. These two, quite different accounts of the origins of firms are examined in Chapters 3 and 4.

In Chapter 5, we focus upon the managers of large corporations and ask what their objectives are likely to be. As we shall see, quite a number of different

Table 1.2 The 100 largest corporations in the world, 2000

Rank	Corporation	Revenues ($ millions)	Employment	Industry	Corporate headquarters
1	Exxon Mobil	210,392	123,000	Petroleum refining	United States
2	Wal-Mart Stores	193,295	1,244,000	Variety stores	United States
3	General Motors	184,632	386,000	Motor vehicles and car bodies	United States
4	Ford Motor	180,598	345,991	Motor vehicles and car bodies	United States
5	DaimlerChrysler	150,070	416,501	Motor vehicles and car bodies	Germany
6	Royal Dutch/Shell Group	149,146	90,000	Petroleum refining	The Netherlands
7	BP	148,062	107,200	Petroleum refining	United Kingdom
8	General Electric	129,853	313,000	Conglomerates	United States
9	Mitsubishi	126,579	42,050	Durable goods-wholesale, nec	Japan
10	Toyota Motor	121,416	215,648	Motor vehicles and car bodies	Japan
11	Mitsui	118,014	33,712	Industrial mach and eq-whsl	Japan
12	Citigroup	111,826	237,500	Finance services	United States
13	Itochu	109,757	36,651	Durable goods-wholesale	Japan
14	Total Fina Elf	105,870	123,303	Petroleum refining	France
15	Nippon Telegraph & telephone	103,235	215,200	Telephone communications	Japan
16	Enron	100,789	20,600	Petroleum, ex bulk statn-whsl	United States
17	AXA	92,782	95,422	Fire, marine, casualty ins	France
18	Sumitomo	91,168	30,715	Durable goods-wholesale, nec	Japan
19	Intl. Business Machines	88,396	316,300	Cmp programming, data process	United States
20	Marubeni	85,351	31,340	Durable goods-wholesale, nec	Japan
21	Volkswagen	78,852	324,402	Motor vehicles and car bodies	Germany
22	Hitachi	76,127	340,939	Electronic computers	Japan
23	Siemens	74,858	447,000	Electr, oth elec eq, ex cmp	Germany
24	ING Group	71,196	92,650	Life insurance	The Netherlands
25	Allianz	71,022	119,683	Fire, marine, casualty ins	Germany
26	Matsushita Electric Industrial	69,475	292,790	Household audio and Video eq	Japan
27	E. ON	68,433	186,788	Conglomerates	Germany
28	Nippon Life Insurance	68,055	68,745	Life insurance	Japan
29	Deutsche Bank	67,133	98,311	Commercial banks, nec	Germany
30	Sony	66,158	181,800	Household audio and Video eq	Japan
31	AT&T	65,981	165,000	Phone comm ex radiotelephone	United States

(continued)

Table 1.2 (Continued)

Rank	Corporation	Revenues ($ millions)	Employment	Industry	Corporate headquarters
32	Verizon Communications	64,707	263,552	Phone comm ex radiotelephone	United States
33	US Postal Service	64,540	901,238	Mail, package, freight delivery	United States
34	Philip Morris	63,276	178,000	Cigarettes	United States
35	CGNU	61,499	72,749	Fire, marine, casualty ins	United Kingdom
36	J.P. Morgan Chase	60,065	98,240	National commercial banks	United States
37	Carrefour	59,888	330,247	Grocery stores	France
38	Credit Suisse	59,316	80,538	Security brokers and dealers	Switzerland
39	Nissho Iwai	58,557	19,571	Durable goods-wholesale, nec	Japan
40	Honda Motor	58,462	115,500	Motor vehicles and car bodies	Japan
41	Bank of America Corp.	57,747	142,724	National commercial banks	United States
42	BNP Paribas	57,612	80,464	Commercial banks, nec	France
43	Nissan Motor	55,077	133,800	Motor vehicles and car bodies	Japan
44	Toshiba	53,827	188,042	Computer and office equipment	Japan
45	PDVSA	53,680	45,520	Petroleum refining	Venezuela
46	Assicurazioni Generali	53,333	57,443	Fire, marine, casualty ins	Italy
47	Fiat	53,190	223,953	Motor vehicles and car bodies	Italy
48	Mizuho Holdings	52,069	31,378	Commercial banks, nec	Japan
49	SBC Communications	51,476	220,090	Phone comm ex radiotelephone	United States
50	Boeing	51,321	198,000	Aircraft	United States
51	Texaco	51,130	19,011	Petroleum refining	United States
52	Fujitsu	49,604	187,400	Electronic computers	Japan
53	Duke Energy	49,318	23,000	Electric services	United States
54	Kroger	49,000	312,000	Grocery stores	United States
55	NEC	48,928	149,931	Computer and office equipment	Japan
56	Hewlett-Packard	48,782	88,500	Computer and office equipment	United States
57	HSBC Holdings	48,633	161,624	Commercial banks, nec	United Kingdom
58	Koninklijke Ahold	48,492	377,000	Food and drug stores	The Netherlands
59	Nestlé	48,225	224,540	Food and kindred products	Switzerland
60	Chevron	48,069	34,610	Petroleum refining	United States
61	State Farm Insurance Cos.	47,863	78,480	Insurance	United States
62	Tokyo Electric Power	47,556	48,024	Electric services	Japan
63	UBS	47,316	71,076	Commercial banks, nec	Switzerland
64	Dai-ichi Mutual Life Insurance	46,436	59,920	Insurance	Japan

Rank	Company			Industry	Country
65	American International Group	45,972	61,000	Fire, marine, casualty ins	United States
66	Home Depot	45,738	230,000	Lumber and oth bldg matl–retl	United States
67	Morgan Stanley Dean Witter	45,413	62,680	Security brokers and dealers	United States
68	Sinopec	45,346	11,173,901	Petroleum refining	China
69	ENI	45,139	69,969	Petroleum refining	Italy
70	Merrill Lynch	44,872	72,000	Security brokers and dealers	United States
71	Fannie Mae	44,089	4,100	Federal credit agencies	United States
72	Unilever	43,974	261,000	Food and kindred products	United Kingdom
73	Fortis	43,831	62,880	Investors, nec	Belgium
74	ABN AMRO Holding	43,390	115,098	Commercial banks, nec	The Netherlands
75	Metro	43,371	179,561	Department stores	Germany
76	Prudential	43,126	21,942	Life insurance	United Kingdom
77	State Power Corporation	42,549	1,137,050	Electric services	China
78	Rwe Group	42,514	152,130	Electric and other serv comb	Germany
79	Compaq Computer	42,383	70,100	Electronic computers	United States
80	Repsol YPF	42,273	37,194	Petroleum refining	Spain
81	Pemex	42,167	135,091	Petroleum refining	Mexico
82	McKesson HBOC	42,010	23,000	Drugs and proprietary-whsl	United States
83	China Petroleum	41,684	1,292,558	Petroleum refining	China
84	Lucent Technologies	41,420	126,000	Tele and telegraph apparatus	United States
85	Sears Roebuck	40,937	323,000	Department stores	United States
86	Peugeot	40,831	172,400	Motor vehicles and car bodies	France
87	Munich Re Group	40,672	36,481	Life insurance	Germany
88	Merck	40,363	69,000	Pharmaceutical preparations	United States
89	Procter & Gamble	39,951	110,000	Soap, detergent, toilet preps	United States
90	WorldCom	39,090	61,800	Phone comm ex radiotelephone	United States
91	Vivendi Universal	38,628	290,000	Conglomerates	France
92	Samsung Electronics	38,491	77,000	Electr, oth elec eq, ex cmp	South Korea
93	TIAA-CREF	38,064	5,975	Life insurance	United States
94	Deutsche Telekom	37,834	227,015	Telephone communications	Germany
95	Motorola	37,580	147,000	Radio, tv broadcast, comm eq	United States
96	Sumitomo Life Insurance	37,536	57,466	Life insurance	Japan
97	Zurich Financial Services	37,431	72,930	Insurance carriers	Switzerland
98	Mitsubishi Electric	37,349	116,590	Semiconductor, related device	Japan
99	Renault	37,128	166,114	Motor vehicles and car bodies	France
100	Kmart	37,028	252,000	Variety stores	United States

Source: Fortune Global 500, Fortune Magazine, July 2001.

hypotheses have been put forward to account for the behavior of professional managers in addition to the standard, textbook assumption that they maximize the profits of their firm.

In the literature dealing with the "Anglo-Saxon corporation" there are only two main actors, the managers who run the firm, and the shareholders who own it. Even in Anglo-Saxon countries there are sometimes additional actors of importance, like banks, however, and in non-Anglo Saxon countries banks, other firms, and the state often substitute for the individual shareholder. In Chapter 6, we discuss the objectives of these other actors. We also describe the different corporate governance systems that exist around the world, and look at some evidence regarding their impacts on corporate performance.

One of the important activities of corporations that might be affected by corporate governance structures and managerial goals is investment in capital equipment. This activity is the focal point of Chapter 7. Mergers and acquisitions can be thought of as another form of investment. In light of their importance for understanding the behavior of large corporations, and the size of the literature that examines them, two chapters are devoted to mergers. Chapter 8 reviews the various hypotheses that have been put forward regarding the causes of mergers. Chapter 9 examines their effects on company performance and social welfare. A brief chapter brings the book to a close.

The "profit motive" is widely believed to be the driving force behind all economic activity in market economies. Although we shall have cause to question whether it is the *sole* driving force motivating corporate decisions, no one including me, would deny the importance of profits as both a measure of company performance and a goal of its owners and managers. Therefore, we begin our excursion in the next chapter by discussing exactly what profits are and how they come about.

2　The nature of profits

The driving force behind the competitive process is often referred to as "the profit motive." Although every first-year student of economics knows that "profits are the difference between revenues and costs," many do not understand why such residuals exist, and why the competitive process tends to drive them to zero. Since we shall devote considerable attention to the workings of the competitive process in a modern capitalist economy, it is useful to pause briefly at this juncture to examine the peculiar characteristics of *profits*. Our discussion draws heavily on the ideas of one of the great Chicago economists Frank Knight.

Uncertainty and profit

Definition. Profit is the residual that exists after all contractual and potentially contractual costs have been met.

In discussing why profits exist, Knight (1921) made the important distinction between *risk* and *uncertainty*. Both words describe situations in which the future is not known with perfect certainty. But in situations that only involve risk, one is able to calculate the probabilities of the different possible unknown future events occurring. For example, the probability of two ones coming up when one throws a pair of dice is 1/36, the probability of a one and a two coming up is 1/18, and so on. It is thus possible to calculate exactly the probability that someone will throw "snake eyes" or a seven on a given roll of the dice. Thus, someone with a lot of money could in principle sell insurance to dice rollers at a casino at a price equal to the amount of money at stake times the probability of it being lost. If a lot of dice rollers bought this insurance, the insurer would break even.

Of course, there is no reason for someone to go into the insurance business if they just break even, and the types of people who frequent casinos are typically *risktakers* who would not be interested in buying insurance if it were available. (Even at casinos some insurance gets sold, however. If a blackjack dealer has an ace showing, the other players can insure against the concealed card's being a ten or a face card.)

In the commercial world, there are many activities that occur with sufficient frequency that probabilities of various events occurring can be calculated and

Table 2.1 Income statement of Small Spill Tanker Company (in $ millions)

Revenues		Expenses	
Oil deliveries	10,000	Wages	6,000
		Fuel	3,000
		Interest	900
		Surplus	100
Totals	10,000		10,000

insurance sold. Oil tankers make thousands of trips each year, and from their experience, the probability of one running aground can be calculated. An oil tanker company can thus buy insurance against one of its tankers having an accident. Now suppose that a very large tanker company chooses not to purchase insurance against possible losses from accidents involving its tankers. Full protection against all losses would have cost it $100 million. It has a lucky year with no losses whatsoever. For the year its income statement looks like that in Table 2.1. As in all income statements, revenues and expenses must be equal.

The entry "Surplus" on the expense side is a sort of fudge factor that ensures that this equality will hold. Had revenues equaled 9,000, surplus would have been set equal to −900. If revenues had been 11,000, surplus would have equaled 1,100.

It is tempting to call this surplus a profit, and this is probably what Small Spill's accountant would call it. But this surplus would not be an economic profit by our definition above. Wages, fuel, and interest are all contractual expenses. The $100 million in insurance is a *potentially* contractual expense. Had Small Spill bought insurance its contractual expenses would have just equaled its revenues. Its economic profits in the oil tanker business for this year are zero. Had its revenues been 11,000, we would say that its economic profits were 1,000.[1]

Suppose, however, that it had not been possible to buy insurance. Small Spill is delivering to Country X that is at war with Y. It runs the danger that Y's submarines will sink its tankers. No insurance company is willing to insure it against the possibility of such losses. Neither it nor any other company has had enough experience in such situations to be able to calculate the probabilities of its tankers getting sunk. Here, Small Spill faces a situation involving genuine uncertainty, and its surplus of 100, if it again should be lucky, should be defined as a profit.

In a world in which no uncertainty exists, in which all unknown events have known probability distributions so that they only involve risk, the free entry and exit of firms should drive all profits down to zero. Wherever entrepreneurs anticipated positive residuals after all contractual and potentially contractual costs had been met, including insurance against all risks, entry would occur and profits would decline. Where negative residuals were anticipated, exit would occur until profits rose to zero.

This uncertainty-based theory of profits provides us with both an ex ante and an ex post theory of profits. Ex ante profits explain the entry and exit decisions of agents. The concept of ex post profits solves the accountant's adding-up problem.

Ex post the difference between revenues and contractual or potentially contractual costs just balances the expenditure and revenue sides of the firm's income
statement.

Mobility and profit

Knight, and many who have followed him, emphasized the willingness to bear
uncertainty among those who took up the entrepreneurial role. But there is another
way to look at entrepreneurship in a theory that makes profit depend on uncertainty.
The flip side of uncertainty is information. The person who *knows* that she will roll
a seven – she knows that the dice are loaded – takes no chance. Thus, an alternative
way of viewing entrepreneurs than as people with a penchant for taking chances
is to view them as people who have *information*, or perhaps just an intuition, that
they can succeed where others fear to try.

Shifting the focus from uncertainty bearing to information possession has the
advantage of helping us identify the persons in a firm who generate its profits –
they will be the people gathering and evaluating information. But the link between
information and uncertainty raises a further question about profits. Information can
be written down and passed on to another person. Why then, can it not be sold?
Why is the reward for having information not a potentially contractual return?

Suppose you visit Warsaw, Poland, on your vacation. You are impressed by
the beauty of the city, by the signs that Western capitalism has taken hold. You
are not surprised to find American Express, Hertz rental car, and McDonalds,
all well represented. But, you are surprised to find that, although there are many
restaurants that make and sell pizza, none provides home delivery. You know that
home-delivered pizza has been highly successful in the United States where it was
first tried, and in Canada, England, and the other countries where it has spread. You
are sure that it would be popular also in Warsaw and the rest of Poland. Question:
how can you profit from this idea, this piece of information, which you have?

You do not have the inclination to start a business on your own, so you approach
the richest man in Warsaw and try and sell him your idea. You begin by telling him
that you have a great idea for making money that you would like to sell to him.
He says, "that's wonderful," what is it? You say its in food retailing. He responds
that Warsaw already has too many food retailers. You object that this one will be
different, it will sell pizza. He replies that three pizzerias went bankrupt last month.
You state that this is a different kind of a pizza restaurant, and offer to write the idea
on a piece of paper and give it to him as soon as he gives you the price that you are
asking. He begins to get angry, and complains you take him for a fool. In frustration
you tell him your idea. He smiles, but says that he is not interested. A week later
you see that he has opened Warsaw's first home-delivered pizza business.

You have learned that information is a very unusual commodity. To sell it you
must describe its content, but then you have given it away. The returns from
information are generally *inappropriable*, and thus not potentially contractual. To
sell information, one usually must effectively give it away. One exception to this
general rule occurs when a new idea can be patented. A patent can be shown to

a potential buyer without destroying its value, because the law prevents anyone from using the patented idea other than its owner. Contracts to transfer ownership of patented information can be written and enforced, and the return from this type of information is therefore not a profit, but a *rent*.

One might argue that a person would not really have to sell a potentially valuable piece of information that she had, but that she could sell her *ability* as a gatherer and evaluator of information. Someone, who had successfully opened other sorts of businesses in the past, might try to convince someone else to buy her idea, or finance her in business on the basis of her past record. But, in situations of true uncertainty, the past will not be a reliable predictor of the future. If potential financiers recognize this, then the holder of a piece of information will only be able to profit from it, by going into the business herself. She will need to *immobilize* herself in the business by taking up the entrepreneurial role.

Information, mobility, and profit

The great Austrian economist Joseph Schumpeter dismissed the notion that profits are due to uncertainty. For Schumpeter (1934, p. 137), "uncertainty had nothing to do with profits." Uncertainty was born by capital, but profits were created by the innovations introduced by the entrepreneur. Schumpeter's belief that capital bears uncertainty rested on the assumption that capital was the least mobile factor. Should grief come to the company, the innovator entrepreneur would be the first one to the door, followed closely by the workers. It would be the owners of immobile capital who would be left to bear the losses from the unexpected troubles of the firm.

Although it is correct to think of the least mobile factor as the bearer of uncertainty, it is incorrect to assume that this factor is inevitably capital. Land can also be highly immobile, not only in the obvious sense that it cannot be moved, but in the sense that it may be dedicated to a particular use. An oil spill can wipe out the value of a particular piece of beach front. Labor, including management, can also be immobile when it develops firm or industry-specific skills and knowledge, that is, specific human capital. For Knight, the entrepreneur was the immobile factor, because the entrepreneur wrote contracts with the other factors *guaranteeing* them their incomes, making the entrepreneur contractually immobile, and thus the bearer of the uncertainties facing the firm.[2]

In our theory, the existence of profit is due to uncertainty, but it is also linked to immobility. In the example above, it is because the entrepreneur cannot sell the information or intuition that she possesses that she has to immobilize herself to obtain a reward for its possession.

Once the link between profit, information, and uncertainty is recognized, it becomes obvious that each individual, and each factor owner is a potential profit recipient. Each agent is perfectly mobile at some points in time; the capital owner before he converts his money into plant and equipment; the college student before she begins to study engineering; the blue-collar worker before he acquires skills in a particular job, buys a home in a given community, and sends his children to a particular school. At these critical junctures, each person makes the entrepreneurial choices of what education to acquire, what firm to join, and where to invest one's money. Those who have good information, or intuition, or just plain luck make the right decisions and earn positive surpluses, those with bad information or luck earn losses in this entrepreneurial function.

Suppose, for example, after taking a course in sociology and studying the factors that lead people to decide to have children, you reach the conclusion that your country will experience a tremendous baby boom in about 10 years. How could you benefit from this knowledge? Well, if there is going to be a baby boom, there is going to be an increase in the demand for obstetricians, so you might try to sell the knowledge to your classmates. (I know a career that you should pursue that will make you a lot of money, and I'll tell you what it is for $100.) But you would immediately confront the approbriability problem with respect to information's value. You might write an article for some career magazine, but this would only earn you a few hundred dollars, assuming it even got published. The only way you could earn a lot of money from your idea, would be to study medicine and specialize in obstetrics yourself, that is, to immobilize yourself in the medical profession. If your prediction proves to be accurate, you will already be delivering babies when the baby boom hits, and can benefit from your knowledge.

Given the time it takes to become an obstetrician, you will be able to charge higher prices for your services, even after it is obvious to everyone that the country is experiencing a baby boom. These above normal returns we would not call a profit, however, because they are not due to uncertainty, but rather to the immobility of factor owners into the profession. The extra returns you earn until the number of obstetricians expands to make the return on this educational investment equal that of other comparable investments, should be called a rent.

These ideas can be summarized in the following way: Let

y_i equal factor owner i's total income,
c_i equal factor owner i's opportunity costs,
r_i equal factor owner i's rent, and
p_i equal factor owner i's profit.

In a world of perfect mobility and perfect competition, where common knowledge of the probabilities of all unknown events exists, neither profits nor rents exist and incomes in one line of activity equal their opportunity costs in the best alternative activity

$$y_i = c_i.$$

In a world of perfect competition in which there is common knowledge of the probabilities of all unknown events, so that there is no uncertainty, but in which immobility of factor owners exists,

$$y_i = c_i + r_i.$$

In a world in which uncertainty and immobility are present,

$$y_i = c_i + r_i + p_i.$$

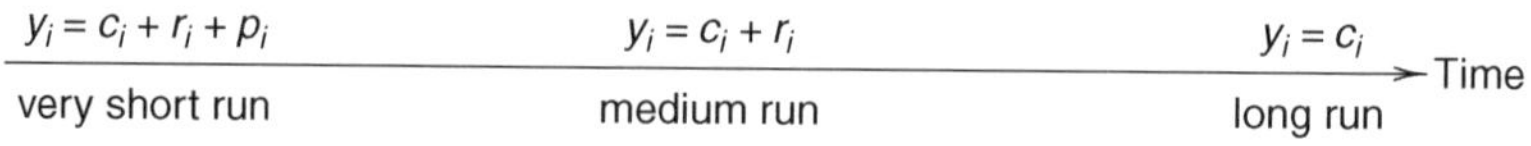

$$y_i = c_i + r_i + p_i \qquad\qquad y_i = c_i + r_i \qquad\qquad y_i = c_i$$

very short run	medium run	long run

→ Time

Figure 2.1 Profits and rents over time.

In the very short run, uncertainty and immobility are both present and a factor's income is likely to have a component of profit and rent to it (see Figure 2.1). Over time information is gathered, uncertainty disappears and so too do profits, but in the medium run immobility may remain, and factor incomes equal opportunity costs plus rents. In the very long run, all factors are mobile, all knowledge is disseminated, and incomes equal opportunity costs. It is this long-run state that exists in the stylized model of perfect competition, of course.

In the world that we live in, the environment is continually casting up unexpected invents, creating new uncertainties, creating new rents. To cope with these uncertainties, we gather information. Uncertainty disappears, profits are converted to rents. In time these too disappear as mobility barriers break down, and the perfectly competitive equilibrium is approached. But new events and new uncertainties will disturb this equilibrium creating new opportunities for profits and new rents. This dynamic view of the competitive process resembles that first described by Schumpeter in 1911. For Schumpeter, the key information being gathered by entrepreneurs was information about innovations. Firms come into existence to exploit some innovative idea of their entrepreneurial founders. Schumpeter's view of firms and competition is discussed in more detail in Chapter 4, but now we turn to an alternative explanation for the creation of firms.

Notes on the literature

In addition to Knight, the link between profits and uncertainty has also been emphasized by Weston (1950) and Bronfenbrenner (1960). For further explication of the nature of profits as presented in this chapter, see Mueller (1976).

3   The nature of the firm

More than 60 years ago Nobel Laureate Ronald Coase (1937) posed the question, why do firms exist? Firms, not to mention giant corporations, are such a familiar part of the economic landscape, that this might seem like a silly question to ask. On the other hand, much of economics is concerned with describing and often celebrating the performance of markets as institutions for allocating goods and services, and thus one might wonder why markets cannot be relied upon as the *only* institutions for undertaking this task. Given the existence of competitive markets with all of their accompanying efficiencies, why are the large, bureaucratic organizations that we call firms or corporations needed? What economic role do they play in the production and allocation of goods and services? The answer that Coase gave has led to the development of a theory of the firm that views it as a *contractual* linking of the laborers, capital owners, managers, and the other suppliers of factor inputs. This theory is the subject of this chapter. We begin by exploring the fundamental characteristics of contracts.

The nature of a contract

Definition. A contract is an agreement between two or more agents specifying certain rights and obligations of each party to the contract, and rewards and penalties for compliance or noncompliance with the contract's terms.

Contracts can be formal, written agreements with most, if not all, terms explicitly stated, or informal agreements with many provisions left implicit. A rental contract, for example, might explicitly specify only the monthly rent, the date that it is due, and the number of months' notice each party must give the other, before breaking the agreement. Implicit might be provisions that the landlord will provide heat, the tenant will not break the windows or damage the walls, and the like. Alternatively, the rental agreement might specify when in the fall the landlord is obligated to begin to supply heat, at what outside temperature heat must be supplied, etc.

Now consider the following commonplace *spot market* transaction. *A* has a stand and sells apples, *B* buys one apple. Such a transaction could be conducted with a contract: *A* agrees to supply *B* one apple, *B* agrees to pay *A*, 0.50. But it would never occur to *A* or *B* to write such a contract. To do so would cost both parties time, and provide neither with any benefits. Such a contract would needlessly raise the costs of making this transaction. Nor would we gain any insight into the fundamental nature of economic exchange by describing this transaction as involving an *implicit* contract.

The situation would be quite different, if *B* wished to purchase a train car full of apples to be delivered one year hence. Both then might prefer a formal written contract specifying the quantity and quality of the apples, date of delivery, and price, to an informal exchange of intentions to conduct the transaction one year later. The important difference between the two transactions is that the second one takes place in the future, and thus involves *uncertainty*. Neither party knows whether next year's apple crop will be good or bad, neither party knows what the spot market price for apples will be next year. Should the spot market price be high, the buyer runs the risk that the seller will choose not to deliver at an informally agreed to price. The opposite risk faces the seller should the spot market price be low. A contract stating price and other relevant dimensions of the transaction can protect both parties from the *opportunistic* behavior of the other party.

Even an informal agreement between the two parties might offer each of them some protection. If they agree to the terms of a future transaction, and "shake hands on it," each might now believe that an *implicit* contract exists, and the existence of this contract plus a sense of duty in both parties to abide by such agreements – to keep their words – might suffice to ensure that the future exchange takes place.

It is important to recognize that the key difference between these two transactions is that the second one takes place in the future, and thus involves uncertainty, and not just the size of the transaction. If *B* wanted to buy a carload of apples from *A* today, no contract would be required. Both would know today's spot market price, *B* could immediately inspect the quality and quantity of the apples. It is uncertainty that creates the need for contracts. If landlords could predict with certainty which potential tenants would pay their rent and which would not, and tenants could predict which landlords would supply heat and which would not, the rental market could function like the spot market for apples without the help of contracts.[1]

In the previous chapter, we saw that economic profits only exist in the presence of uncertainty. Uncertainty gives rise to actions that can potentially generate profits. We now have seen that uncertainty explains why contracts exist. This leads us to expect that there must be some relationship between profits and contracts in the contractual theory of the firm – and there is. The key issue to be resolved in the contractual theory of the firm is how the revenues of the firm, including the profit residual, get divided.

The uncertainty inherent in future transactions can be divided into two broad categories: uncertainty about the future behavior of the parties to the contract, and uncertainty about future *states of nature*, events beyond the control of the parties of the contract. The first form of uncertainty gives rise to provisions in the contract specifying the obligations of each party, and the penalties for not executing these obligations. Uncertainty over states of nature gives rise to provisions in the contract that are contingent on a given state of nature. All insurance contracts are of this contingent form – company C agrees to pay D up to x in the event that D's house is struck by lightening.

If the firm is a contractual joining of certain factor owners, and all contracts exist because of uncertainty, and all uncertainties addressed by contracts are of the two types just mentioned, then the provisions of the contract defining a firm must concern one or both of these two kinds of uncertainty. Each uncertainty gives rise to a different sort of contract, and a different rationale for the existence of firms. We take up next those contracts that arise because of uncertainty over states of nature.

The firm as an insurance contract

Assume that for whatever reason N workers and M capitalists have come together to form a firm. The capital stock is fixed as is the number of workers. Labor and capital are the only two inputs, and they produce output which generates an annual revenue of R. This revenue is not a constant, however, but varies with demand conditions. We shall symbolize this variability by designating revenue as R_s, with the s indicating that revenue is a random variable depending on the state of nature, that is on demand conditions.

The workers are paid a wage w, which may also be dependent on the state of nature and is thus written, w_s. The rest of the revenue of the firm, $R_s - w_s N$, is divided equally among the M capital owners. The Pareto optimal contract for dividing the revenue of the firm between capital owners and workers must be such that it is not possible to increase the utility of one group without reducing someone else's utility. For simplicity, let us assume that all workers have the same utility functions, U_L, and that all capitalists have the same utility functions, U_K. We can determine the characteristics of the Pareto optimal contract then by maximizing the utility of the members of one group, say the capitalists, while holding the utility of the other group fixed. That is, the Pareto optimal contract must be such as to maximize (3.1)

$$O_L = EU_K \left(\frac{R_s - w_s N}{M} \right) + \lambda \left[EU_L(w_s) - \overline{U}_L \right], \tag{3.1}$$

where E symbolizes the mathematical expectation of the future values of U_L and U_K, and $\overline{U}_L$ the fixed level of utility at which the worker's expected utility is held. Maximizing (3.1) with respect to w_s, we get

$$\frac{-U'_K N}{M} + \lambda U'_L = 0, \tag{3.2}$$

from which we obtain

$$\frac{U'_L}{U'_K} = \frac{N}{\lambda M}. \tag{3.3}$$

Both the number of workers, N, and the number of capital owners, M, are assumed to be constant. The Lagrangian multiplier λ is also a constant, and thus, equation (3.3) requires that the ratio of the marginal utility of income of a laborer to that of a capitalist in the firm also be a constant.

Equation (3.3) requires that the ratio of the marginal utility of income for a laborer to that of the capitalist remains constant in the face of changes in the state of nature, as for example shifts in the firm's demand schedule. If both workers and capitalists have diminishing marginal utilities of income, then this condition requires that any increases or decreases in firm revenues be shared by the workers and capitalists. The optimal contract is a *profit-sharing contract*. An individual who has diminishing marginal utility of income is unwilling to accept fair gambles, because the gain in utility if she wins will be less than the loss if she loses. If both workers and capital owners are risk averse, they can gain expected utility by agreeing to share the ups and downs of the firm's revenue. The Pareto optimal contract dividing the firm's revenues is a form of insurance contract.

Now consider the optimal contract, when one party is risk neutral, while the other remains risk averse. Assume that the capitalists have constant marginal utilities of money, and the workers continue to have diminishing marginal utilities. With U'_K constant, the only way that equation (3.3) can be satisfied, when revenues vary, is for the workers to be paid a fixed wage, and capitalists receive the entire residual income. The workers' marginal utilities of income do not change because their incomes do not change. The capitalists' marginal utilities do not change, because they are risk neutral and thus have the same marginal utility regardless of their income. The most frequently observed contract in which the workers are paid a fixed wage and the capitalists receive the entire residual income is the Pareto optimal contract, if workers are risk averse and capitalists are risk neutral.

While taking risks even at unfavorable odds – gambling – can sometimes be fun, introspection and considerable casual observation suggests that most people, most of the time are risk averse in their choices. Is it reasonable, therefore, to assume that capital owners do not have these sorts of preferences? If not, what accounts for the ubiquity of the fixed wage contract?[2]

The famous Chicago economist Frank Knight (1921), whose theory of profit was discussed in the previous chapter, did argue that entrepreneurs were an unusual breed of animal with a penchant for taking risks, and perhaps this is also true of capital owners. But the assumption that the capital owners of a particular firm have constant marginal utilities with respect to their income from that firm can be rationalized in a more plausible manner.

The modern capitalist is a stockholder, who holds a diversified portfolio of shares, or shares in a mutual or pension fund, which in turn is a diversified portfolio. The variation in the returns of any one item in that portfolio has a very small impact on the variance in the returns on the entire portfolio. An individual might be risk averse, and thus wish to avoid variations in the returns on her portfolio of shares, and yet appear as risk neutral with respect to the variation in returns on any single share owing to the small impact a single share's performance has on the total portfolio. Indeed, *the only reason for holding a portfolio of shares is because one is risk averse.* Thus, paying workers fixed wages and having the capital owners receive the residual income, becomes the Pareto optimal payment contract of the firm even when both capitalists and workers are risk averse, if each worker receives a large fraction of his total income from the firm, and each capitalist receives but a small fraction of her income from a given firm.

Capital owners can optimally absorb all of the risks of demand shocks facing a firm, because they can effectively "buy insurance" in the capital market against the risks facing the firm. This kind of market solution for spreading the risks facing the firm is clearly superior to using the worker–capitalist contract within a given firm, because it allows the risks of the individual firm to be spread across a much wider group of individuals.

Many of the risks of business life are specific to given firms or industries. An unusually hot summer raises the demand for mineral waters, soft drinks, and beers. A sharp increase in the price of oil depresses the demand for automobiles and steel. Thus, if workers in a steel mill wished to protect themselves against the ups and downs of their firm and industry, it seems unlikely that they would consider first the capital owners in their firm, since the fortunes of both are so highly intertwined. Far better would be to approach workers in other firms or industries, or other capitalists. This consideration suggests that capital and labor would not come together to form a firm, *just to pool the risks* associated with their sources of income. Given that a firm has formed for some other reason, on the other hand, capitalists and workers may choose to write a contract for dividing the revenue that spreads the risks of the firm across both groups, when superior alternatives are not offered by the market. But they would never form a firm just for this reason. Our quest for an explanation for why firms exist and the nature of their contractual relationships must go further.

The firm as a coordination contract

Suppose that there are two weavers in a remote village. Each spends his time weaving and selling his cloth. Each earns on average $400 per week. The weavers discover, however, that if they work together as a team, one specializing in weaving and the other in selling, they can average $1,000 per week. Together they can earn more than apart, so it obviously pays for them to work together. The question now arises, how to divide the average income of the team of $1,000 between the two. Since the team only *averages* $1,000 per week, they cannot agree on fixed amounts that sum to $1,000, since they will not always have enough to cover these amounts. A *sharing* contract again seems in order with α going to one member of the team, and $1 - \alpha$ going to the other. So long as $0.4 \leq \alpha \leq 0.6$, both members of the team are at least as well off as when they worked alone, or so it would appear.

But in this case appearances might be deceiving. When a weaver works alone, the loss in income when he takes a break for coffee, goes for lunch, or takes a day off to go fishing is borne entirely by himself. Each weaver can be expected to take time off for coffee, lunch, fishing, and the like, such that the marginal utility from these breaks, call it the marginal utility of leisure (MU_L) just equals the marginal utility of the lost income from the lost output from not working (MU_Y). But when the two weavers work as a team, the loss of income of one of

Table 3.1 Prisoners' dilemma with respect to shirking

		Weaver Column			
		Does not shirk		*Shirks*	
		1		3	
Weaver Row	Does not shirk	10 utils	10 utils	6 utils	12 utils
		2		4	
	Shirks	12 utils	6 utils	7 utils	7 utils

the weavers from taking a coffee break is only a fraction, α, of the loss in income to the team.

Instead of choosing a level of leisure such that $MU_Y = MU_L$, this member will choose leisure such that $\alpha MU_Y = MU_L$. The price of leisure for each member of the team has fallen, and each accordingly consumes more. The end result is that each finds himself worse off in the teamwork situation, than he had expected to be.

Once the two weavers form a team and institute a sharing contract, they find themselves in a *prisoners' dilemma* with respect to shirking (consuming leisure). This prisoners' dilemma is depicted in Table 3.1. Since the utility of each team member depends on both his income and his leisure, the entries in the matrix are defined in utility units, "utils." When each member of the team works as hard in the team as he was working by himself, the total income of the team is $1,000, and this leads, let us say, to them each achieving a level of utility of 10 utils under the assumption that they have the same utility functions and share the revenue equally ($\alpha = 0.5$). This outcome is depicted in square 1. If Column continues to work at the same level, but Row begins to take longer breaks (shirks), Row's utility rises as the extra utility from shirking offsets his share of the loss in team income. Column consumes no extra leisure and receives less income and is worse off (square 2). Square 3 depicts the symmetric outcome with Column shirking and Row not shirking. When both members shirk the outcome is in square 4.

There are three properties of this game which are important for our analysis of the firm. (1) There are gains from cooperation, the movement from square 4 to square 1. If the two weavers can agree not to shirk, they both can be better off. (2) There are incentives not to cooperate, to cheat on any agreement to cooperate – the gains to one member from movement from square 1 to either square 2 or 3. (3) The gains from cooperation can only be achieved in the context of the game. We have built this condition into the example by assuming that the two weavers are isolated in a remote village. The gains from cooperation that they experience are gains from specialization. If a perfectly competitive market for wholesale cloth existed, however, the gains from specialization could be achieved without forming a team. One person could specialize in weaving and sell his cloth in the wholesale market, the other could specialize in selling and buy his cloth in the wholesale market. The absence of a wholesale market forces the weavers into teamwork cooperation to achieve the gains from specialization. A necessary condition for prisoners' dilemma-teamwork situations to arise in production is some sort of "market failure" that forces factor owners to cooperate in teams to produce at maximum efficiency.

To achieve Pareto optimal levels of effort from both members of the team, they must be induced not to shirk, to cooperate in team production. We describe three different situations under which this might occur.

Both team members immobile

The benefits to each team member from cooperation seem so obvious, and in many situations so large, that the reader may think it unlikely that the cooperative outcome, square 1, would not emerge. But, in fact, in single plays of the game, quite the opposite is the case. If each player chooses whether to cooperate (not shirk) or not independently of the other, then not cooperating, shirking, is the *dominant* strategy. Regardless of what Column does, Row is better off if he chooses not to cooperate. The same holds true for Column, and herein is the heart of the *dilemma*. Rational, independent decisions by each player lead them irrevocably to an outcome, which is collectively irrational.

If both team members are immobile, that is to say it is costly for them to leave the town or find comparable employment opportunities outside of the team, both individuals face the same prisoners' dilemma week after week. If each acts independently, each rationally chooses not to cooperate and the outcome in square 4 reoccurs week after week.

Now suppose one member of the team, while enjoying one of his extra long coffee breaks, reflects on why it is that his realized utility within the team, is not as high as he expected it to be when he joined. He observes that he is enjoying much more on-the-job leisure than before, but his weekly income is lower than he had expected it to be, and as a consequence his combined utility from leisure and income is not as high as he thought it would be. The thought occurs that maybe the other member of the team is also consuming far more leisure now than he was before, and that the less-than-expected income comes about because of the more-than-expected consumption of leisure by both parties. It occurs to him that if he and his team partner would both refrain from shirking, both would be better off. How to bring this outcome about?

One possibility, which does not rely on direct communication between the players, is for each of them to recognize that because of their immobility they really face not a single prisoners' dilemma game as depicted in Table 3.1, but a prisoners' dilemma *supergame*, that is an indefinite sequence of games identical to Table 3.1. Having recognized the supergame nature of the situation, each player can now choose a supergame strategy to try and induce cooperation from the other player. One such strategy would be a matching strategy, often also called the tit-for-tat strategy, as depicted in Table 3.2. Players' R and C face a sequence of identical prisoners' dilemma games, $1, 2, 3, 4, \ldots$. Player R chooses the sequence of strategies M_i such that R will play in any round i, the identical strategy that C played in round $i - 1$. That is R will cooperate in round 3, if C cooperated in

Table 3.2 A prisoners' dilemma supergame

Game	1	2	3	4	5	6	7	8	...
Player R		M_1	M_2	M_3	M_4	M_5	M_6	M_7	
Player C									

round 2. Such a strategy effectively rewards C for cooperating in a given round by R's cooperating in the next round, and punishes C for not cooperating by subsequently not cooperating. If C cooperates in the first round, R will cooperate in the second, and in every subsequent round so long as C continues to cooperate. If both players adopt this matching strategy, and both choose to cooperate in the first round, mutual cooperation continues indefinitely.

Axelrod (1984) has described prisoners' dilemma situations in which cooperation has emerged without direct communication even between armies facing one another in war. Normally, however, communication is possible and its use seems a more natural way for cooperation to arise. One team member approaches the other and says, "If you cut down on your shirking, I'll cut down on mine."

Agreements such as these are easier to enforce, the smaller and more stable the group is. Thus, we expect mutual monitoring and cooperation to appear in small firms with stable memberships. Lawyers and doctors are among the most immobile of all occupations, in general, and we often find them organized into partnerships in which all members use *voice* to ensure cooperation, and the revenues of the firm are shared. By voice we mean various command and democratic procedures in contrast to the use of *exit* as is common in market transactions.

One team member mobile, one immobile

Consider now the impact on the contractual relationship when one member of the team becomes mobile. A factory opens in a nearby town and begins hiring weavers at a wage of $500. This event changes the relationship between the team members dramatically. Where before the weaver in the team might have received anything between $400 and $600, now he must be paid at least $500. The survival of the firm becomes much more important to the immobile member of the team, the seller, whose income will revert to $400 if the weaver exits and the firm folds. Because the weaver can always get a job in the neighboring town at $500, he may begin to take greater chances at shirking. Anticipating this the seller takes on more of a monitoring role. The seller may choose to pay the weaver a fixed wage equal to the weaver's opportunity cost, and keep the entire residual. The seller stipulates the hours the weaver must work, the duration of coffee and lunch breaks, and checks to see that the weaver does not break the rules. The seller becomes the monitor and residual claimant policing the contract by voice, the weaver receives a fixed wage and polices the contract by the threat of exit. A situation of mutual trust and cooperation is replaced by one of indifference and suspicion. Knowing that

Table 3.3 Alternative control patterns in the firm

		Mobility patterns		
		Symmetric immobility	Asymmetric mobility	Symmetric mobility
		1	2	3
No economies of monitoring	Interpersonal relationships	High trust	Low trust/Impersonal	Impersonal
	Control devices	Voice	Voice/exit	Exit
	Contract form	Profit sharing	Residual claimant/fixed payment	Residual claimant/fixed payment
		4	5	6
Economies of monitoring	Interpersonal relationships	Very low trust	Low trust/impersonal	Impersonal
	Control devices	Voice	Voice/exit	Exit
	Contract form	Profit sharing or residual claimant/fixed wage	Residual claimant/fixed payment	Residual claimant/fixed payment

the contract is of less importance to the weaver than it is to the seller, the seller continually suspects that the weaver is shirking or in some other way cheating on the contract. The weaver on the other hand is indifferent as to what the seller does, so long as he receives his fixed wage. The characteristics of the new contract are summarized in Table 3.3, square 2, and can be contrasted with those in which the two team members are both immobile (square 1).

Both team members mobile

If the seller can also take a job in the neighboring town at a wage of $500, the survival of the firm becomes a matter of indifference to both team members. Both police the terms of the contract by the threat of exit. We have the situation of square 3 in Table 3.3.

Economies of monitoring

The mobile members of a team can police their part of the contract by the threat of exit. Exit being costly, the immobile members must resort to voice. Such a division is natural, *so long as there are no economies of monitoring*. But such economies often exist. It is much easier for the seller to know when the weaver has been shirking – there is no cloth – then it is for the weaver to know when the seller has been shirking. Perhaps the seller did not shirk, but there simply were no customers that day, or none willing to buy the cloth in any event.

When one member of the team has a natural advantage in monitoring the contract, or significant scale economies exist, the tendencies depicted in squares 1 through 3 may be reinforced, or the link between immobility and voice may be upset. If both members of the team are immobile, and the seller can monitor the weaver, but the weaver cannot monitor the seller, the situation of mutual trust of square 1 may disappear (square 4). If with asymmetric mobility it is the *mobile* member of the team who is in a position to monitor, suspicion and distrust may be maximal (square 5). As always, full mobility solves all problems even when there are gains from specialization in monitoring (square 6).

Cheating on insurance contracts

Cheating can also take place on insurance contracts. Suppose, for example, that there are no gains from specialization, and thus no efficiency reason for the two weavers to form a team. From time to time, however, the weavers become ill or their machines break down. To protect themselves against these temporary losses in income, the weavers might agree to pool their incomes each week and share them as a way to insure against the risks of getting sick or machine breakdown. Once a sharing contract exists, however, the same incentives to shirk arise. Each weaver now has an incentive to feign illness, to claim that his machine has broken down. Such cheating on insurance contracts is so common that it has a special name, *moral hazard*. Insurance contracts, like all other sharing contracts, encourage cheating.

The nature of the firm

We are now in a position to answer the question Ronald Coase posed over 60 years ago. What is the essential nature of the firm? In answering this question, Coase observed, "It can, I think, be assumed that the distinguishing mark of the firm is the supersession of the price mechanism." We have emphasized in our example of the two weavers, the necessity of the absence of a wholesale market for cloth, so that the weavers are forced to cooperate to achieve the gains from specialization. Coase's stress on superseding the price mechanism captures this notion of market failure. Firms are not the only institutions that arise for dealing with market failures, however. The normative case for government also rests on the existence of market failure. Indeed, if the word "firm" is replaced with "government" in the above quotation, the statement makes equal sense and is equally valid. Governments are institutions for achieving Pareto optimal allocations of resources in the presence of market failures in *consumption*. Firms are institutions for achieving Pareto optimal allocations of resources in the presence of market failures in *production*.

In a subsequent, equally classic paper, Coase (1960) demonstrated that the existence of a market failure did not necessarily call for the intervention of government. If the smoke from A's burning trash discomforts B, B need not call out the troops, B might simply approach A and ask A not to burn the trash, or offer A a bribe not to burn the trash. Externalities and other market failures require agreements (contracts) between the concerned parties to achieve Pareto optimality, not necessarily government intervention.

Our example of the two weavers resembles on a smaller scale "the putting out system" that evolved in England prior to the industrial revolution. Each step in the production of clothing – raising sheep, spinning yarn, weaving cloth, etc. – might be undertaken by a separate person, typically working alone in his cottage. The goods were moved along from one stage to another by a manager–entrepreneur. The different people in the production chain were neither separated by impersonal markets, nor joined together in a single firm. Rather they were *contractually* linked to achieve the productive gains from specialization. The interdependence among the different stages in production made all vulnerable to disruptions at any stage, and thereby imposed significant *transaction costs* on the manager–entrepreneur to ensure a steady flow of goods through the system. The firm, a gathering of all stages at a single place under a single manager, emerged out of the putting out system as a way to reduce the transaction costs of production.[3]

We can now define the firm.

Definition. A firm is an organization for achieving the gains from cooperation in production, whose members are joined by informal contract.

Firms differ from other forms of cooperation in production by the nature of the contract that joins its members. If General Motors takes out a loan from Citibank to finance an investment, this loan will take the form of a formal contract specifying when repayment will be made and at what interest rate. We do not say that Citibank and General Motors constitute a single firm. If the central headquarters of General Motors provides the Pontiac division funds to finance an investment, the terms of repayment, and penalties for nonpayment, are likely to be implicit. We do not call General Motors' central management and the Pontiac division two separate firms. The salient characteristic of a firm as an organization for cooperation in production is the *informal* and *implicit* nature of its contract.

Hierarchy in the firm

The more formal and explicit a contract is, the easier it is to determine whether its terms have been violated. An important advantage of formal contracts is that they can be more easily monitored by independent third parties. If A contracts with B to deliver a carload of apples of specified quality to B on November 15, for a price of $10,000, then B can take A to court should A fail to deliver the apples, and A can take B to court, if upon delivery A refuses to pay the $10,000. In contrast, if the agreement between A and B is merely verbal, "sealed with a handshake," a judge may find it impossible to determine the "terms" of the initial agreement, and therefore impossible to arbitrate it.

Formal contracts require more transaction costs (e.g. time) to write initially, and may involve substantial ongoing costs, if the "rights and obligations" that they govern cannot be accurately predicted in advance. It would be prohibitively costly, if not impossible, to specify in advance all of the tasks that a secretary might be asked to do – how many letters will have to be typed, how many phone numbers dialed, etc. Thus, the specific duties of a secretary are often left rather vague at the time he is hired. The implicit contract under which a secretary works is that he will do what his boss tells him to do. But what if the boss asks the secretary to crawl out on the window ledge of their 107th story office, and wash the windows? The secretary might object that this task is not what the secretary envisaged doing when he took the job, this task is not part of "the contract." But, since the terms of the contract are very vague, it may be very hard to determine what is part of the contract. Can the boss ask the secretary to wash the windows from inside the office? Dust the shelves?

Informal contracts involve lower initial costs of writing. Because of their lack of specificity, however, they are more difficult to monitor by impartial third parties. Monitoring must fall to the parties to the contract themselves. With opportunistic individuals, such internal monitoring of the contract can be a source of conflict. Such conflicts may generate large "transaction costs" ex post, when disagreements arise between the parties over the terms of the contract. Such disagreements have figured prominently in the literature on the firm. We shall discuss two examples to help illustrate the essential features of the problem.

Conflicts between the firm's team members

Capitalist and worker

In the classical theory of Smith and Ricardo, the capitalist owned the physical capital of the firm, the machines, and gave orders to the workers who operated them. The worker's "contract" was in fact, as the economist John Commons (1924, p. 285) once described it, "not a contract, [but] a continuing implied *renewal* of contracts at every minute and hour, based on the continuance of . . . satisfactory service . . . and compensation." Thus, in the classical theory the monitoring role fell appropriately to immobile capital, and any disagreements over the terms of the contract would be settled by the capitalist. The worker protected himself from opportunistic interpretations of the contract by the capitalist through the threat of or actual exit.

As our above discussion suggests, such an arrangement should work fine, *so long as workers remain highly mobile*. But, as Karl Marx so forcefully pointed out, when "an army of unemployed" exists, the workers cannot costlessly move from one firm to another should they not like the way their contract with a capitalist is being interpreted by her. High unemployment destroys the worker's ability to use exit to enforce his side of the contract, and encourages the worker to strengthen his ability to use voice. The struggle of workers throughout the latter half of the nineteenth and much of the twentieth centuries to form unions and to induce government to legitimate and protect them can be interpreted in part as a struggle to replace exit with voice in the monitoring of the capitalist–worker contract.

The workers' movement in the United States made its greatest strides during the Great Depression, when unemployment rates rose to 25 percent of the work force.

Congress passed legislation that defined and protected workers' rights to form unions and to bargain collectively with managers. The workers' contract became a written contract, specifying in great detail procedures for discharging and promoting workers, the duties of different categories of workers, their direct and indirect compensation, etc. The contract between capitalist (management) and labor today is a much more formal and explicit contract than that described above by John Commons three-quarters of a century ago. Accordingly, in 1935 the US Congress created the National Labor Relations Board, a quasi-judicial third party agent, to arbitrate contractual disputes between management and labor. Thus, today in the United States the contract binding capital and labor is in many cases a formal contract, capable of third party arbitration.

The same is true in all developed countries and in many developing countries. In many enterprises in Germany and Austria workers are able to exercise "voice" through the process of co-determination (*Mitbestimmung*). Workers are represented in councils in which formal democratic procedures are used to make decisions of particular importance to the workers. Japanese firms have sought to avoid the high transaction costs of contracting and the arbitration of contracts that characterizes Western employment relationships by allowing workers to participate informally in making the decisions that affect them. The workers inability to use exit as a control strategy is recognized and allowed for by providing life-time employment with well-established procedures for advancement.

The manager–shareholder conflict

The joint-stock company, as Adam Smith called it, has evolved over the last two centuries out of the business partnership. At first the number of shareholders in a joint-stock company was small, and usually included the entrepreneur founder, who would also be the firm's chief executive officer. Corporate charters, the constitutions of the corporations, defined the economic activities of the company, and could not easily be changed. Major decisions required the unanimous approval of all shareholders. Thus, in the early stages of the corporation's development, when markets for shares were thin or nonexistent, stockholders relied on voice mechanisms to police the terms of their implicit contract with managers.

Over time capital markets developed, shares could be bought and sold quickly, and shareholders began to rely more and more on exit as a means of control. Large companies came to have large numbers of shareholders, each of whom held but a small fraction of a company's shares. Most important decisions were made by management. Proposals to the shareholders required only a simple majority of their votes for approval.

In October of 1929, however, many shareholders in North America discovered that they were not as mobile as they had thought they were. They could not get to the telephone fast enough to sell their shares and avert a dramatic decline in their wealth. In the aftermath of the Great Crash, much soul searching took place as to "what had gone wrong" prior to the Crash. In some cases it was discovered that managers had engaged in actions of a questionable ethical and even legal nature, actions that enriched the managers at the expense of their shareholders. Although the sums involved were typically not large enough to have harmed the shareholders significantly, the fact that they were harmed at all, on top of the large losses they had experienced as a result of the Crash, led to similar demands as those made by labor for government action to strengthen the hands of shareholders relative to managers.

Perhaps no contractual linkage in the firm is vaguer than that between shareholders and managers. A common share entitles its holder to a share of the proceeds from dissolving the company, but conveys no specific rights with respect to the ongoing operations of the enterprise. The *implicit* contract between managers and their shareholders is that managers work hard and generate large economic profits for the firm, that the managers honestly report these profits to the shareholders, and that they pay out as large of a share of these profits to the shareholders as is in the shareholders' best interests. Since all of the money generated by the firm that is not paid out to shareholders is potentially available in one form or another to the managers, an obvious and potentially large conflict exists between the interests of shareholders and those of the managers. With all of the authority to interpret the contract lying with the managers, the danger exists that managers interpret the contract in a way of maximal advantage to themselves.

Changes in the laws governing the manager–stockholder contract passed during the Great Depression strengthened the shareholders' ability to use both voice and exit to monitor this contract. Managers were for the first time *required* to report the sales, costs and profits of their firms, and to hire certified, independent accountants to verify the authenticity of these numbers. Specific information concerning the corporation's operations was also required at the time of any new listing of common shares. As with the monitoring of the worker–manager contract an agency, the Securities and Exchange Commission, was created to help police the manager–shareholder contract.

Despite these measures and others, which have been taken subsequently, the potential conflict between managers and shareholders remains an ongoing issue in the governance of large enterprises in North America and around the world. Regulations governing the shareholder–manager contract exist in every country, but in many they are much weaker than in the United States. For example, managers in the United States must declare the number of shares in their company, which they and members of their family own, their compensation from the company, and similar data regarding the managers' financial stake in the company. In other countries, like Germany, managers need not tell the owners of their company what their salaries are. For companies organized as GmbHs, they need not even declare sales and profits. Policing managerial actions with so little information is rather difficult.

Conclusions

Firms exist to achieve the gains from cooperation among factor owners in production. To avoid opportunistic behavior by individual factor owners, this behavior must be monitored, and rewards and penalties meted out. Who does the monitoring and how each individual is rewarded or punished depends on the relative mobilities of each factor owner, and the costs of monitoring. These interrelationships among the factor owners are defined by contract.

The contracts that link factor owners in production may be formal or informal. Formal contracts have the advantage of being capable of third-party monitoring. Usually we do not think of the individuals and organizations that are linked by formal contracts as being part of the same firm. Rather these contracts define *inter*firm transactions of the same type as occur between firms in the market. The main difference between these transactions and normal, spot market transactions is that they involve uncertainty in some nontrivial way. This uncertainty typically arises, because some portion of the transaction takes place in the future, as when a firm borrows money from a bank and repays it over time.

The salient characteristic of the firm is that its factor owners are linked by *informal* contracts. As they are informal, these contracts are difficult for independent third parties to monitor. The contracts linking the firm's factor owners must be arbitrated by the factor owners themselves. When an individual whose rewards are determined by a contract is also in a position to arbitrate the contract, the potential for self-serving opportunistic behavior is obviously present. Actual or suspected opportunistic behavior by one party to the firm's contract is a constant danger and source of conflict, given the nature of the firm's contract.

The history of the firm, and its modern manifestation the corporation, is one of trying to find the minimum cost contractual relationship among factor owners for achieving the gains from their cooperation. The putting out system with its arms-length transactions between independent, but contractually linked producers, gave way to the factory to reduce transaction costs. The very informal and vaguely defined contracts between managers and workers, and managers and stockholders that existed at the beginning of this century have by now given way to much more formal contracts, contracts, which can be and are monitored by a third party, and this third party is most often the government. The result is, of course, that the transaction costs of contracting within the firm have risen tremendously. The *raison d'être* of the firm, its low transaction costs from informal contracts, has been partially removed. This outcome is almost inevitable, given the teamwork nature of the production process, and the opportunistic nature of individuals.

The history of the firm and its likely future is a never-ending struggle to balance the transaction cost savings from informal contracts, against the conflicts and transaction costs to which these conflicts give rise. Faced with the higher transaction costs of organized labor and government regulations, some firms have simply migrated to regions or countries in lower stages of development, where workers are willing to accept employment on the terms of the traditional employment contract as described above by Commons. Other firms have given workers a share in monitoring and control by introducing some form of co-determination. But democratic decision-making procedures of this type have their own transaction costs. No organizational structure can do away with the transaction costs of coordinating team production. The task is to identify those organizational structures that keep these costs to a minimum.

Notes on the literature

Coase's (1937) article is the seminal contribution to the contractual theory of the firm. Following Coase the most important contribution to this literature is by Williamson (1975). The role of transaction costs and the informal nature of the contract joining the participants in the firm, and thus the need for hierarchy, is emphasized by Williamson (1985).

Alchian and Demsetz (1972) emphasize the teamwork nature of production, and thus the incentives to shirk. The role of managers in their theory of the firm is to police shirking by the other team members. Alchian and Demsetz assume that the managers and all other factor owners are perfectly mobile. Their model of the firm thus belongs to square 6 in our Table 3.3, and resembles the market with all members of the firm able to protect their interests by the threat of exit.

Stephen Marglin (1974) argues that the putting out system did not disappear because it involved higher transaction costs than the factories that replaced it. Rather, Marglin argues, the managers who ran the factories, the bosses, obtained utility from being bosses, and thus installed the hierarchical organizations that we observe today. As noted above, Herrigal (1996) has also questioned in the context of Germany's economic development whether the putting out (*Verlag*) system was inefficient.

Questions of moral hazard and monitoring in the firm have been dealt with more recently by Grossman and Hart (1986) and Hart and Moore (1990).

The distinction between exit and voice is taken from Hirschman (1970).

Berle and Means (1932) first documented the existence of a "separation between ownership and control," and discussed the conflict between managers and shareholders, which it caused. Their book also contains a detailed history of the evolution of the corporation.

This chapter relies heavily on the arguments and examples presented by FitzRoy and Mueller (1984).

4   The Schumpeterian firm

> We were engineers and we had a big dream of success. We thought that in making
> a unique product we would surely make a fortune.
>
> (Akio Morito, 1988, pp. 64–5)

In the 1950s, Edwin H. Land invented a process for developing film in a camera
immediately after a picture has been taken. To market this revolutionary invention
he founded the Polaroid Company. Several companies were founded in the 1950s
by scientists and engineers from the Bell Laboratories, where the transistor was
invented, because they thought that they could profitably develop and manufacture
transistors in this rapidly expanding industry. Akio Morito cofounded Sony after
the Second World War, because he thought that there would be a market for tape
recorders in post-war Japan. None of these firm start-ups seems to be well described
by the statement that their founders foresaw ways to economize on transaction
costs.

Schumpeter depicted the birth of a firm as the result of the innovative idea of
some would-be entrepreneur.[1] The birth of many firms seems linked to some innovative idea of its founder, and thus for many firms Schumpeter's explanation for
why firms exist offers an alternative and perhaps a more accurate characterization;
and many economists have approached the study of the birth and evolution of firms
and industries with a Schumpeterian perspective. In this chapter, we review this
literature.

The product life cycle

Most industries go through what are typically called "product life cycles." Klepper
and Graddy (1990) have studied the pattern of product life cycles of 46 products.
Their findings are summarized in Figure 4.1. During the first stage, the industry
comes into existence and begins to grow. Stage 1 of the product life cycle ranges
from a mere two years to over a half century, with a mean of 29 years. During
stage 1, the number of firms in an industry increases on average by nearly four
per year.

Stage 2 of the product life cycle consists of a so-called shakeout stage, which is
much shorter than stage 1, averaging scarcely more than a decade. Companies exit

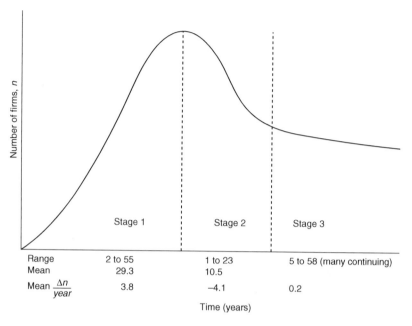

	Stage 1	Stage 2	Stage 3
Range	2 to 55	1 to 23	5 to 58 (many continuing)
Mean	29.3	10.5	
Mean $\frac{\Delta n}{year}$	3.8	−4.1	0.2

Time (years)

Figure 4.1 Three stages of a product's life cycle.
Source: Adapted from Klepper and Graddy (1990).

during the shakeout phase at an even faster rate than they entered. Stage 3 in the figure covers the stage of maturity. Many of the industries in the Klepper/Graddy sample were still in this stage so that the mean length of this stage could not be computed. The upper limits of this stage are probably well over half a century.

Other authors break the product life cycle into four or five stages:[2]

1   *The innovation stage.*   This stage occurs when the first firm enters (creates) an industry. Thus, all industries begin as monopolies, and by definition the innovation is made by a firm outside of the industry. In some cases like nylon, the innovation is protected by a patent and the innovator remains a monopolist for many years. In others, like the automobile, imitators appear almost immediately. In many important instances during the twentieth century, industries have been launched by inventions developed by small firm or an individual inventor. Famous examples of radical new products invented by individuals would include: F.G. Banting – insulin; L. Biro – the ballpoint pen; C. Carlson – the photocopy machine; A. Fleming – penicillin; K. Gillette – the safety razor; E.J. Houdry – catalytic cracking; C. Munters – gas refrigeration; H. von Ohain – jet engine; and E.A. Thompson – automobile transmissions.[3] Often, at this stage, R&D outlays are minimal. It is uncertainty over the success of the innovation, not the size of the investment needed that acts as a deterrent to entry at the innovation stage.

2 *The imitation stage.* Once an industry has been launched by the introduction of a new product, imitators appear rapidly and often in great numbers, if the product appears likely to have a great demand. Most imitators focus on variations in product designs. Product improvements are frequent, output grows and prices fall. Figures 4.2 and 4.3 reproduce the findings of Klepper and Graddy with respect to output and price changes during the first years of a product's life. As the industry expands, its output grows dramatically at the beginning, but its rate of growth declines quickly. Prices fall continuously over the first years of a product's life, but the rate of decline slows as the product ages. During the imitation stage new developments continue to come from firms that are initially outside of the industry and R&D costs continue to be modest. The innovation and imitation stages make up stage 1 in Figure 4.1.

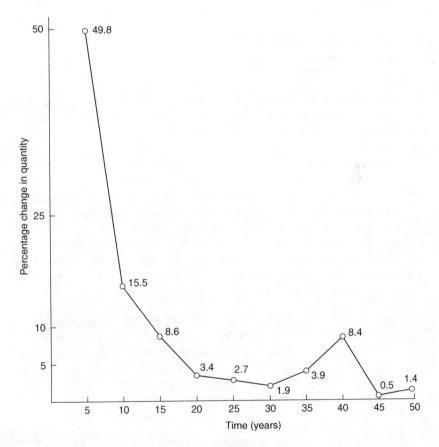

Figure 4.2 Changes in output over a product's life cycle.

Source: Adapted from Klepper and Graddy (1990, table 4).

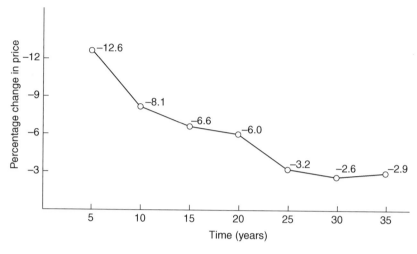

Figure 4.3 Percentage changes in prices over a product's life cycle.

Source: Adapted from Klepper and Graddy (1990).

3   *The shakeout stage.* At some point in time in a product's life cycle, the market begins to select its favorite product designs. Some firms have also selected superior production or distribution techniques, or have made greater improvements than others. Those firms that have selected the "right" product designs or production process survive, the others depart. As Figure 4.1 suggests, departures during this shakeout phase of an industry's life cycle are often rapid and numerous. At this stage, entry stops and all innovations begin to come from firms already inside of the industry. Where technology is important, R&D begins to become an entry barrier as insiders have accumulated considerable knowledge about their products and production techniques, knowledge that new entrants could only acquire through considerable investments in R&D. R&D also tends to shift from an emphasis on improvements in product design to improvements in the production process.

4   *Maturity.* Following the shakeout period, the industry stabilizes and enters a mature phase in which the number of sellers and industry concentration do not change dramatically. In industries where technology is important, R&D constitutes a significant entry barrier as the gap in accumulated knowledge between insiders and outsiders grows ever larger. R&D is concentrated on cost reducing innovations and minor improvements in product design. This mature phase of the product life cycle may go on indefinitely.

5   *Decline.* For those products that eventually get replaced by entirely new products – the vacuum tube, the manual typewriter – a fifth and final stage of decline takes place in which the number of firms falls through horizontal

mergers, voluntary exits and bankruptcies. Output falls, and concentration rises. What R&D there is in the industry is undertaken by insiders, of course, but R&D expenditures begin to decline as the time horizons of those left in the industry begin to shorten. Very often this period of decline takes place not because a product is totally displaced technologically like the manual typewriter and the slide rule, but because of international competition. As a product's technology matures, further improvements in product design and production become more and more difficult to bring about, and the high-wage, high-R&D industrial countries lose their competitive advantage over low-wage, low-R&D developing countries. Production moves "off-shore." Examples of these industries would include textiles and shoe manufacturing in the United States and several West European countries. Occasionally, a country loses out to foreign competition, because its domestic producers have failed to adopt some important production technique or product design. An example of this is television manufacturing in the United States. US television set producers were slow to introduce solid state technology into their television receivers, and thus lost their domestic market to Japanese producers (see, Klepper and Simons, 1999). Stages 4 and 5 of a product's life cycle are encompassed in the third stage in Figure 4.1.

The causes of shakeouts

An explanation for why revolutionary innovations like the automobile, penicillin, and the personal computer spark great bursts of imitative activity and entry is not difficult to find. The potential profits for a successful entrant seem enormous, and many risk- (uncertainty-) taking entrepreneurs who think that they have a good idea are willing, indeed eager, to take the plunge. Nor is it difficult to understand why an industry matures and perhaps eventually enters into a period of decline. Eventually, all of the possible designs for a sweater have been tried, the process of knitting them has been refined about as far as it can go. Less obvious is the reason why it also seems inevitable that an industry passes through a shakeout phase on its way to maturity. Why does an industry shakeout so often result in only a handful of surviving companies and a very high industry concentration ratio rather than 50 or 100 producers, each profitably ensconced in its own chosen niche?

The most obvious answer to this question is that the technology of production upon which an industry eventually settles involves significant economies of scale, and thus that there is "only room in the industry" for a handful of minimum average cost firms. This obvious answer is most certainly wrong, however. Engineering estimates of minimum efficient size dating back to Bain's (1956) classic study have shown that concentration levels in most industries are far higher than are needed to ensure that every producer has reached the minimum point on its average cost curve.[4] Estimates of minimum efficient size using other methodologies, as for example the survivor technique, imply even *smaller* scale economies (e.g. Saving, 1961). Some alternative explanation must be found for why during the shakeout stage so many industries appear to "overshoot" the concentration levels needed to achieve static efficiency. In this section, we briefly discuss three hypotheses and some evidence.

Hypotheses

The exogenous-technological-shock hypothesis. Jovanovic and MacDonald (1994) have hypothesized that shakeouts occur following major technological innovations that are more or less exogenous to the industry. Some companies are success-ful in adopting the new technology, others not, and thus a shakeout ensues. Jovanovic and MacDonald also assume that the technological breakthrough raises the minimum-efficient-size of a firm in the industry.

The dominant-design hypothesis. Utterback and Suarez (1993) have hypo-thesized that during the imitation stage of an industry's life cycle many different product designs appear. Some of these prove to be more popular than others. Even-tually, the market settles in on a particular product design, and those firms that chose the wrong design depart. The shakeout stage is thus caused by the market's selection of a particular product design.

The economies-of-scale-in-R&D hypothesis. Where Utterback and Suarez emphasize the importance of advantages in product design, Klepper (1996) has stressed the importance of cost advantages in explaining industry shakeouts.[5] An innovation that reduces the unit costs of production by $1 saves a firm producing a million units $1 million. The same innovation saves a firm producing 10 million units $10 million. Thus, the nature of cost-reducing innovations gives rise to an important form of economies of scale in R&D. Since the early entrants into an industry generally have larger outputs than later entrants, they have greater incen-tives to spend money on introducing cost-reducing innovations. Early entrants that are successful in innovating obtain a further advantage over late entrants, which allows them to expand their outputs and thereby further increases their incentive to invest in cost-reducing innovations. As an industry matures and settles in on a few product designs, cost differences begin to dominate product differences, and the firms which have been unsuccessful in lowering their costs are driven out of the industry.

Evidence

Klepper and Simons (2000b) have tested the three hypotheses about shakeouts by examining the histories of four industries in the United States: automobiles, tires, televisions, and penicillin. Figure 4.4 plots the number of firms in each industry against time. It can easily be seen that each industry went through a shakeout phase: automobiles starting around 1912, tires around 1920, televisions around 1950, and penicillin around 1952.

Klepper and Simons focus upon the hazard rates of exiting when testing the three hypotheses.[6] They argue that the hazard rates of early entrants into an industry should not fall prior to the beginning of the shakeout stage and should gradually

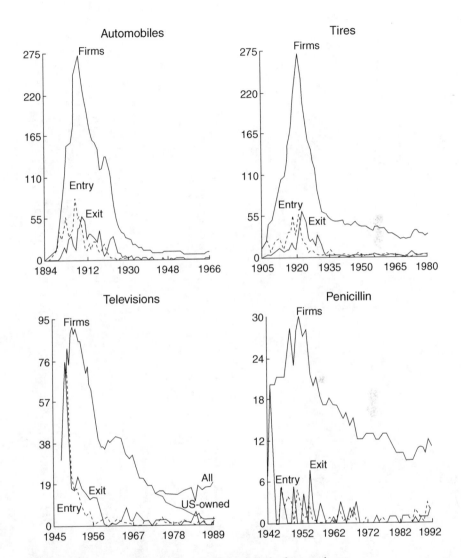

Figure 4.4 Number of producers, entry, and exit in the four products.

Source: Klepper and Simons (2000b).

approach zero. Late entrants into the industry should, in contrast, see their hazard rates rise during the shakeout. Figure 4.5 plots smoothed hazard rates for three cohorts of entrants in the four industries. As can easily be seen, the hazard rates for the latest cohort of entrants all rise dramatically when the shakeout periods begin, while the hazard rates of the earliest entrants taper off toward zero in most cases. Television sets are somewhat of an exception in that the hazard rate of the

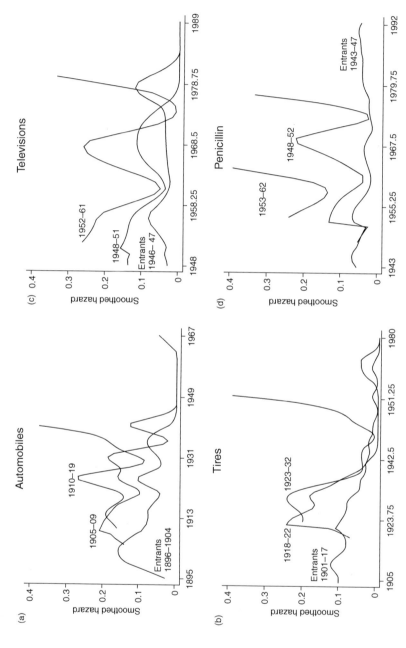

Figure 4.5 (a) Smoothed hazard plot for automobiles. (b) Smoothed hazard plot for tires. (c) Smoothed hazard plot for televisions. (d) Smoothed hazard plot for penicillin.

Source: Klepper and Simons (2000b).

earliest entrants bulges upward in the 1970s as the domestic manufacturers fall prey to the Japanese. The earliest producers of penicillin have a near constant hazard rate from the birth of the industry. These results clearly indicate that the earliest entrants into these industries had important survival advantages over the late entrants. Indeed, late entrants almost invariably disappear entirely.

Klepper and Simons present additional evidence in support of the economies-of-scale-in-R&D hypothesis. Early entrants, for example, are found to be more likely to produce important subsequent innovations. Success in surviving is also linked to success at innovating, which helps explain the link between survival success and early entry. Some of these findings seem to contradict the other two hypotheses about the causes of shakeouts. For example, a major innovation might be expected to impact all incumbent firms in the same way, independent of when they entered an industry, and one might even argue that late entrants should have an advantage over early ones in choosing a successful product design, since they have an opportunity to observe the market's reaction to the early entrants' choices. Thus, the strong superiority of early entrants in terms of survival chances seems to fit the predictions of the economies-of-scale-in-R&D hypothesis best – at least in industries where technological factors are significant.[7]

Entry and exit

The patterns of entry and exit observed over an industry's life cycle generally accord with what economic theory leads us to expect. Firms enter an industry in the stages when expected profits are high, they exit when profits expectations collapse. Little entry occurs after entry barriers become substantial.

Of necessity the literature on product life cycles consists of case studies of individual products. To trace an industry's history back to its very beginning and document all of the entrants and departures over perhaps 100 years or more requires much time and detective work. Although enough case studies have now been completed to allow us to be fairly confident that the "stylized facts" presented in the two previous sections are common to most if not all industries, one would like to have some reassurance that the process of entry and exit just described holds for a broader cross-section of industries. This section reviews the literature that focuses on the entry and exit process by looking across industries at a particular point in time rather than at a particular industry over time.

The facts

Entry is significant

Table 4.1 presents mean entry rates into four digit SIC industries over the period 1963–82 in the United States as reported by Dunne *et al.* (1988) (hereafter, DRS). Entry is defined as construction of a new plant by a New firm (NF); construction of a new plant by an existing firm diversifying into the industry, Diversifying firm (DF); or the transfer of an existing plant into the industry by an existing firm

Table 4.1 Entry rates for the United States, 1963–82

Method of entry	Time period				Mean of census	Mean per year
	1963–67	*1967–72*	*1972–77*	*1977–82*		
Entry rate						
Total	0.307	0.427	0.401	0.408	0.386	0.081
NF	0.154	0.250	0.228	0.228	0.215	0.045
DF	0.028	0.053	0.026	0.025	0.033	0.007
Transferring plant	0.125	0.123	0.146	0.154	0.137	0.029
Output shares						
Total	0.136	0.185	0.142	0.169	0.158	0.033
NF	0.060	0.097	0.069	0.093	0.080	0.017
DF	0.019	0.039	0.015	0.020	0.023	0.005
Transferring plant	0.057	0.050	0.058	0.057	0.056	0.012

Source: Dunne, Roberts, and Samuelson (1988, table 3).

diversifying into the industry (Transferring plant). The data come from the US Census of Manufacturing and thus measure entry over a four- or five-year period between two censuses. Thus, the data *understate* the amount of entry taking place between any two census years, because they omit entrants, which enter and exit between the two census years. Nevertheless, the data reveal a substantial amount of entry on average in any time period. In 1982, for example, 40.8 percent of the plants in an average 4-digit industry were owned by a firm that was not operating in the industry in 1977.[8] Twenty-one and a half percent were new plants built by NFs. The sixth column in the table presents the annual average of the mean entry rates for each census interval.[9] Taking into account the downward bias in this figure due to the exit of new entrants before they can be counted, one can easily conclude that on average one out of every ten plants in an industry at the end of a year was not in the industry at the beginning of the year.

The bottom portion of Table 4.1 reports the shares of industry output accounted for by new entrants. One can readily see that new entrants make up a much larger percentage of the population of firms in an industry than their share of its output. Although 40.8 percent of the plants in an average industry in 1982 were not present in 1977, they accounted for only 16.9 percent of its output.

The mean entry rates reported in Table 4.1 conceal a tremendous range across industries going from a low of zero in some 4-digit tobacco industries to a high of over 90 percent in printing – nine out of ten plants in the industry were not there five years earlier (DRS, table 5).

A similar pattern of entry rates to that reported for the United States has also been recorded for Canada. Between 1971 and 1982, on average, 4.3 percent of the plants in a Canadian industry were owned by either a firm that had entered an industry by building a plant or by acquiring one (Baldwin, 1995, p. 16). This figure should be compared to the sum of the NF and DF rows in Table 4.1 (5.2 percent).[10] New entrants in Canada are smaller than incumbents as is true in the United States.

Table 4.2 Exit rates for the United States, 1963–82

Method of exit	Time period				Mean of census	Mean per year
	1963–67	1967–72	1972–77	1977–82		
Entry rate						
Total	0.308	0.390	0.338	0.372	0.352	0.074
1963 firms	0.308	0.224	0.103	0.082	0.179	0.038
NF		0.087	0.134	0.173	0.131	0.026
DF		0.011	0.024	0.022	0.019	0.004
Transferring plant		0.068	0.076	0.096	0.080	0.016
Output shares						
Total	0.144	0.191	0.146	0.173	0.164	0.034
1963 firms	0.144	0.126	0.056	0.061	0.097	0.020
NF		0.032	0.050	0.061	0.048	0.010
DF		0.005	0.013	0.014	0.011	0.002
Transferring plant		0.027	0.028	0.038	0.031	0.006

Source: Dunne *et al.* (1988, table 4).

The 4.3 percent of all plants in any year that enter an industry account for only 0.9 percent of its employment.

Exit is significant

Table 4.2 presents mean exit rates as reported by DRS. Exit rates have been computed according to the three entry categories employed in Table 4.1. Since DRS did not know how the plants that existed in an industry in 1963 had entered it, they treat these plants as a separate category. As can readily be seen, exit rates although smaller on average than entry rates, are nonetheless substantial. By 1982, 37.2 percent of the plants that were in an average industry in 1977 had left it.

The bottom portion of Table 4.2 reports the shares of industry output accounted for by the exiting plants. Entering plants are smaller on average than incumbent plants, and the same holds true for exiting plants. The 37.2 percent of all plants in an average industry that exited between 1977 and 1982 accounted for only 17.3 percent of its output.

Audretsch's (1991) figures for NFs are less dramatic than DRS's figures for new plants, but they nevertheless imply a high mortality rate for NFs. Audretsch traced the 11,154 firms that came into existence in 1976 and entered the manufacturing sector up through 1986. Within 10 years almost 65 percent of them disappeared.

Once again the data for Canada paint a similar picture. Between 1971 and 1982, on average 5.3 percent of the plants in a Canadian industry closed down. These plants accounted for 1.2 percent of industry employment (Baldwin, 1995, p. 16). The comparable figures for the United States from Table 4.2 would be 6.8 percent and 3.2 percent, if one equates output shares in the United States to employment shares in Canada.

Table 4.3 Correlations between output shares of entrants and exits United States, 1963–82

Entrants time period	Entrants time period			Exits time period			
	1967–72	*1972–77*	*1977–82*	*1963–67*	*1967–72*	*1972–77*	*1977–82*
1963–67	0.721	0.697	0.598	0.741	0.722	0.681	0.571
1967–72		0.804	0.692		0.770	0.800	0.691
1972–77			0.759			0.788	0.758
1977–82			10.00				0.804

Source: Dunne *et al.* (1988, tables 6 and 7).

Entry and exit are highly correlated

Table 4.3 presents correlation ratios for entry in one census period and entry and exit in various later census periods. Looking first at the correlations between entry rates and entry rates presented in the left part of the table, we see that entry rates into industries are highly correlated. Even after 15 years have elapsed, the correlation between entry rates is nearly 0.6 (1963–67 and 1977–82). Industries for which entry is easy and attractive in one five year period continue to experience much entry over time.

The second thing to note is that *exit* rates are also highly correlated with entry rates. Those industries that are seeing large numbers of firms rushing in, witness at the same time large numbers of firms rushing out. Industries with modest amounts of entry also have modest amounts of exit. This latter finding is *not* what we would expect from the product life-cycle histories reviewed above. These histories would lead us to expect industries in the early stages of their life cycles to have much entry and little exit, in the shakeout phase much exit and little entry, and in the maturity stage little entry and exit. A positive correlation would be expected only for mature industries, and even here one might not expect high correlations, since with both entry and exit rates low, both may be dominated by random factors producing low correlations. What then explains the high correlations observed in Table 4.3?

Part of the answer does lie in the fact that at any point in time most industries are in the mature phases of their life cycles, and thus the inverse correlation that one expects to hold in the early phases is not observed. The second part of the explanation relies on the evidence presented in Tables 4.1 and 4.2. *On average* entry and exit rates are much higher than many of the case histories of individual industries lead one to expect. This is probably due to the fact that the scholars who have conducted theses case studies have chosen "interesting" industries to study – industries with sophisticated technologies and which in their mature phases have been populated by some of the most important, and hence biggest, firms in the economy. These two properties of the industries usually examined in product life-cycle studies result in there being little entry and exit in the mature stage of the cycle. Many "less interesting" industries like furniture, textiles manufacturing, and lumbering, do not have technologically complex products and production processes, however. Entry barriers are low even though these are very mature industries. Numerous optimistic managers of existing firms and starters of new ones continue to test their luck by entering these industries with most of them soon exiting them. In table 5 of their article, DRS print the 4-digit industry entry and exit rates for the lowest and highest deciles for each 2-digit SIC industry. As noted tobacco products is an industry for which the entry and exit rates in the lowest decile are near zero. The same is true for transportation equipment. But in the 2-digit furniture industry, the entry and exit rates in the *lowest* decile are 0.28 and 0.32, in the highest decile they are 0.69 and 0.62. It is industries like these that lead to the high correlations reported in Table 4.3.

Old means big and rare

The last set of facts that we will examine from the DRS study is quite consistent with the picture of an industry's evolution painted by the product life-cycle literature. There, we saw that the survivors of a shakeout tended to be among the earliest entrants and the largest companies at the time of the shakeout. Although the *number* of survivors from any entry cohort must inevitably diminish over time, the size of the survivors grows. The DRS data cover a much shorter time span than the life of the typical industry, nevertheless, they too reveal the same tendency for age to be correlated with size.

Figure 4.6 plots, for five census years, the average size of a plant from a given entry cohort relative to the average size of all companies in the same industry in the same year. The plants held by firms that existed in 1963 are treated as one

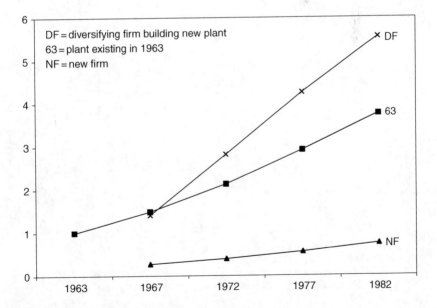

Figure 4.6 Average size of surviving firms from 1963–67 cohort.

Source: Dunne *et al.* (1988, table 10).

entry cohort and labeled 63. Their mean size relative to their industries in 1963 is 1.0, of course, since they constitute the population of plants in an industry. The mean size of the survivors rises to equal 3.76 times the size of the average plant in each respective industry in 1982. NF is the plot of mean plant sizes for plants opened by NFs between 1963 and 1967. At the end of this census interval plants opened by NFs are only 0.27 times the size of the average plant. Surviving plants owned by these NFs also grow in relative size over time, but by 1982 they have still obtained only a relative size of 0.75 of the size of an average plant. Plants opened by existing firms diversifying into an industry (DF) start their lives larger than the average plant (DF = 1.41 in 1967), and grow to be much larger fairly quickly (DF = 5.55 in 1982). We have not plotted the sizes of plants entering between 1963 and 1967, which already existed but switched product lines. Their sizes resemble the pattern for DF, except that they are roughly twice as large in any year.

The high correlations between entry and exit rates in Table 4.3 suggest a kind of revolving door pattern in which today's new entrant becomes tomorrow's new exit. The correlation might also come about, however, because the new entrants *displace* large numbers of incumbents. How quickly is the entry of a firm followed by its exit?

Very quickly. Figure 4.7 plots the exit rates for the same three cohorts of firms presented in Figure 4.6. By 1967, 42 percent of the firms operating in an average industry in 1963 had left it. By 1982, 81.5 percent had left. By 1972, 64 percent

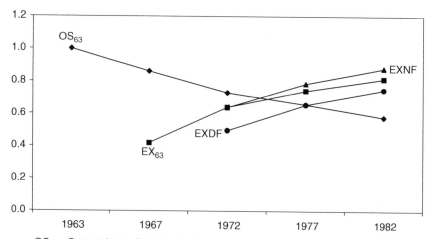

OS₆₃ = Output share of 1963 cohort
EX₆₃ = Cumulative exit rate of 1963 cohort
EXDF = Cumulative exit rate of diversifying firms buiding new plants, 1963–67 cohort
EXNF = Cumulative exit rate of new firms from 1963-67 cohort

Figure 4.7 Output shares and cumulative exit rates by cohort.

Source: Dunne *et al.* (1988, tables 9, 11).

of the NFs from the 1963–67 cohort were gone, by 1982, 88 percent. Even plants opened by diversifying companies had a 75 percent attrition rate between 1967 and 1982.

As time passes the number of survivors from a given cohort dwindles while their average size grows. What is the *net* effect on the output of a given cohort of entrants? The line labeled OS_{63} in Figure 4.7 gives an answer to this question for the cohort of firms in existence in 1963. The attrition rate for firms more than offsets the growth in relative size of the survivors. Over time the fraction of an industry's output accounted for by a given cohort of entrants declines.[11]

Explaining entry and exit

Consider an industry in which each firm's total cost function has the following form

$$TC = S + cx, \tag{4.1}$$

where x is output. Entry can then be expected to take place until n firms are in the industry, and the condition $\pi_n \geq S > \pi_{n+1}$ is fulfilled. Prior to reaching n firms, it is reasonable to assume that the rate of entry is greater, the greater the excess profits in the industry are over S. If E_t represents entry in year t, then we might write an entry equation as

$$E_t = \alpha(\pi_{t-1} - S), \tag{4.2}$$

where π_{t-1} is industry profits in year $t - 1$.

Entry depresses profits so we can write

$$\pi_t = \pi_{t-1} - \beta E_t. \tag{4.3}$$

Substituting from equation (4.2) into (4.3) and a little manipulation gives us

$$\pi_t = (1 - \alpha\beta)\pi_{t-1} + \alpha\beta S. \tag{4.4}$$

Equation (4.4) has been most frequently estimated with cross-sectional industry data with the lagged profits term being dropped. A vector of measures of sunk costs and other entry barriers are substituted for S, and some measure of industry concentration is added to capture the potential for collusive behavior in the industry. The fit to these models is generally rather good except for the concentration variable, which usually has the predicted positive coefficient, but is often of borderline significance.[12]

The time dimension must be explicitly specified in the entry equation, of course. Entry in period t is positively related to current profits in the industry and negatively related to the height of entry barriers and sunk costs. Variants on equation (4.2) have been estimated in numerous studies. The pioneering effort was by Orr (1974). Several measures of barriers to entry had the predicted negative effect on entry and were highly significant. The profits variable was *not* significant, however. Entry did not appear to respond to differences in industry profit levels, once account was taken of differences in the heights of entry variables.

This latter, somewhat surprising finding has been reestablished in numerous studies. Geroski (1991, ch. 4), for example, uses data from the UK to estimate variants on equations (4.2) and (4.3) that include several lagged values of both the relevant right-hand side variables and the dependent variables. Although profitability does have a positive and significant coefficient in the entry equation, the R^2 for the equation is a modest 0.08. The R^2 for the profits equation is much higher, but most of the explanatory power comes from the fixed industry effects. Entry that lagged one and two periods has the predicted negative effect on industry profits, but is not highly significant. Profit differences across industries are significant, persist over time, and are not greatly affected by the entry of new firms. Acs and Audretsch (1990) found that the entry of NFs was not significantly related to industry price–cost margins in the United States. The same is generally true for Canada (Baldwin, 1995, ch. 14). When a measure of profitability is significant in an entry equation, it invariably has the predicted positive sign, but it often is not statistically significant and even when it is, it is often not economically significant. NF entry into industries does not seem to have the kind of equilibrating effect on profits that economic theory leads one to expect.[13]

The results with respect to firm and plant exits are a bit more supportive of the predictions of economic theory. While NF start-ups were not significantly related to industry price–cost margins in the data of Acs and Audretsch (1990), *net* entry rates were. Thus, the chances of entering an industry and surviving do improve if one enters an industry with high profitability. Conversely, exit rates are inversely correlated with industry profitability. As noted above, however, the single most important variable in explaining industry exit rates today, are industry entry rates yesterday. The hazard rates of new entrants are very high.

What are we to make of these findings? If new entrants possessed rational expectations, then the same variables that explain gross entry rates should determine net entry. This is not generally the case, and so we must reject the hypothesis that the entrepreneurs who start NFs have rational expectations. They appear to consider carefully neither the heights of industry entry barriers nor the levels of industry profits, when deciding to enter. Each entrepreneur appears to be marching to his or her own drum and focusing most heavily upon what they believe to be their competitive advantage over their rivals. These economic factors do play their predicted roles in determining who survives, however. Firms that enter industries with low profitability, high entry barriers, and with high numbers of other entrants are less likely to survive.

First-mover advantages and dynamic competition

As we have seen above, one empirical regularity of a product or industry's life cycle is that the firms that eventually emerge as the industry leaders tend to be among the first to enter the industry. This phenomenon is so frequent that it has been dubbed "the first-mover's advantage." Just what the first-mover's advantage is, is often not clear, however. The industry studies, which we have discussed so far, have tended to concentrate on industries in which technological innovations have been important, and have given technological explanations for first-mover advantages. Technology is not a factor in all industries, however. Campbell's Soup has been the dominant wet soup producer in the United States for nearly a century, but it is difficult to categorize soup production as a high-tech industry. What factors explain its relative success? In this section, we examine several explanations for the advantages of first-movers. They can be divided into four demand-related advantages, and four cost-related advantages.

Demand-related advantages

Set-up and switching costs

Perhaps the easiest first-mover advantage to understand occurs when there are set-up and switching costs. Switching costs can take the form of transaction costs from switching brands, learning costs, or seller-induced costs like contractual costs (Klemperer, 1987). To play video games on a television set, one needs a small computer that attaches to the set, and a video cassette with a particular game on it. The first game one buys costs the price of the computer, P_c, plus the price of the game, P_g. All subsequent games cost only P_g. To switch to a second manufacturer's games requires buying the second manufacturer's computer. Thus, on the margin each game sold by the first-mover costs P_c less than a similar game from a second mover. Once one has accumulated several games from the first-mover, an additional switching cost arises to replace its computer should it break down with that of a rival, because one then loses access to the stock of games one owns.

Another example of a product with measurable switching costs is computers. Once one has become accustomed to one company's software, the costs of learning a different software discourage switching to another manufacturer's computer.

Network externalities

The value of a telephone increases with the number of users who are connected to the same system. The value of a credit card increases with the number of stores, restaurants, etc., which accept this card, which in turn depends on the number of possible customers holding the card. These products are characterized by network externalities.[14] If N is the number of users of a product with network externalities, then its value to individual i, U_i, is increasing in N, $U_i = U_i(N), U_i' > 0$, and so too therefore, is i's willingness to pay for the product. Once a first-mover has established a large network for a product with positive network externalities, the potential demand for a second-mover's product lies far below that of the first-mover.

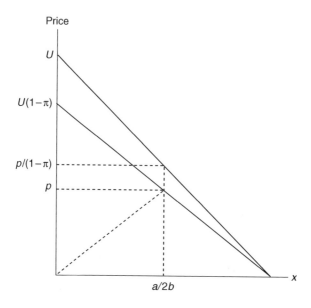

Figure 4.8 Demand schedules with quality uncertainty.

Buyer inertia due to uncertainty over quality

Consider a new product of a given quality. The amount of utility each purchaser of the product would get if he purchased it, U, is defined by the demand schedule $U = a - bx$. The utility each purchaser gets net of price P (consumers' surplus) is then $U - P$. When the new product appears, consumers are uncertain of the product's quality, however, and thus discount the utility that they expect to receive by $(1 - \pi)$. The demand curve facing the firm that introduces the new product is thus $U' = U(1 - \pi) = (a - bx)(1 - \pi)$ (see Figure 4.8).[15]

Once the product is tried, its buyers experience its quality, and their demand for it shifts up to the undiscounted demand schedule. Thus, all buyers who try the product in the first period are willing to pay a higher price for it in the second and all subsequent periods. The innovating firm's optimal strategy is to charge some price P in the first period, and to raise this price to $P/(1 - \pi)$ in all subsequent periods. At price P, the firm's output in the initial period is given by

$$P = U' = (a - bx)(1 - \pi), \tag{4.5}$$

or

$$x = \frac{a}{b} - \frac{P}{b(1 - \pi)}. \tag{4.6}$$

For simplicity let us assume that the only costs of producing the product are the sunk costs of developing it, that is, that there are zero marginal costs (or that the demand schedules in Figure 4.8 are drawn net of constant marginal costs). Let the innovating firm have a time horizon of t periods after the initial period in which it introduces the product. Ignoring discounting, the problem of the innovating firm then becomes to maximize

$$\Pi = Px + t\frac{P}{1-\pi}x. \tag{4.7}$$

Substituting for x from equation (4.6) we get

$$\Pi = \left(1 + \frac{t}{1-\pi}\right)P\left(\frac{a}{b} - \frac{P}{b(1-\pi)}\right), \tag{4.8}$$

which yields as a first order condition

$$\frac{d\Pi}{dP} = \left(1 + \frac{t}{1-\pi}\right)\frac{a}{b} - \left(1 + \frac{t}{1-\pi}\right)\frac{2P}{b(1-\pi)} = 0, \tag{4.9}$$

from which we obtain

$$P = \frac{a(1-\pi)}{2}, \qquad x = \frac{a}{2b}. \tag{4.10}$$

Equation (4.10) defines the profit maximizing price and quantity of a monopolist with the first period demand schedule $P = (a - bx)(1 - \pi)$, with $P/(1 - \pi)$ being the profit-maximizing price for the higher demand schedule that exists in all subsequent periods. If the expected profits from the prices and quantities defined in equation (4.10) exceed the costs of developing the new product, it will pay the firm to introduce the new product. Note that its optimal strategy in entering is one which we often observe – initially offering the product at a lower price. This strategy sometimes appears as "introductory trial offers," or coupons for discounts off the list price, or refunds from the manufacturer, or sometimes even free samples.

Now consider the situation faced by a firm contemplating imitating the first-mover, and entering in some subsequent period. Let us suppose that it can produce a product identical in quality to the innovator's for the same investment. Since the consumers are uncertain about the quality of the imitator's product, it potentially faces the same, discounted demand schedule that the innovator faced. None of the consumers along this demand schedule between the outputs $a/2b$ and a/b have tried the innovator's product, and so they can be induced to purchase it, if the imitator charges an initial price less than $a(1 - \pi)/2$.

All consumers to the left of output $a/2b$ know the quality of the innovator's product. They will switch to the imitator's product only if the *net* of price utility they expect from it exceeds the known consumer's surplus they enjoy from the innovator's product. Thus, the number of customers that the imitator woos away from the innovator is also given by the schedule $P = (a/2 - bx)(1 - \pi)$, and is shown by the dotted line from the origin in Figure 4.8. This line is obviously just the lower demand schedule to the right of $a/2b$ flipped over so that it makes the same angle with the horizontal. The imitator's total quantity demanded is the sum of the demand schedule for the consumers to the right of $a/2b$ and those to the left. Designating the imitator's price as P_2, its demand becomes

$$P_2 = \frac{a(1-\pi)}{2} - \frac{b(1-\pi)x}{2},$$

(4.11)

from which we obtain first period prices and quantities of

$$P_2 = \frac{a(1-\pi)}{4}, \qquad x_2 = \frac{a}{2b},$$

(4.12)

with P_2 rising to $a/4$ in all subsequent periods. If the innovator's price remains at $a/2$, its output falls from $a/2b$ to $a/4b$. It retains the quarter of the market with the greatest willingness to pay for the product, and the greatest consumers' surplus. Because of the latter, these consumers are unwilling to take a chance on the imitator's product. Since the innovator's price is twice that of the imitator, it makes the same profits per period as the imitator.

Thus, the imitator in this simple example would supply the same output as the innovator originally supplied, but at half of its price. Obviously, its per period profits would be half of those that the innovator enjoyed prior to the imitator's arrival. Should the expected value of these profits not exceed the costs of developing the product, the second firm would be deterred from imitating even though it could produce the identical product at the same costs as the innovator.

In addition to predicting low initial prices, this model predicts another characteristic of markets with dominant first-movers – they charge higher prices for their product than other firms in the market. Buyers of the first-mover's product stick to it after entry occurs, because they are uncertain of whether the new entrant's product would provide as much consumers' surplus over the purchase price as the pioneer brand's product. This behavior is often observed in the pharmaceutical industry. A newly developed drug is given a brand name – Prozac. Imitator drugs and generics enter with lower prices than the pioneer drug and capture increasing shares of the market. The pioneer maintains its price at or near its initial, high level gradually forfeiting market share.[16] Most drugs are infrequently purchased, however, so that consumers have little opportunity or incentive to experiment with alternatives, and if a consumer finds a particular drug efficacious, she has little incentive to try another brand. Application of the model to prescription drugs is complicated by the fact that the consumer of the drug typically does not select it, and may not even pay for it. The persons who select the product, the physicians, have even less incentive to try a new drug than do consumers, once they have ascertained that the pioneering brand is efficacious.

The fast-food chain McDonalds might be regarded as another example that fits the Schmalensee model. Although hamburgers and french fries have been around for a long time, McDonalds pioneered in distributing them through small, no frills outlets that promised quick service and uniform quality. In the beginning, it charged much lower prices than food of comparable quality that was sold at traditional coffee-shop-type restaurants. Other fast-food chains have copied McDonalds, but it still appears to maintain a first-mover advantage, particularly outside of the United States, because the traveler/customer is certain about the quality/price relationship she will find in a McDonalds outlet.

Although these examples seem to fit the Schmalensee model, many markets in which first-mover advantages are significant, do not fit it very well.[17] Coca-Cola, Hershey's chocolate, Wrigley's chewing gum, and Campbell's soups are all examples of first-mover products that have enjoyed market leadership positions and high profits for decades in the United States. Yet, there are very few adult Americans who have not tried the competitors' colas, chocolate bars, gums and soups, and who in the United States has not been in a Burger King, a Burger Chef, and some of the other fast food chains, as well as in McDonalds? If the other products are of similar quality, then some other explanation for the resiliency of the first-movers' market positions, prices, and profits must be found than that buyers are unsure of the quality of the second-movers' products.[18]

Buyer inertia due to habit formation

Behavioral psychologists explain habits as the result of operant conditioning. I commit an action purely by chance. If it is positively reinforced, the probability of my committing the action goes up; if I am punished for the action, the probability of my committing the action falls. The more frequently an action is rewarded and the greater the rewards, the more frequently it is repeated. Most of us smile and say hello when we meet someone out of habit, because this action has frequently been positively reinforced by the behavior of those we have met in the past.

Each time a product is consumed that provides greater utility than its cost, this action is positively reinforced. So long as purchasing the product continues to yield utility surpluses, this action is reinforced and becomes a habit, that is, one buys the product almost without thinking. Such behavior can be modeled as follows: Let π_{iKt} be the probability that i buys product K at time t. Let U_{iKt} be the utility i experiences from buying K at t, and P_{iKt} be the price i pays for K at t. Then i's consumer's surplus from buying K is

$$C_{iKt} = U_{iKt} - P_{iKt}. \tag{4.13}$$

Behavioral psychology predicts that π_{iK} is higher, the more frequently the purchase of K has been rewarded in the past. This might be captured as

$$\pi_{iKt} = \pi_{iK}\left(\sum_{j=0}^{t-1} C_{iKj}\right), \qquad \pi'_{iK} > 0. \tag{4.14}$$

Actions that are not committed cannot be reinforced, actions that are not reinforced are extinguished (performed less frequently) over time. Thus, reinforcement of an action in the distant past should have a weaker impact on the probability of committing the action today than its recent reinforcement. We can capture this feature by adding a depreciation factor, λ_{iKt}, to equation (4.14), $1 > \lambda_{iKj+1} > \lambda_{iKj}$.

$$\pi_{iKt} = \pi_{iK}\left(\sum_{j=0}^{t-1}\lambda_{iKj}C_{iKj}\right). \tag{4.15}$$

The term in parentheses in equation (4.15) resembles a stock of some sort, and we might think of it as a stock of goodwill created by the cumulated consumer surplus individual i has experienced. Indeed, we might place this stock of goodwill in a utility function and model i's choice as the outcome of a maximization decision. The notion that i is consciously maximizing some sort of function is totally alien to the principles of behavioral psychology, but it is possible to reconcile behaviorist's predictions with the assumption that people act *as if* they were maximizing a particular objective function.[19]

Equation (4.15) or its utilitarian equivalent imply that an individual's consumption choice today is a function of both her past consumption of the product and its past prices. The lower a firm's prices have been in the past, the greater the cumulative goodwill (positive reinforcement), and the higher the probability of repeat purchase. As with the quality-uncertainty explanation for consumer inertia, the habit-formation explanation predicts that a new product is introduced at a low price or with special offers to get people to try the product and develop the habit of buying it. First-movers have the opportunity to condition consumer buying habits before second-movers arrive.

But, habits do get broken, of course, and new ones get formed. The advantage of the pioneer brand should be weaker, the bigger the likely gain from switching brands is, and the weaker the habit of buying the pioneer brand is. The potential gain from switching brands should be roughly proportional to the size of the expenditure made on the product. Since the strength of a habit depends on the frequency with which it is reinforced, pioneer brands of frequently purchased, small expenditure products should have the greatest first-mover advantages from buyer inertia. Soft drinks, candy, chewing gum, soups, and fast foods fit this description nicely.

Goods of this type, variously referred to as *experience goods* or *convenience goods*, are also the ones for which a high correlation between advertising and profitability has been found.[20] They are called experience goods, because the consumer learns about the quality of the brand from his experience in consuming it, rather than say by reading an article in a magazine like *Consumers' Reports* that evaluates its quality. This learning by experiencing can create the kinds of habits just described.

Advertising often achieves its effect at the subconscious level. One observes young, happy people drinking a particular brand of soft drink in a television advertisement. One does not consciously believe that drinking this brand will make one young and happy, but subconsciously one associates positive things like being young and happy with the brand. This good feeling one gets when one consumes the soft drink acts as a *secondary reinforcer* and strengthens the habit of buying the product.

Advertising is often modeled by assuming that it builds up a stock of goodwill. Here again there is a link between ones's cumulative experience with the product and one's cumulative receipt of advertising messages.

Our fourth explanation for first-mover advantages thus rests on the psychological behavior of the consumer. The consumer is not the rational utility maximizer whom we meet in economics textbooks, ever ready to switch to a competing brand at the drop of a price. Instead, he is a creature of habit, who routinely purchases the same products even though others that would provide comparable levels of utility are offered at the same or lower prices.[21]

Supply-related efficiency advantages

Each first-mover advantage, which is related to the structure of demand has its analogue related to the structure of costs.

Set-up and sunk costs

To the extent that some costs like R&D and advertising are sunk, an incumbent firm faces lower costs than a potential entrant, because the incumbent can ignore the sunk costs when choosing its optimal output and price combination, where the potential entrant must incur both. The latter's total costs are thus

$$TC = S + C(Q),\qquad\qquad(4.16)$$

where S are sunk costs, and Q is output. Because the incumbent firm can ignore S, it may be able to choose price and quantity combinations, which fail to cover the potential entrant's TC.[22]

Network externalities and economies

A firm that develops a new product may be able to develop contractual links to suppliers of important inputs. These have been commonly discussed in the industrial organization literature as entry barriers related to vertical integration. Examples would be ALCOA's development of bauxite reserves and rubber companies contracting for natural rubber sources. These network linkages generally have a sunk-cost component to them. ALCOA discovered certain bauxite deposits and owned the right to them. The second firm in the industry had to incur the exploration investments of finding new deposits.

Scale economies

If it takes time to install capacity, and there are economies of scale in production, then the first firm in an industry has more time to expand and achieve these scale economies.

A particularly important form of scale economy in explaining first-mover advantages occurs with respect to R&D (Klepper, 1996). This first-mover advantage was discussed above as an explanation for why early entrants into an industry are more likely to survive the shakeout phase of an industry's life cycle. We shall not discuss it further here, therefore.

Learning-by-doing cost reductions

A new product often requires a new production technique. New machinery and new production, assembly, or packaging lines may also be required. Experience with production may suggest ways to reorganize an assembly line, or redesign a machine to improve efficiency. The more experience an organization has with production, the more opportunities it has to recognize cost-reducing improvements.[23]

Since experience accumulates with production, learning-by-doing cost reductions depend on the cumulative output of the firm, and time. Designating AC_t as the firm's average costs in year t, and Q_j its output in year j, learning-by-doing advantages imply the following relationship

$$AC_t = f\left(\sum_{j=0}^{t} Q_j, t\right), \tag{4.17}$$

where the partial derivatives of $f(\cdot)$ with respect to both arguments are negative.

Because the innovating firm is the only producer until the first imitator appears, it must enjoy some first-mover advantage from learning by doing. This advantage should be greater, the more complicated the new production process is, and the greater its departure from existing practices is. This advantage should be greater, the longer the innovating firm remains alone in the market, and the more rapidly it grows initially. Aircraft require the kind of complicated production process in which learning advantages should be present, and these advantages have indeed been found to be significant in this industry (Alchian, 1963). Considerable evidence of learning-curve advantages has been accumulated.[24] Indeed, the recent literature on learning-by-doing and dynamic economies suggests the potential for significant first-mover advantages, even when the first-mover has *not* chosen the optimal product or production process design from the set of initial candidates (Arthur, 1989; David, 1985, 1992; Silverberg *et al.*, 1988).

Summary

First-mover advantages arise either because of certain characteristics of a product's demand structure or of its cost function. On the demand side, the first-mover can have an advantage, because its product was the first one buyers tried, and thus they incurred the (sunk) set-up costs if any exist, or by trying it have removed uncertainty over its quality. The other first-mover advantages on the demand side are related to the total output of the first-mover (network externalities) or its cumulative sales (habit-driven advantages).

The mere passage of time can also give a first-mover a cost advantage to the extent that the production function has a sunk-cost component or there are dynamic learning economies. Average costs fall with output if there are scale economies, and with cumulative output in the presence of learning-by-doing economies. These relationships can be summarized by letting P be the price the representative consumer i is willing to pay for a unit of firm f's product at t, and C_{ft} be f's average cost at t.

$$P_{it} = P_i\left(Q_f, \sum_{j=0}^{t-1} \lambda_{ij} Q_{ij}, t\right), \quad C_{ft} = C_f\left(Q_f, \sum_{j=0}^{t-1} Q_{fj}, t\right),$$

where the partial derivatives of P with respect to all three arguments are positive, and the partial derivatives of C with respect to all three arguments are negative.

First-mover disadvantages

Although many of the arguments underpinning the existence of first-mover advantages can be expressed through tight analytic modeling, the arguments regarding the disadvantages of being a first-mover are based more on observation and ex post deductions than on modeling.

We have already noted that the learning advantages of a first-mover are so powerful that its costs may fall way below those of new entrants, even if it chooses a second-best product design or production technique. Such a choice leaves open the door to a second mover's overtaking the first-mover and surpassing it, if it finds a way to overcome the first-mover's initial cost advantage.

Large, bureaucratic firms have difficulties processing the massive amounts of information that flow through them (Williamson, 1967). These hierarchical liabilities are likely to be particularly acute in processing the rich flow of information that is generated by the R&D laboratory. Add to these problems syndromes like the "not-invented-here" bias that induce large companies to pass up or fail to see the potential of products and processes developed outside of the company, and one has an explanation for the well-documented superiority of small firms over large ones in coming up with important inventions and innovations (Mueller, 1962; Jewkes *et al.*, 1969; Pavitt *et al.*, 1987).

Finally, one has the fact that a firm in the mature phases of its life cycle is often governed by the interests of its managers, which do not always include the relentless improvement of efficiency and technical progress. Managers of large, mature firms may prefer to substitute the relative simple strategy of growth through merger for that of developing new products or improving existing ones (Mueller, 1969, 1972); or perhaps just to pursue the quite life: should any of these tendencies takeover the first-mover after it has established a dominant position in a market, its dominant position can become vulnerable.

The persistence of profits

In the Schumpeterian image of dynamic competition industries are born out of radical innovations, followed by the entry of imitating firms with an erosion of profits and eventual return to the zero profit state of a competitive equilibrium. We have seen that the innovation/imitation sequence is observed in many industries, with considerable entry often occurring during the imitation phase. But we have also seen that following a shakeout period in which considerable exit occurs, industries typically enter into a relatively stable and tranquil period in which comparatively little *net* entry occurs, and market structures change very slowly. We have also seen that first-movers in an industry can have significant advantages over the firms that follow them. These observations raise the following questions: Does the process of dynamic competition eventually lead the profits of all firms to converge on a normal level? If it does, how long does this convergence take?

To answer these questions we can think of a company i's return on capital in year t, π_{it}, as being composed of three parts, the competitive return on capital c, a firm specific permanent rent r_i, and a firm specific short-run rent, s_{it}, that with time is expected to become zero.

$$\pi_{it} = c + r_i + s_{it}. \tag{4.18}$$

The answers to our questions regarding the efficacy of dynamic competition thus boil down to determining (1) whether permanent rents r_i exist, and (2) how quickly the s_{it} become zero. Several studies have investigated these questions for different countries and different time periods using variants on the following model.[25]

Short-run rents are assumed to dissipate according to the following equation

$$s_{it} = \lambda s_{it-1} + \mu_{it}, \quad 0 \le \lambda < 1. \tag{4.19}$$

Assuming that equation (4.18) holds in every period, it can be used to remove s_{it-1} from equation (4.19), and with a little rearranging we obtain

$$\pi_{it} = (c + r_i)(1 - \lambda) + \lambda \pi_{it-1} - \mu_{it}. \tag{4.20}$$

All studies have found that short-run rents erode rather quickly with a typical estimate of λ being at most 0.5. At most only half of this year's short-run rents persist until next year. After four years, less than 10 percent of a given short-run deviation of profits from their long-run level is expected to remain.

On the other hand, all studies have found that large numbers of firms have permanent rents, r_i, that differ significantly from zero. Morever, a large fraction of these permanent rents are *negative*. While some firms seem to have returns on capital that are permanently greater than those of the average firm, others have permanent returns that are below average. We shall review several hypotheses as to why this can occur in later chapters. We turn next to a discussion of whether these persistent differences across firms can be explained by the first-mover advantages discussed above.

First-mover advantages and the persistence of profits

Table 4.4 lists the 81 companies from a sample of 551 firms that were projected on the basis of data from 1950 through 1972 to have a return on capital 50 percent or

Table 4.4 Companies with projected profits (π_{ip}) ≥ 0.50. M_{50} is market share in 1950. π_{50} and π_{94} are deviations from mean profit/assets ratios in 1950–52 and 1993–94

1972 Name	M_{50}	π_{50}	π_{ip}	π_{94}
Amalgamated Sugar	2.4	−0.12	0.53	
Amerace Esna	2.7	−0.51	0.54	
American Cyanamid	9.0	0.03	0.56	
American Home Products	4.8	0.10	1.71	1.37
Arrow-Hart	2.9	0.48	0.81	
Avon Products	n.a.	0.12	2.93	1.52
Basset Furniture	1.2	0.37	1.18	0.24
Beatrice Foods	3.5	−0.07	0.63	
Black & Decker	17.4	0.17	0.69	−0.10
Briggs & Stratton	n.a.	0.76	1.33	1.16
Bristol-Myers	5.6	−0.04	1.51	1.61
Brown-Forman Distillers	3.8	−0.07	0.67	1.28
Campbell Soup	63.2	0.05	0.56	0.67
Caterpillar Tractor Co.	48.2	0.05	0.72	0.29
Central Soya	3.2	0.29	0.59	
Champion Spark Plug	7.7	0.71	0.62	
Chesebrough-Pond's	n.a.	0.39	0.93	
Coca-Cola	30.2	0.34	0.98	2.24
Collins & Aikman	1.3	−0.37	1.49	0.02
Columbia Broadcasting System	n.a.	−0.31	0.56	
Consolidated Foods	n.a.	−0.44	0.58	0.03
Conwood	6.0	−0.26	0.72	
Corning Glass Works	30.6	0.27	0.76	−0.39
Crown Cork & Seal	3.2	−0.58	0.55	−0.06
Diamond International	19.6	−0.06	0.63	
Diebold	n.a.	−0.25	0.54	0.41
Du Pont	23.6	0.46	0.91	−0.01
Eastman Kodak	32.4	0.13	1.42	−0.14
Emerson Electric	5.6	−0.06	1.14	0.83
Emhart	5.2	−0.53	0.81	
Ethyl	n.a.	−0.18	0.51	0.54
Gardner-Denver	6.0	0.29	0.70	
General Motors	47.4	0.54	0.78	−0.20
Gerber Products	37.4	0.18	0.92	
Gillette	43.4	1.41	1.58	0.85
Hershey Foods	38.1	0.64	0.72	0.63
Heublein	n.a.	−0.41	0.78	
Hiram Walker	8.5	0.31	0.50	
Hoover	13.1	−0.02	0.66	
IBM	47.9	0.01	1.10	−1.40
Inspiration Consoliated Copper	2.2	0.16	0.58	−0.43
Kayser-Roth	1.2	−0.47	0.79	
Kellogg	20.5	0.82	1.20	1.77
Eli Lilly	8.8	0.27	1.61	0.20
Magnavox	1.8	0.39	1.20	

(*continued*)

Table 4.4 (Continued)

1972 Name	M_{50}	π_{50}	π_{ip}	π_{94}
Maytag	14.3	0.96	2.37	0.11
Melville Shoe	2.9	0.57	0.78	
Merck	7.8	0.10	2.12	1.05
Minnesota Mining & Mfg.	15.8	0.41	1.16	0.73
Monroe Auto Equipment	n.a.	−0.25	2.04	
Morton-Norwich Products	n.a.	0.27	0.88	
Nalco Chemical	n.a.	0.50	1.14	
Northwestern Steel & Wire	3.3	0.33	0.99	0.06
Noxell	n.a.	1.05	0.99	
Peter Paul	3.4	0.06	1.00	
Polaroid	n.a.	0.46	0.94	0.06
Procter & Gamble	29.9	0.37	0.86	0.05
Purolator	n.a.	0.43	1.15	
R.J. Reynolds Industries	23.3	−0.22	1.11	
Richardson Merrell	2.1	0.22	0.66	
Roper	8.4	−0.24	0.53	
Royal Crown Cola	n.a.	0.62	0.94	
Schering-Plough	n.a.	−0.03	1.17	2.51
G.D. Searle	n.a.	1.22	1.95	
Smith Kline & French Labs.	2.0	0.83	2.18	
Square D	6.6	0.55	1.76	
Stanadyne	3.3	0.02	0.81	
Sterling Drug	4.5	0.17	1.34	
Stewart-Warner	4.2	−0.18	0.59	
Tecumseh Products	38.7	0.78	0.93	0.39
Texaco	6.9	0.24	0.52	0.03
Textron	1.4	−0.67	0.88	−0.13
Thomas & Betts	n.a.	0.50	1.08	−0.13
United States Tobacco	10.9	−0.07	0.97	
Upjohn	2.0	−1.00	1.43	0.58
V. F. Corporation	n.a.	−0.05	2.60	0.78
Warner-Lambert	1.8	−0.46	1.30	0.69
Whirlpool	14.8	0.40	0.70	−0.03
Wm. Wrigley Jr.	52.8	0.44	0.63	2.67
Xerox	n.a.	−0.28	1.00	−0.58
Zenith Radio	6.1	0.33	0.97	−2.34

more above that of the average firm in the sample (see column, π_{ip}). As one looks through the table one finds many firms with persistently above normal profits that would seem to benefit from the first-mover advantages discussed above. Coca-Cola had a profit rate of 34 percent above that of the average firm in the sample in the years 1950–52 (π_{50}), and was projected to earn a return on capital 98 percent above the average into the indefinite future. Its profits in 1993–94 were 224 percent more than the average firm in a large sample of manufacturing companies (π_{94}). It had 30 percent of the soft drinks market in 1950, about what it has today.

Gillette was the leading producer of safety razors and blades in 1950 with 43.4 percent of the market, and remains so today. Its return on capital was almost 150 percent higher than the average at the beginning of the period (1950–52), and was some 85 percent higher 40 years later (π_{94}). As one looks through the table one observes many companies which were, and often still are, leaders in markets for convenience and experience goods – American Home Products (over-the-counter drugs), Brown-Forman Distillers, Campbell Soup, Kodak (film), Diamond International (matches), Gerber Products (baby food), Hershey Foods (chocolate), Kellogg (breakfast cereals), Noxell (cosmetics), Peter Paul (candy), Procter & Gamble (soaps, toothpaste, and other drugstore and supermarket products), R.J. Reynolds (cigarettes), and Wm. Wrigley Jr. (chewing gum) – the kinds of small expenditure, frequent purchase items for which habits once formed and then reinforced by advertising can produce significant first-mover advantages. In other cases one observes firms which may have benefitted from learning-by-doing cost savings, or the costs-savings generated from more intensive R&D efforts to introduce cost saving innovations (Caterpillar Tractor, Central Soya, Du Pont, General Motors, IBM, Maytag, Whirlpool, and Zenith Radio). In some cases, the reported market shares for 1950 understate the extent to which a firm dominated a market, or a market niche. Maytag had only 14.3 percent of the major appliance market, but was the second leading producer of washers and dryers, with considerable first-mover advantage in this submarket. Liquor, cosmetics, and pharmaceutical companies typically have brands in distinctive submarkets in which they are the dominant sellers. Peter Paul's small share of the candy market understates the uniqueness of its chocolate-covered cocoanut bars, and the market advantage this uniqueness yields.

When looking at Table 4.4, it is interesting to observe that many of the firms that survived the shakeout phases of their industries' life cycles and survived the first three quarters of the twentieth century were not able to convert their first-mover advantages into persistently above normal profits. None of the leading tire and steel manufacturers appears in the table, only one automobile company is present. Only in the pharmaceuticals' industry do first-movers seem to have been able to both *survive* and *prosper* after the Second World War.

Several of the companies listed in Table 4.4 no longer exist as independent entities, and several no longer enjoy the substantial difference in profitability from the average that they once did. But in many cases, these developments do not reflect the kind of "perennial gale" of competition that Schumpeter described. The most frequent cause for the disappearance of a large company is a merger. Although mergers occasionally take place to remove a company facing bankruptcy from the market, this is fairly rare. Most acquired companies in the United States have been normal, healthy firms.[26]

The biggest change since 1972 in the economic environment affecting the profitability of US companies has been the growth of competition from abroad. The gale of creative destruction that eroded the profits of General Motors came not from newly formed or existing American firms, but from European and Japanese companies, first-movers in their home markets that chose to take on giant American companies. Had American car buyers waited for internally generated competition to erode General Motors' market share and profits, they might still be waiting.

In some markets, the Schumpeterian scenario has been observed. IBM would appear to have enjoyed significant first-mover advantages in the market for mainframe computers. It was slow to innovate in the personal computer market, however, and saw both its share of the computers' market and its profits fall. As so often occurs, the significant innovations in personal computers that have displaced mainframes did not come from firms that were major producers of main frames. Thus, the history of the US economy since the Second World War reveals some markets in which Schumpeterian competition has destroyed the high profits of the market leaders, and others where it has not.

Evolutionary models of firms and industries

Alfred Chandler (1992), the Harvard business historian, has said that of the four approaches to the study of firms – neoclassical, principal–agent, transaction costs and evolutionary – he found that the neoclassical models "contribute little" to our understanding of the development of the modern, capitalist corporation, the evolutionary approach arguably the most. Many of the studies already discussed in this chapter have employed or been inspired by the evolutionary approach. We close this chapter by describing just what this approach is.

Evolutionary theory offers not just an alternative perspective on firm and industry growth and development, but an alternative paradigm. To appreciate both the novelty and the potential importance of the evolutionary approach, therefore, it is useful to review the main elements of the neoclassical approach so as to be able to contrast the two.

The elements of neoclassical economics

Neoclassical economics rests on two sets of assumptions: one involving the behavior of individual actors, and the other on the operation of the institutions in which individuals act. With respect to individuals, neoclassical economics assumes that they *rationally* seek to advance their self-interest. The rationality assumption in turn is operationalized by positing that individuals *maximize* a particular objective function. The arguments of this function are chosen according to the goals posited for the agent, whose behavior is modeled. Consumers maximize their utility, which is a function of their consumption bundle. Workers maximize their utility, which is a function of their income and leisure. Entrepreneurs maximize the profits of their firms.

The second pillar of neoclassical theory is the assumption that the institutional settings in which individuals interact – markets – produce equilibria. Demand equals supply, the profits of the industry are zero. The two pillars of neoclassical analysis, maximizing individual behavior and equilibrium generating markets, produce two equations – the first-order condition from the individual's maximizing decision and the equation defining the market equilibrium – that are then used to derive predictions and "to solve" the problem that led to the model's construction.[27] The attraction of this methodological approach is that it can combine rigor with simplicity, and often does seem to describe reasonably accurately phenomena that we observe. *But* it does not always do so, and there are some questions, particularly of a dynamic nature, for which neoclassical models seem particularly ill-suited.[28]

It is here that evolutionary models offer their greatest promise.

The elements of evolutionary economics

Evolutionary models relax or outright abandon both pillars of neoclassical theory. At the level of the individual, most evolutionary models retain the assumption of self-interested behavior, although evolutionary theorists are willing to assume a wider array of goals for individuals than are neoclassical theorists, and thus can more readily accommodate the kinds of managerial motivation described in Chapter 5. Evolutionary models do assume, however, that individuals are goal oriented, and that these goals are closely related to the interests of the actors.

Evolutionary models depart radically from neoclassical models, however, with respect to the postulate of rationality and its implication of maximizing behavior. Evolutionary theory, like transaction costs economics, stresses the bounded rationality of individuals. To cope with the complexities individuals encounter they often adopt *rules of thumb* or *routines*. These routines replace the first order conditions derived under maximizing assumptions.

The equilibrium conditions that form the second analytic pillar of neoclassical models are replaced in evolutionary models with dynamic equations like those that describe a Markov process

$$y_t = \alpha y_{t-1} + \mu_t, \tag{4.21}$$

where y_t is some variable of interest in period t, and μ_t is a random error.

These differences have important implications for the kinds of questions the two approaches are able to answer. For example, consider the question of predicting the effect of a horizontal merger in a given industry on social welfare. This question is well-suited to the application of neoclassical economics. The researcher begins by first choosing what she believes to be the appropriate oligopoly model, for the industry – say the Cournot model. An assumption is made about the goals of the firms, most likely that they maximize profits, and with these the equilibrium outputs and price can be determined both before and after the merger. Given these it is quite straightforward to compute the welfare loss from any price increase caused by the merger. In contrast, a practitioner of evolutionary economics is much more likely to be interested in tracing out the effects of a whole series of mergers over time on the concentration levels of an industry, or of the entire economy.

Winter's (1984) analysis of Schumpeterian innovation processes provides a good illustration of evolutionary modeling. Winter seeks to model and compare Schumpeter's description of the innovation process in his early work, *The Theory of Economic Development* (1911, 1934), with his later views as expressed

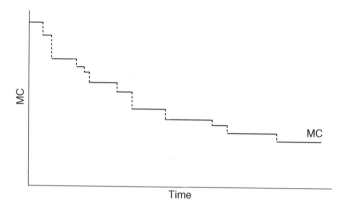

Figure 4.9 MC over time with Schumpeterian innovation.
Source: Adapted from Winter, 1984.

in *Capitalism, Socialism and Democracy* (1950). In the earlier work, Schumpeter stressed the role of the entrepreneur who introduces radical innovations thereby creating both NFs and whole new industries. In the later work, Schumpeter argued that the innovation process had been taken over and routinized by the giant corporations. Winter's modeling of these two views of the innovation process can be likened to someone searching for needles in a haystack. Upon each needle is written a cost-reducing innovation. Under the entrepreneurial innovation process, each innovation is a radical departure from all previous processes in use. If, at any point in time, an innovation is discovered with lower costs than any existing process, it is adopted and defines the level of costs in the industry until a new and superior cost-reducing innovation is found. The evolution of the industry's cost structure under these assumptions looks something like that depicted in Figure 4.9. Marginal costs (MC) remain constant over a stretch of time until a needle is found with a lower cost process written on it. At this time the innovation is adopted and costs sink to the new level where they remain until an innovation is found with even lower costs. It displaces the previous innovation and so on.

The process of innovation is, of course, stochastic. Sometimes a very long interval may exist between the discovery of superior innovations, sometimes the interval is quite short. At first the average time between discoveries is fairly short, and some of them result in substantial cost reductions. With time it becomes more and more difficult to find a needle containing a lower cost than the process already in existence. The average interval between innovations increases and the average fall in costs declines over time.

The process of routinized innovation in large companies is different. Here, each discovery constitutes an *improvement* on the existing cost structure rather than a complete displacement of it. Cost reductions occur more smoothly and are of smaller size.

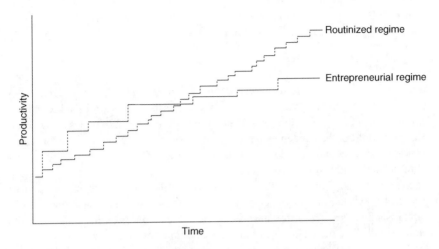

Figure 4.10 The evolution of productivity in two Schumpeterian regimes.
Source: Adapted from Winder, 1984.

Winter incorporates these and other assumptions about the innovation process into his simulation models and derives several interesting findings. One of these is illustrated in Figure 4.10. Although productivity tends to increase faster at first in an industry populated by entrepreneurial firms, the steady progress that large corporations make through their R&D programs is such that they eventually overtake and surpass the entrepreneurial industry's productivity level.

Schumpeter's depictions of the capitalistic innovation process can be interpreted as accurate descriptions of corporate capitalism at two points in its evolution – at the beginning of the twentieth century when the corporate landscape was dotted with entrepreneurial/family led companies, and in the middle of the twentieth century when the large, R&D-conducting corporations towered over the landscape. It is also possible to interpret these two models as descriptions of a single industry at different points in its life cycle – the entrepreneurial stage characterizing its early phases, routinized R&D characterizing its mature phase. The product life-cycle literature reviewed above is consistent with this interpretation. Viewed in this light, we see that *both* descriptions of the innovation process are valid for any given industry at different points in its life cycle, and for different industries at a given point in time.

Research by Pavitt *et al.* (1987) is consistent with this interpretation. They discovered that the size distribution of the firms that accounted for 4,378 significant innovations in the United Kingdom since the Second World War was U-shaped. Firms with fewer than 1,000 employees accounted for only 3.3 percent of the R&D undertaken in the United Kingdom, but 34.9 percent of the major innovations. At the same time, however, the 100 largest UK companies accounted for an equally large fraction of significant innovations. The left-hand-side of the U is presumably made up of the kind of entrepreneurial firms that Schumpeter first wrote about almost 100 years ago, the right-hand-side of the U by corporations who have successfully routinized the innovation process.

Conclusions

Why did communism collapse in Eastern Europe in 1989 and in the Soviet Union in 1991? Certainly, an important part of the answer was that it was a colossal economic failure. When one asks why it was an economic failure, or in what ways it was an economic failure, the concepts that we usually use to study economic performance in neoclassical economics do not seem appropriate. Certainly, most enterprises were not too small to take advantage of static scale economies, since they were often much bigger than in the West. Peter Murrell (1990) has shown that the relative prices of goods exported from communist countries looked similar to those from capitalist countries. The problem was not one of the planners failing to set "relative prices right." The most significant failings of communism appear to have been in the form of X-inefficiency and dynamic inefficiency. Production in the communist countries took place far inside of the potentially available isoquants, and these isoquants shifted inward at a far slower pace than in the West. Explanations for this are not the main fare of neoclassical economics. They belong more to transaction costs economics, and to Schumpeterian or evolutionary economics.

These literatures contain fewer QEDs per page than appear in orthodox neoclassical economics. In their place one often finds essentially historical accounts of how firms or industries have evolved, or simulations of their future evolution. From these the analyst attempts to obtain an understanding of how competition functions as a dynamic process. This seemed to Schumpeter the most important aspect of the competitive process, and still seems so to many of his followers today.

Notes on the literature

For an excellent survey of many of the themes discussed in this chapter, see Richard Caves (1998).

David Mowery and Nathan Rosenberg (1998) provide a readable history of innovations in three major sectors of the US economy over the twentieth century. They highlight the relative roles of small and large firms in this process. Alfred Chandler's *Scale and Scope* (1990) is a more sweeping history of the evolution of the giant corporation in the United States, Germany, and the United Kingdom.

After Schumpeter, Richard Nelson and Sidney Winter must be deemed the undisputed fathers of evolutionary economics and their *An Evolutionary Theory of Economic Change* (1982) remains the classic treatment of the subject.

5   The managerial corporation

The separation of ownership from control

The corporate form as we know it today is the product of an evolutionary process that began in England as early as the seventeenth century. In most of the early corporations, ownership claims were held by a handful of individuals, some of whom also participated in management. The initial corporate charters were very specific with regard to the kind of activities the corporation could engage in. If the management of a company founded to make rifles wished to diversify into making pots and pans, or to purchase another company that made pots and pans, it would require the approval of its shareholders. Moreover, decisions like this typically required the *unanimous* approval of the shareholders. Even one shareholder's vote could block a merger. This tight control by shareholders characterized corporate structures in the United States as late as the mid-nineteenth century.

At that time there were also no organized markets for exchanging ownership claims. Shares were transferred to relatives or sold to friends. Shares were not widely distributed and most owners actively participated in the control of the firm. Control of corporations was by *voice* rather than by exit, and rested in the hands of corporate owners.

Innovations like the steam engine and the open hearth furnace for making steel greatly expanded the optimal size of firms in many industries, and created entirely new industries like the railroads with giant firms and giant demands for capital. To satisfy these demands large numbers of shares were issued and shareholder numbers grew. Toward the end of the nineteenth century, organized markets to exchange shares opened in New York and in the capitals of Europe.

To attract corporations and the jobs and taxes they bring with them, many state legislatures rewrote their laws regarding incorporation, allowing corporations to write broad charters and thus granting considerable authority to managements. The unanimity rule was replaced by the simple majority rule and many important decisions like mergers no longer required the approval of the shareholders. As their numbers grew, shareholders increasingly relied on the *exit* option to express their pleasure or displeasure with "their" managers' decisions. Control via voice nominally shifted to the boards of directors, but they typically contained and were dominated by the managers themselves. Thus, over the latter half of the nineteenth and beginning of the twentieth centuries control of corporations shifted into the hands of their managers.

In 1932, Adolph Berle and Gardiner Means published a book in which they recounted the corporation's evolution, and documented the extent to which effective control had shifted from shareholders to managers. They argued that managers were in effective control of a company whenever its outstanding shares were so widely dispersed that no single person or group held 20 percent or more of the outstanding shares. Forty-four percent of the largest 200 corporations at that time, with 58 percent of their assets, met this criterion.

As the twentieth century enfolded and corporations continued to grow, and the second and third generations of their founding families reduced their shareholdings, the extent of the separation of ownership from control, which Berle and Means first documented, advanced. Using the lower cut-off of a 10 percent concentration of shares in a single group's hands, Robert Larner (1966) found that by the mid-1960s control of some 75 percent of the 200 largest US corporations had fallen to management.

Similar figures have been reported for UK corporations (Florence, 1961; Prais, 1976), so that by the 1960s or 1970s, in the United States and the United Kingdom, it is safe to say that well over half of the largest corporations were effectively controlled by their managers. The same could not be said for other countries in Europe, however, at least if the criterion for management control is that no single person or group owns, or can cast the votes for a large fraction of the companies' shares. In Continental European countries, family control of even quite large companies is still the general rule. In Germany, the large banks and other financial institutions control many of the largest companies. Large Italian firms rely heavily on bank borrowing for capital, and in this country banks also typically exercise considerable influence on corporate decision-making. Nevertheless, it is also true that in each of these, and most of the other European countries, corporations can be found where ownership and control are separated as in the United States.

In the last quarter of the twentieth century, two developments have taken place that arguably reduced the extent of a separation of ownership from control in the United States. The first was the hostile takeover wave of the late 1980s, when managements were replaced, ostensibly because of their poor performance owing to the discretion provided to them by the separation of ownership from control. Fearful of losing their jobs, corporate managers responded by substituting corporate debt for equity thereby increasing the fraction of outstanding shares that they themselves held. The second development has been the tremendous growth of pension funds, mutual funds, and other institutional holdings that has concentrated share holdings in the hands of the managers of these funds. Shareholdings in the United States today are more concentrated than Larner found in the early 1960s.[1]

The existence of a separation between ownership and control gives rise to what has come to be called the *principal–agent* problem. We turn now to a general analysis of this problem.

The principal–agent problem

Many persons who must make a decision, as say whether to purchase a car or not, often feel that they lack the information to make the "optimal" decision. In this situation, they may turn to someone whom they think is more knowledgeable on this matter – a friend who has recently purchased a car, a car salesperson, or a magazine that tests cars. In doing so, the car buyer enters into a principal–agent relationship, where the buyer is principal and the person consulted is the agent.

Everyone confronts numerous principal–agent situations everyday. You arrive at the railway station in an unfamiliar city and take a taxi to your hotel. In doing so you rely on the driver's knowledge of the city and honesty to choose the shortest route to the hotel. You are feeling ill and go to a doctor. You rely on the doctor's knowledge and honesty to diagnose your illness correctly and prescribe a painless and inexpensive cure for it. The goals of your agent may be different from yours, however. Both the taxidriver and the doctor may behave *opportunistically*. The taxidriver may set the meter at a high rate and take a circuitous route to the hotel. The doctor may recommend an appendectomy, where a simple laxative would have sufficed. The problem all principals confront in principal–agent situations is how to align the interests of the agent with those of the principal.

The separation between ownership and control gives rise to a classic principal–agent problem. The stockholder wants her agent–manager to maximize the value of her shares. The manager may be better off pursuing some other strategy. In this section, we examine the salient features of this principal–agent situation.[2]

Let $X = (x_1, x_2, \ldots, x_n)$ be a vector of inputs with, say, x_1 being blue-collar workers, x_2 secretaries, x_3 electricity, x_4 company cars, etc. The company's revenues and total costs are a function of these inputs, $R(X)$ and $C(X)$. Suppose that the company comes into existence, chooses a vector of inputs, obtains the revenues generated, and then goes out of existence giving all of the profits, $(\pi(X) = R(X) - C(X))$, to the firm's owners. The value of the ownership claims on the firm is then equal to these profits, $M(X) = \pi(X)$, ignoring discounting.

Consider first the situation in which there is no principal–agent problem. The top manager supplies all of the capital and is owner–manager of the firm. The vector of inputs that maximizes the profits of the firm maximizes the owner–manager's wealth. Call this vector X_W. The owner–manager may very well *not* choose this vector, however. Suppose, for example, that profits are maximized with the choice of a Volkswagen as the sole company car. If the owner–manager is wealthy enough to have several luxury cars for his private use, why should he have a single functional car for his professional use? Why should he ride in a Volkswagen to the office, and a Mercedes to the opera? We can expect the utility-maximizing owner–manager to use some of *his residual income* to engage in on-the-job consumption, to increase those elements in the vector of inputs that give him personal utility.

Let us define $D(X)$ as the amount of discretionary expenditures that the owner–manager makes, that is, inputs that provide him utility at the expense of his profits. We can measure this discretionary expenditures as simply the difference between

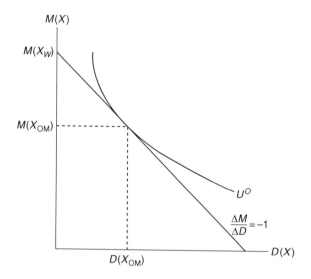

Figure 5.1 Optimal consumption of discretionary inputs for owner–manager.

the actual value of the company's shares and their potential maximum

$$D(X) = M(X_W) - M(X).$$ (5.1)

The owner–manager faces a trade-off between his wealth as owner and his on-the-job consumption as manager (see Figure 5.1). Both his final wealth and his on-the-job consumption give him positive utility. The owner–manager has normal convex-to-the-origin indifference curves as in Figure 5.1, and chooses the discretionary expenditures, $D(X_{OM})$, that allow him to reach his highest indifference curve. At this discretionary consumption the firm has a market value $M(X_{OM}) < M(X_W)$.

Now consider the situation in which the top manager does not own all of the company's shares. Suppose that he sells the fraction $(1 - \alpha)$ and retains α fraction for himself. Suppose further, that the capital market buys this $(1 - \alpha)$ fraction of shares at the same price as implied by $M(X_{OM})$. Thus, if the manager continued to consume $D(X_{OM})$ the outcome would be as before.

But, if the manager owns only α fraction of the shares his "budget constraint" line is not as before. Instead of having a slope of -1, as in Figure 5.1, where each dollar of discretionary consumption D lowers the manager's wealth by a dollar, it has a slope of $-\alpha$ as in Figure 5.2. Each dollar of D now costs the manager αD dollars of lost wealth ($0 < \alpha < 1$), not one dollar. This fall in the "price of D" leads to greater consumption of it, with $D(X_\alpha)$ being purchased, and the manager enjoying a higher level of utility because of the "subsidy" provided by the shareholders who absorb $(1 - \alpha)$ fraction of each dollar of the manager's discretionary consumption.

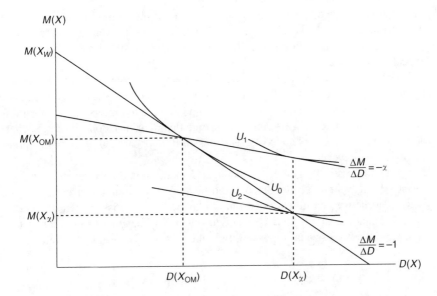

Figure 5.2 Consumption of discretionary inputs for manager owning α-fraction of shares.
Source: Adapted from Jensen and Meckling, 1976.

Rational shareholders will not provide this subsidy. If they have rational expectations, they realize that the manager will consume more D when he pays only α fraction of its cost than when he pays for all of it. They realize when they purchase the shares that they are not worth the price that produces $M(X_{OM})$, because the manager will not constrain his discretionary consumption to $D(X_{OM})$. The *rational expectations* assumption implies that the shareholders correctly predict the manager's choice of $D(X_\alpha)$, when he retains α fraction of the shares. The announcement of the sale of $(1 - \alpha)$ of the shares results in an immediate fall in their price to a level consistent with the manager's choice of $D(X_\alpha)$, $M(X_\alpha)$ as depicted in Figure 5.2. If we assume that shareholders have rational expectations, then the only possible equilibria are points on the original budget constraint line with a slope of -1. If we also assume utility maximization on the part of managers, then their indifference curve must be tangent to their budget constraint line with slope $-\alpha$, as depicted in Figure 5.2.

Two important implications follow. (1) Rational expectations result in the manager bearing *all* of the costs of his extra consumption of D, the costs of the principal–agent problem emerging from the sales of shares. The fall in market value of the firm from $M(X_W)$ to $M(X_\alpha)$ comes *before* the manager sells the shares. (2) Therefore, the manager will not sell the shares. His utility if he does, U_2, is lower than if he does not, U_0.

Obviously we have explained too much. We have explained away the issuance of corporate shares. But before discussing this anomaly, note the importance of the result. To the extent that the capital market is characterized by rational expectations, managers have an incentive to curtail their discretionary expenditures from their optimal value, and to inform shareholders that they have done so. The capital market eliminates the principal–agent problem under the rational expectations assumption.

Given the above analysis, how do we explain the widespread issuance of shares? Something must be missing from the discussion, or one of the assumptions must be wrong. One possibility, of course, would be that the managers could constrain their consumption to $D(X_M)$ *and* demonstrate that they have done so, that is, that no principal–agent problem exists. This possibility appears unlikely for the large corporation, however.

A second possibility is that the manager does not possess sufficient capital to finance the company's production possibilities. In such a situation, an entrepreneur with an attractive investment opportunity may be forced to issue shares and bear the full agency costs of their issuance to obtain any benefits from creating the company. We discuss a third possibility in the section "The firms life cycle."

The goals of managers

As discussed in the section on "The separation of ownership from control," the top managers in many of the largest corporations in the United States own tiny fractions of their companies' shares, perhaps as little as 0.1 percent and seldom as much as 2 or 3 percent. The previous section demonstrated that in equilibrium the slope of a manager's indifference curve equals the fractional level of his shareholdings, a number perhaps as small as 0.001. The slope of the manager's indifference curve also equals the marginal rate of substitution of D for wealth. The obvious implication is that managers of the largest US corporations carry their on-the-job consumption to nearly the satiation point, to a point where their marginal utility from additional D is near zero. This analysis thus implies the potential existence of a huge principal–agent problem between shareholders and managers in large corporations with widely dispersed ownership, and raises the question of just what it is in D that managers consume in excess. This question was first addressed in the so-called managerial-discretion literature which preceded the development of principal–agent models. We now review some of the hypotheses put forward in this earlier literature.

Leisure

Other than income, perhaps, the most obvious item that managers may pursue in excess is leisure.[3] To see what is involved here let us begin by considering the effort/leisure choice of an owner–entrepreneur. In Figure 5.3, hours of leisure per day for the owner–entrepreneur are depicted along the horizontal access from zero to a maximum of twenty-four. Hours of work are then measured from right to left.

As the owner–entrepreneur devotes effort to managing the firm, the difference between revenues and contractual costs $(R - C)$ grows reaching perhaps a maximum where fatigue leads the owner–manager to make errors. The difference

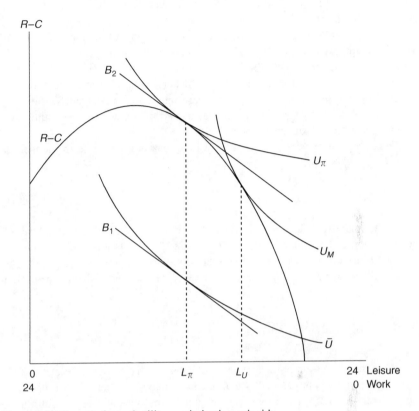

Figure 5.3 When profits and utility maximization coincide.

between revenues and contractual costs is *not* the economic profits of the firm, how-ever, because it does not take into account the outside opportunities of the owner–manager. Since both residual income and leisure can be presumed to be arguments in the owner–manager's utility function, her opportunity costs can be depicted by the indifference curve $\overline{U}$, representing the utility that the owner–manager can earn at her next best employment opportunity. The profits of the firm for each number of hours worked are then the distance between the $R - C$ and $\overline{U}$ curves.

Given the assumption of diminishing marginal returns to hours worked, the $R - C$ curve starts steeper than $\overline{U}$ where they cross on the right. The gap between them grows until the level of leisure/work is reached where the slopes of the two curves are equal, L_π. This level of work/leisure produces the maximum profits for the firm. A profit-maximizing owner–manager consumes L_π hours of leisure per day.

The first thing to note about this choice is that it seems highly unlikely that it would correspond with the utility maximizing choice of an owner–manager. The $R - C$ curve represents her opportunity set. Her utility maximizing leisure choice corresponds to the highest obtainable indifference curve along the $R - C$ curve.

This might easily be the indifference curve U_M and the level of leisure L_U would maximize her utility.

Now consider the implications of the owner–manager's utility maximizing decision coinciding with the profit-maximizing choice, U_M is tangent to $R - C$ at L_π (see U_π). For the profit-maximizing choice of an owner–manager to coincide with utility maximization for large numbers of owner–managers and all sorts of firm-specific opportunity sets, it must be the case that owner–managers' indifference curves have identical slopes along any vertical straight line. Such a condition can be interpreted in two different ways.

First, suppose owner–manager utility functions are separable in income and leisure

$$U(\pi, L) = u(\pi) + v(L). \tag{5.2}$$

Since the quantity of leisure consumed does not change along a vertical straight line in Figure 5.3, the marginal utility of leisure, MU_L, cannot change. But for the slopes of all indifference curves to be the same along a vertical straight line, the marginal utility of profits for an owner–manager, MU_π, must also remain constant, since

$$\text{slope of indifference curve} = -\frac{\Delta\pi}{\Delta L} = \frac{MU_L}{MU_\pi}. \tag{5.3}$$

Thus, under the assumption that owner–managers have separable utility functions, their leisure choices will simultaneously maximize both their utilities and their firms' profits, only if owner–managers have constant marginal utilities of money. No matter how much money an owner–manager has, she still gets the same satisfaction from a bit more, and she works just as hard to get it.

Notice that the parallel lines B_1 and B_2 resemble budget constraint lines for the owner–manager. If money and leisure are normal goods for her, she will consume more of each as her budget line shifts outward. If leisure were an inferior good, she would consume less as her budget line shifted outward. For the optimal choice with expanding opportunities to be a *constant* level of consumption, leisure must be just on the border between being a normal or an inferior good.[4]

Although some owner–managers may be workaholics as these considerations imply, one assumes that many are just normal people, who indulge in some additional leisure as their incomes grow. If this is true of owner–managers, for whom each dollar reduction in profit because of increased leisure consumption implies a dollar loss in income, what will be true of those managers, who own only a tiny fraction of a company's shares? How much additional leisure will a manager consume, if each dollar's fall in profits due to increased leisure causes the manager to lose but a few cents in income?

Leisure is one candidate for inclusion in a manager's objective function in addition to the profits of the firm.

Sales

William Baumol once observed that whenever he asked a business manager how business was, the manager responded by describing recent movements in sales. A manager's first thought was of sales rather than of profit. This observation led Baumol to postulate that managers maximized the *sales* of their firm not its profits (Baumol, 1967).

Baumol postulated that managers felt obliged to earn a reasonable or normal profit rate, and determined what this rate should be by looking at what other similar firms (say companies in the same industry) were earning. Managers sought to maximize their company's sales subject to the constraint that its profits did not fall below this normal or minimally acceptable level. The choice is depicted in Figure 5.4.

Let X be the firm's output. Its profits reach a maximum at output X_π. A sales-maximizing management expands its output to X_s, however, if it feels constrained to earn no more than $\bar{\pi}$ in profits.

If the sales maximizer expands output by cutting price, its demand elasticity may fall as output expands, as for example when it faces a straight line demand schedule. If its demand would become inelastic before the output X_s is reached, the sales maximizer will cut price only to the point where its demand elasticity is unity. In this situation, its profits would exceed $\bar{\pi}$, and its sales would fall short of X_s.

Sales can be expanded in other ways than just by cutting price, however. The firm may engage in advertising beyond the profit-maximizing level, for example.

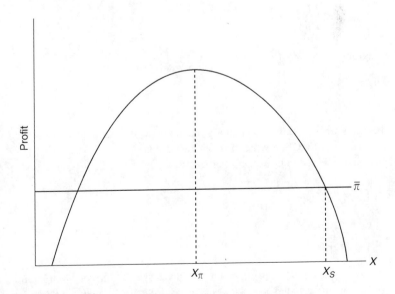

Figure 5.4 Sales maximization.

Given the many options like advertising that firms have to expand sales, we do not expect a sales maximizer to choose outcomes that result in profits greater than $\bar{\pi}$.

Baumol's sales maximization hypothesis advances a plausible goal for managers, and is analytically tractable (see following section). Without knowing why and how managers decide on $\bar{\pi}$, however, we do not have a full explanation for what drives managers' decisions. We shall try to supply a full explanation below, when we take up the growth-maximization hypotheses.

Sales maximization analytics

Managers wish to maximize sales revenue, R, subject to the constraint that profits not fall below $\bar{\pi}$. Let us write R as a function of both output X and advertising A, $R = R(X, A)$. If production costs are $C(X)$, the revenue maximizing firm's goal becomes the maximization of R subject to the constraint $\pi = \bar{\pi}$. Writing this as a Lagrangian we obtain

$$O_R = R(X, A) + \lambda[R(X, A) - C(X) - A - \bar{\pi}]. \tag{5.4}$$

Maximizing with respect to output gives

$$\frac{\partial O_R}{\partial X} = \frac{\partial R}{\partial X} + \lambda \frac{\partial R}{\partial X} - \lambda \frac{\partial C}{\partial X} = 0, \tag{5.5}$$

from which it follows that

$$\frac{\partial R}{\partial X} = \frac{\lambda}{1 + \lambda} \frac{\partial C}{\partial X}. \tag{5.6}$$

The Lagrangian constant $\lambda > 0$, and thus

$$\frac{\partial R}{\partial X} < \frac{\partial C}{\partial X}. \tag{5.7}$$

At the sales-maximizing output marginal revenue is less than marginal costs. Output is greater than that which maximizes profits.

Maximizing (5.4) with respect to A we obtain

$$\frac{\partial R}{\partial A} + \lambda \frac{\partial R}{\partial A} - \lambda = 0, \tag{5.8}$$

$$\frac{\partial R}{\partial A} = \frac{\lambda}{1 + \lambda}. \tag{5.9}$$

Since the profit-maximizing management invests in advertising only until the last dollar of advertising produces one more dollar of revenue ($\partial R/\partial A = 1$), equation (5.9) implies that a sales maximizer advertises more than a profit maximizer.

Staff and emoluments

Oliver Williamson once observed that white-collar employment for some companies with volatile demand schedules varies more over the business cycle than their blue-collar employment. Since blue-collar workers are essential to producing output, this observation led to the inference that white-collar workers are to some degree *less essential* than blue-collar workers. White-collar workers are in part a luxury which managements indulge in when times are good, and cut back when times are tough. The kind of white-collar workers that Williamson had in mind here would be secretaries, managerial assistants, and the like. People, who could relieve managers of some of their duties and make their work more enjoyable.

Williamson (1963, 1964) added to these the other good things in life from which managers can obtain pleasure (luxurious offices, fancy company cars, etc.), and put forward the hypothesis that managers gained utility from the staff and other emoluments of the firm, and purchased these in excess.

The problem is illustrated in Figure 5.5. Up to a point, adding staff and emoluments, S, increases profits. An efficient manager needs administrative support, and some emoluments – like a company car – can increase a manager's efficiency. But eventually staff and emoluments increase costs by more than the extra revenues that they generate and profits fall. (A Volkswagen as a company car may increase profits, a Rolls Royce reduces them.)

If managers get utility from profits as well as S, perhaps because their incomes or their job security are tied to profits, then managers have the usual convex to the origin indifference curves. With a concave profit function serving as

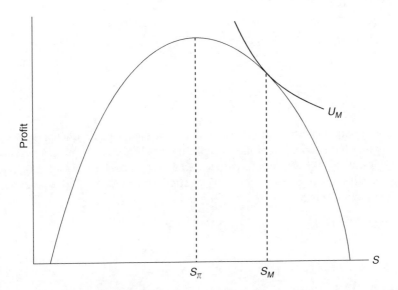

Figure 5.5 Staff and emoluments.

the opportunity set, utility-maximizing managers choose more than the profit-maximizing level of S (S_M rather than S_π). A reduction of profits due to a demand shift shrinks the managers' opportunity set from say π_1 to π_2, and leads to the staff reductions that Williamson observed.

"Consumption" of staff and emoluments is a plausible managerial goal, and Williamson (1964) provided empirical support for his hypothesis. "Excess consumption" of staff and emoluments is unlikely to be of quantitative significance for the *top* managers of large corporations, however. The profits of these firms run into the billions, and a few extra secretaries and a Rolls Royce or two will not have much impact on them. If the pursuit of staff and emoluments extends through all levels of the corporate pyramid, however, it will have a great impact. Thus, the significance of managerial consumption of staff and emoluments is linked to the idea of internal control loss, also developed by Williamson (1967, 1970, ch. 2). But this leaves open what it is, that the top managers pursue. We propose an alternative goal in the section on "Growth." But first we examine the analytics of the pursuit of staff and emoluments.

Staff and emoluments analytics

Let a manager's utility function contain both profits, π, and staff and emoluments, S, with $\pi = R(X, S) - C(X) - S$. The manager chooses X and S to maximize his utility, that is, his objective function is

$$O_S = U(R(X, S) - C(X) - S, S). \tag{5.10}$$

Maximizing first with respect to output we obtain

$$\frac{\partial O_S}{\partial X} = \frac{\partial U}{\partial \pi}\frac{\partial R}{\partial X} - \frac{\partial U}{\partial \pi}\frac{\partial C}{\partial X} = 0. \tag{5.11}$$

From which follows

$$\frac{\partial R}{\partial X} = \frac{\partial C}{\partial X}. \tag{5.12}$$

This is a very important result, for it states that managers, who pursue S in excess of what maximizes profits, behave nonetheless in their price and output decisions as profit maximizers. *All standard price theory developed under the profit-maximization assumption is directly applicable to S-oriented managers.*

Maximizing equation (5.10) with respect to S yields

$$\frac{\partial O_S}{\partial S} = \frac{\partial U}{\partial \pi}\frac{\partial R}{\partial S} + \frac{\partial U}{\partial \pi}(-1) + \frac{\partial U}{\partial S} = 0. \tag{5.13}$$

From which we obtain

$$\frac{\partial R}{\partial S} = 1 - \frac{\partial U/\partial S}{\partial U/\partial \pi}. \tag{5.14}$$

Profit maximization requires that $\partial R/\partial S = 1$, and equation (5.14) implies that $\partial R/\partial S < 1$, which is to say that the manager purchases staff and emoluments beyond the level that maximizes profits as we saw in Figure 5.5. Indeed, equation (5.14) merely states algebraically what we see in Figure 5.5. Rewriting equation (5.14) as

$$\frac{\partial R}{\partial S} - 1 = -\frac{\partial U/\partial S}{\partial U/\partial \pi},$$
(5.15)

we have on the right-hand side of equation (5.15) the slope of the manager's indifference curve, and on the left-hand side the slope of the profit function – the change in revenue with respect to a change in S less the reduction in profit caused by increasing S (1.0).

Growth

Robin Marris (1963, 1964, 1998) postulated that managers were not interested in maximizing the size of their companies, but rather their growth rates. Managers might seek to expand or maintain their company's growth to obtain both the pecuniary and the nonpecuniary benefits that accompany growth (Marris, 1964, ch. 2).

One of the iron laws of hierarchical organizations is that bosses get paid more than the people whom they supervise. This law implies that a person's income is higher, the higher up in the hierarchy that person is. A large increase in the size of a corporation eventually increases the number of levels in its hierarchy. A manager at a particular level should see the number of levels grow beneath him, and thus his salary also. As we shall see in the section on "Managerial compensation" a strong link does exist between how much managers are paid and the size of their companies. This link can explain why managers would maximize sales as Baumol postulated or growth in sales as Marris did.[5]

In many companies, openings in the managerial ranks are typically filled by promoting people from within the organization (Doeringer and Piore, 1971). The faster a firm is growing, the more the openings that appear above him in the hierarchy, and the better are his chances for promotion. This link between growth and the likelihood of being promoted gives managers an additional pecuniary reason to see that their company grows fast.

Reaching the top of the hierarchy of a large corporation can bring fame and fortune to a manager. In economics, we focus heavily upon the financial motives for certain actions. Workers are interested in income and leisure, and that is all. Investors are interested in income and risk. It is natural therefore in considering why managers might wish to see their firm grow faster to postulate that it is simply and solely because they will earn more. But managers of large corporations have sufficiently large incomes that further increases may not seem that important to some. Nonpecuniary goals like the power and prestige of running a giant corporation may take hold. The CEO of the 10th largest company in the United States is much more likely to see his face on the cover of *Business Week* than is the CEO of the 1,000th largest company. If having one's picture on the cover of a wide circulation magazine gives a person utility, then he will pursue those strategies that make this more likely.

At the beginning of the twentieth century, when managerial capitalism was in its infancy, Joseph Schumpeter expressed with eloquence the importance of nonpecuniary goals to the men, who were founding the enterprises that were to grow into Europe's and America's industrial giants.[6]

> First of all, there is a dream and the will to found a private kingdom, usually, though not necessarily, also a dynasty. The modern world really does not know any such positions, but what may be attained by industrial or commercial success is still the nearest approach to medieval lordship possible to modern man. Its fascination is specially strong for people who have no other chance of achieving social distinction. The sensation of power and independence loses nothing by the fact that both are largely illusions. Closer analysis would lead to discovering an endless variety within this group of motives, from spiritual ambition down to mere snobbery. But this need not detain us. Let it suffice to point out that motives of this kind, although they stand nearer to consumers' satisfaction, do not coincide with it.
>
> Then there is the will to conquer: the impulse to fight, to prove oneself superior to others, to succeed for the sake, not of the fruits of success, but of success itself. From this aspect, economic action becomes akin to sport – there are financial races, or rather boxing-matches. The financial result is a secondary consideration, or, at all events, mainly valued as an index of success and as a symptom of victory, the displaying of which very often is more important as a motive of large expenditure than the wish for the consumers' goods themselves. Again we should find countless nuances, some of which, like social ambition, shade into the first group of motives. And again we are faced with a motivation characteristically different from that of "satisfaction of wants" in the sense defined above, or from, to put the same thing into other words, "hedonistic adaption."
>
> Finally, there is the joy of creating, of getting things done, or simply of exercising one's energy and ingenuity. This is akin to a ubiquitous motive, but nowhere else does it stand out as an independent factor of behavior with anything like the clearness with which it obtrudes itself in our case. Our type seeks out difficulties, changes in order to change, delights in ventures. This group of motives is the most distinctly anti-hedonist of the three.
>
> (Schumpeter, 1934, p. 93f.)

Marris suggested that the constraint on managerial pursuit of growth was the threat of takeover and dismissal. This threat increases as managers in pursuit of growth invest at greater levels than would maximize shareholder wealth. Excessive investment causes the firm's market value to fall below its potential maximum reducing the *valuation ratio*, V, the ratio of the firm's market value to the book value of its assets. When this valuation ratio falls far enough, the firm becomes an attractive target for some wealth-seeking outsider, who can toss the management out, reverse its policies and obtain the gain from raising the firm's market value. Marris introduced both the threat of takeover as a constraint on managerial discretion and the valuation ratio as a statistic for measuring that constraint. Subsequently, Tobin (1969) introduced the q-ratio in which the book value of assets in Marris' V is replaced by their replacement costs. Most empirical works now use Tobin's q. We shall refer to both.

To see what is involved in managerial pursuit of growth consider the following simple model. The firm's profits in year t equal the return, r, on its capital at the end of period $t - 1$

$$\pi_t = r K_{t-1}. \tag{5.16}$$

Investment in year t is the change in capital stock between $t - 1$ and t

$$I_t = K_t - K_{t-1}. \tag{5.17}$$

The firm faces a set of investment opportunities, which are growing at a constant rate. The managers make a once and for all decision of how much of each year's profits to invest and how much to pay out as dividends. Let b be the fraction of profits that are retained and reinvested, and therefore $(1 - b)$ the dividend payout ratio. Then

$$I_t = b\pi_t \quad \text{and} \quad D_t = (1 - b)\pi_t. \tag{5.18}$$

But then

$$I_t = br K_{t-1},$$

and

$$K_t = K_{t-1} + br K_{t-1} = (1 + br)K_{t-1}. \tag{5.19}$$

Thus, the firm's growth rate is the product of its retention ratio and its return on capital, $g = rb$.

The market value of the firm at any point in time is the present discounted value of its future dividends

$$M_0 = \sum_{t=1}^{\infty} \frac{D_t}{(1 + i)^t} = \sum_{t=1}^{\infty} \frac{(1 + g)^t D_0}{(1 + i)^t}, \tag{5.20}$$

where i is the firm's discount rate or cost of capital. If $i > g$ (5.20) simplifies to (dropping the 0 subscript)

$$M = \frac{D}{i - g} = \frac{(1 - b)r K}{i - rb}. \tag{5.21}$$

The market value of a firm at any point in time is a function of its current capital stock, the returns on that capital, its retention ratio, and its cost of capital.

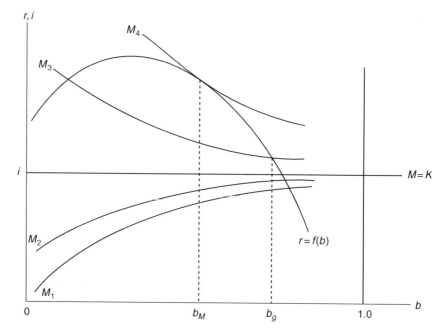

Figure 5.6 Growth maximization subject of a takeover constraint.

Assuming that after some point there are diminishing marginal returns to investment, the opportunities facing a firm look like those depicted in Figure 5.6. Each M_i curve represents combinations of b and r that yield a given market value. Holding the retention ratio b fixed higher curves involve higher rates of return and higher market values ($M_1 < M_2 < M_3 < M_4$). The horizontal line through $r = i$ represents a market value for the firm equal to the value of the capital stock K. M_i above this horizontal are greater than K, below are less than K. Since the present value of a stream of zeros from now to infinity is zero, the market value of a firm that pays zero dividends is simply the value of its capital stock. Thus, all market value curves converge on K as b approaches 1.0.

If a firm's management maximized the firm's market value, it would choose the retention ratio that allowed it to reach the highest iso-market value curve along its opportunity set $r = f(b)$. That would be curve M_4 with a retention ratio of b_M. A management that valued the growth of the firm, because of the personal benefits it produced, would select a higher retention ratio. If it feared a takeover should its market value fall below M_3, but not above it, it would select b_g. Alternatively, one could think of the M_i curves in Figure 5.6 as indifference curves for managers, whose utility depends only on the firm's market value. Indifference curves for managers who obtain utility from both higher market values (greater security from takeover), *and* growth have a greater tilt to the right than the M_i

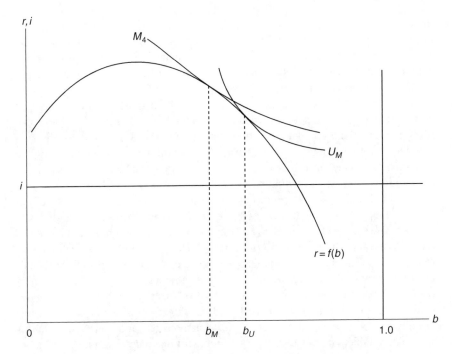

Figure 5.7 Utility maximization by growth-oriented managers.

curves. In choosing a retention ratio that allowed them to reach the highest level of utility along $r = f(b)$, they would again choose a higher b than b_M, say like b_U in Figure 5.7.[7]

The conflict between a growth-oriented management and its shareholders thus reduces to disagreement over the firm's retention policies. The management pays too little in dividends, retains and invests too much, and grows too fast. Although it is possible that managers might on occasion also pursue excessive growth by issuing debt or equity,[8] such a policy could not be successfully pursued indefinitely. The need to pay interest on the debt would prevent managers from indefinitely using it to finance projects that did not cover the interest. Issuing equity to finance such projects would lower the value of outstanding equity. Continual resort to the equity market to finance low return projects would lead the market to discount the newly issued shares *before* they were bought.[9]

Finally, it should be noted that a growth-maximizing management, as one which gains utility from staff and emoluments, chooses price and quantity so as to maximize short-run profits (Williamson, 1966). Since the managers seek investment funds to obtain growth, they do not pass up short-run opportunities to increase their ability to invest and grow. Thus, all of neoclassical price theory is applicable to a growth-maximizing management.

The firm's life cycle

In the Marris growth model, managers choose a retention ratio, which determines the firm's return on capital, and capital, sales, profits, dividends, and investment all then grow indefinitely at the same rate. This steady-state view of firm growth contrasts starkly with the Schumpeterian view presented in the previous chapter. The Schumpeterian firm starts with the expectation of earning high returns and the successful few do. Growth and returns eventually decline, however. Although many enter into a long period of maturity in which their markets and their own sales grow at roughly equal rates, declining growth threatens all and some succumb to that threat. In this section, we explore the implications of combining the Schumpeterian view of firm life cycles with the hypothesis that managers of large corporations often are growth maximizers.[10]

Consider Figure 5.8. CF_y represents the cash flow (profits plus depreciation) of a small, young firm. Its managers perceive that it has attractive investment opportunities. The expected marginal rate of return for the young firm (mrr_y) intersects the CF_y line above the firm's cost of capital i_y. The young firm pays no dividends, reinvests all of its cash flow, and raises additional capital externally. Ownership of the young firm is likely to reside in a few hands with the entrepreneurial founder(s) owning a large fraction of shares. Those who do own shares at this time have gambled on the firm's becoming a success, and wish to see it raise external capital as cheaply as possible. No conflict exists between managers and shareholders at this time. Shareholders do not fear that managers will try to grow too fast, but rather that the firm will not be able to exploit its investment opportunities to the fullest.

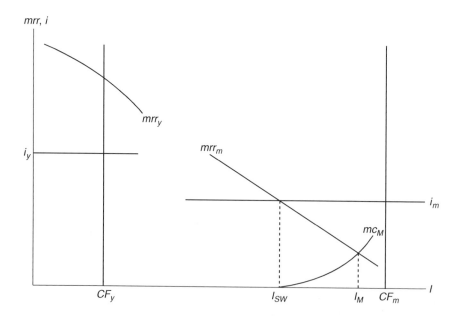

Figure 5.8 Investment choices over the firm's life cycle.

As we saw in Chapter 4, the perceptions of the founders of new firms about their ultimate success are frequently ill-founded. But those companies that do succeed see their cash flows grow tremendously. The cash flow for a mature firm, CF_m, is placed to the right in Figure 5.8. The break in the bottom horizontal line indicates that the cash flows of the truly successful giant company are far greater than for the cash-short younger company. The cost of capital for the mature company, i_m, is drawn lower than that for the young one to represent the different opportunities for raising external capital generally faced by new firms.

Of course, a successful company's investment opportunities grow as well as its cash flows, but usually not as rapidly. At some point in the company's life cycle, it finds itself in the situation depicted on the right-hand side of Figure 5.8. The mature firm's marginal returns on investment schedule intersects its cost of capital to the left of the CF_m line. If its management maximizes the shareholders' wealth, it invests I_{SW} and pays $CF_m - I_{SW}$ in dividends. By the time that the successful company has grown this large, its numbers of outstanding shares and shareholders have expanded tremendously. Ownership has become separated from control, and managers have the discretion to advance their own welfare at the shareholder's expense.

The cost of capital for a shareholder-wealth-maximizing company is the return its shareholders can earn by investing in other companies of comparable risk. But for the management that derives benefits from the firm's growth, the shareholder's opportunity costs are of consequence only to the extent that they influence the threat of takeover. This threat is zero, let us assume, if the managers maximize shareholder wealth, but rises as they go beyond that level. We depict the marginal *psychological* cost of investing beyond I_{SW} from the perception of higher probabilities of a takeover as mc_M. The mature company's managers trade off shareholder wealth for growth by investing $I_M > I_{SW}$ and paying less in dividends.

There are a couple of observations to be made concerning this life-cycle variant of the growth-maximization hypothesis. First, if one looks at a cross-section of firms, it is not necessarily the fastest growing firms that harm their shareholders through the excessive pursuit of growth. The fastest growing firms in the economy are generally among the youngest firms, and as we have seen, no manager–shareholders' conflict is likely to exist for them. Where this conflict is most acute is for the very mature firms, for which the growth rate that would maximize shareholder wealth is zero or negative. Here the prospects of managers are not of expanding hierarchies, expanding salaries, and expanding opportunities for promotion, but rather of contracting opportunities and, except for those at the very top, even of being released from a shrinking firm. Faced with this specter, many company managers seek ways to expand their company.

The life-cycle model implies that the level of dividends that maximizes shareholders' wealth is zero for an initial set of years followed by a gradually increasing dividend pay-out ratio. The growth-maximizing management also pays dividends, but it pays less than the optimal level. Thus, the conflict between managers and shareholders appears only slowly over time, as a somewhat slower expansion of the dividend payout ratio than is in the shareholders' best interests. Appearing only slowly, it may be difficult to detect.

A company faced with a slow-growing or declining market has two choices for avoiding stagnation and decline: it can expand its share of this market, or diversify into new ones. Growth can be sustained indefinitely only through diversification. Thus, we expect the maturing company to resort to internal diversification by developing new products and/or external diversification through mergers. Even in a steady-state world, a company must (continually) diversify to sustain a growth rate above that of its company's market. If growth through diversification is pursued to advance only the managers' welfare, we expect investments in diversification to have low returns. We will see in Chapter 9 that this has by-and-large been the case.

We are now in a position to present the third reason promised in the section, "The principal–agent problem" for why external capital markets cannot effectively constrain the managers of large corporations. Companies resort to external equity markets most heavily when they are young, have attractive investment opportunities, and are short of cash. The chief threats to shareholders' wealth at that time are not managerial consumption, but the risks of the market including the possible failure of the company. The principal–agent problem is likely to be most acute, however, when corporations are large and mature. But in this phase of their life cycle managers do not rely on the equity market for funds, but rather use their internal fund flows. For the capital market to constrain today's actions of the managements of large mature corporations, it would have to offer lower prices for the shares they issued 50 or 75 years ago. Anticipating this managers at that time would have constrained not only their own discretionary on-the-job consumption, but also that of all future generations of managers including the present one. What such constraints could be and how they might be enforced is not obvious. We conclude that the external capital market is not likely to be an effective constraint on the managers of a large, mature corporation. Jensen and Meckling, the developers of the capital market constraint hypothesis, admitted as much when they observed that:

> One of the most serious limitation [sic] of the analysis is that as it stands we have not worked out in this paper its application to the very large modern corporation whose managers own little or no equity.
>
> (Jensen and Meckling, 1976, p. 354)

Constraints on managerial discretion

In addition to an efficient capital market ruled by rational expectations, four other constraints on managerial opportunism have been discussed in the literature. We now discuss each of these.

Product and factor markets

In an economy with perfectly competitive markets, any factor that fails to receive its opportunity costs from one firm withdraws to another. A management's discretion to pursue anything but mere survival in the industry depends on their being enough "slack" in the competitive process for it to divert the firm's revenues to its own goals, or simply to enjoy more leisure. To the extent that competitive forces and the antitrust authorities maintain a tight competitive environment, managers will be unable to deviate from doing anything other than maximizing their firm's profits, if they wish it to survive.

As discussed in the previous chapter, several studies from a variety of countries have found that a significant fraction of firms seems capable of earning above normal returns on capital, virtually indefinitely. The competitive process does not appear to be sufficiently Darwinian to eliminate all corporate rents. Managers at the top of a company with large permanent rents have the resources to pursue their own interests if they so choose.[11]

The market for managers

Because the pursuit of their own goals by middle managers reduces profitability, top management can be expected to introduce controls and monitoring procedures to constrain this behavior. Middle managers who creatively and energetically maximize profits are more likely to be promoted. These middle managers are also more attractive candidates for jobs at other firms. A young manager seeking to rise to the top of her present employer, or to be hired for higher positions by some other companies can probably follow no better strategy than trying to maximize her company's profits, unless ordered to do otherwise.

Even a young president of a small to medium sized company may aspire to be appointed as top manager by the board of directors of a larger firm, and strive to increase those chances by making the profits of his present company as conspicuously large as possible. But the president of a large company, who has reached his fifties, as most have, is not likely to be greatly concerned about his *next job*. He has made it to the top, to the place where he always wanted to be. His thoughts are more likely to be of what he should do with his authority in this position, than of his chances of getting a different position. If expanding the size and growth of the company can bring personal rewards, he may be inclined to do so. Perhaps, on the other hand, this becomes the time to "cash in" on his past hard work by claiming a higher salary and more leisure. The absence of strict shareholder control allows him some latitude to follow these alternative goals. Even a well-functioning market for managers at the lower and middle management levels leaves the possibility of the pursuit of other objectives open to higher level managers.[12]

The market for corporate control

A common share has value for two reasons: (1) it is an ownership claim on the dividends paid by the firm, and in the case of its dissolution on the value of its assets, and (2) it confers a right to vote on certain organizational and strategic corporate decisions. Even if the former attribute and an efficient capital market do not suffice to constrain managerial discretion, the latter alone might.

In a zero-transaction-costs world even a slight deviation of a company's market value from its potential maximum would lead someone to purchase a controlling interest in it and remove the management, alter its policies, and claim the wealth gain from bringing the company to its maximum value. Marris (1963, 1964) postulated that this threat of takeovers was the chief constraint on managerial pursuit of growth, but that it was sufficiently loose to allow managers to deviate significantly from shareholders'-wealth-maximizing policies. Henry Manne (1965) coined the term "market for corporate control" to describe this process, and argued that this "market" did provide sufficient discipline to constrain managers effectively.

When Marris and Manne first discussed this process hostile takeovers were sufficiently rare, at least in North America, that it was difficult to determine how tight the takeovers' constraint was. In the merger wave at the end of the 1980s, hostile takeovers became more frequent and conspicuous and the impression grew that they were a powerful constraint on managers.

Despite some headline making hostile takeovers in the late 1980s, they remained a tiny fraction of all corporate acquisitions during this period (Bhagat *et al.*, 1990). Moreover, in response to the intensified threat of takeover, managements brought pressures on state legislatures to pass laws making hostile takeovers more difficult. Such laws now exist in all but a handful of states (Romano, 1987; Roe, 1993b). Thus, very few hostile takeovers have occurred in the United States since 1990.

Contractual constraints

The principal–agent contract

The principal–agent problem was introduced earlier in this chapter. The principal–agent literature has proposed a *contractual* solution to the principal–agent problem.[13] The principals (shareholders) would like to see their agents (the managers) maximize their wealth. But they do not have sufficient information to insure that the managers do so. They try therefore to design an employment contract that gives the managers incentives to maximize shareholder wealth. One such contract would assign all profits to the managers, but require that they pay a fixed payment to the shareholders. By making this payment large enough, the shareholders can ensure that the expected incomes of the managers, if they maximize the firm's profits, are just equal to their opportunity costs, that is, the minimum needed to retain them at their managerial job.

Although such a contract has ideal *incentive* effects – managers receive all of the residual income and thus have no incentive to shirk – it is suboptimal as an insurance contract. All of the risks of the enterprise are borne by managers.

If we assume that managers are risk averse and shareholders risk neutral, then the optimal *insurance* contract gives all of the residual income to the shareholders and a fixed income to the managers.[14]

The *Pareto optimal* contract must balance the gains from allowing risk-neutral shareholders to claim the residual income, against the positive incentive effects of having the managers receive all of the residual income. It is the optimal compromise between the optimal insurance and incentive contracts.

If shareholders – the principals – actually wrote the managers' employment contracts, we might be satisfied with such a compromise. As we shall see in the next section, however, a significant part of the real world managerial discretion problem arises because the shareholders do not write the managers' employment contracts. The managers do.

The basic principal–agent model

The problem faced by the principal is that she cannot observe perfectly the actions of the agent. To capture this fact, assume that the profits of the firm depend on both the efforts of the agent, e, and random shocks that are independent of the agent's actions, u, where u has an expected value of zero, $E(u) = 0$.

$$\pi = e + u. \tag{5.22}$$

Exerting effort causes disutility, while managers get positive utility from their income, y. For simplicity, assume that the disutility of effort can be measured in the same units as income, and write the agent's utility function as

$$U = U\left(y - \frac{de^2}{2}\right), \tag{5.23}$$

where d is a scalar that measures the disutility of effort of a particular agent.

To induce the agent to exert effort the principal must tie the agent's income to the profits of the firm. Let us assume that the principal accomplishes this with the following, simple linear compensation contract

$$y = \alpha + \beta\pi. \tag{5.24}$$

Given this compensation contract the agent's expected utility then becomes

$$E(U) = E\left(U\left[\alpha + \beta\pi - \frac{de^2}{2}\right]\right) = E\left(U\left[\alpha + \beta e + \beta u - \frac{de^2}{2}\right]\right). \tag{5.25}$$

The agent chooses effort to maximize equation (5.25)

$$\frac{dE(U)}{de} = U'(\cdot)\left(\beta - \frac{2de}{2}\right) = 0. \tag{5.26}$$

Since the marginal utility of income is positive, equation (5.26) implies

$$\beta = de \quad \text{or} \quad e = \frac{\beta}{d}. \tag{5.27}$$

The agent exerts greater effort, the more closely his income is tied to profits, and the smaller his level of disutility, d, from exerting effort.

A key assumption in the model is that the principal is risk neutral. We can capture this by assuming that the principal chooses a contract to maximize her expected income – the profits of the firm less what she pays the agent, $E(\pi - y)$. Replacing π and y we get

$$E(\pi - y) = E(e + u - \alpha - \beta e - \beta u). \tag{5.28}$$

Since β is a constant and $E(u) = 0$, (5.28) simplifies to

$$E(e + u - \alpha - \beta e - \beta u) = e - \alpha - \beta e. \tag{5.29}$$

The principal knows that the agent chooses effort to maximize his utility, and thus we can substitute from (5.27) into (5.29) to get the principal's expected income

$$E(\pi - y) = (1 - \beta)\frac{\beta}{d} - \alpha. \tag{5.30}$$

To induce the agent to work for the firm, he must be offered a contract that promises him at least the same level of expected utility, $\overline{U}$, as he can obtain at his next best employment

$$EU\left(\alpha + \beta e + \beta u - \frac{de^2}{2}\right) = EU\left(\alpha + \frac{\beta^2}{d} + \beta u - \frac{\beta^2}{2d}\right)$$

$$= EU\left(\alpha + \beta u + \frac{\beta^2}{2d}\right) \geq \overline{U}. \tag{5.31}$$

To obtain the Pareto optimal contract we can maximize the expected income of the principal as given in (5.30) subject to the constraint that the agent's expected utility as given in (5.31) equals his opportunity costs, $\overline{U}$, that is, maximize

$$L = (1 - \beta)\frac{\beta}{d} - \alpha + \lambda\left[EU\left(\alpha + \beta u + \frac{\beta^2}{2d}\right) - \overline{U}\right]. \tag{5.32}$$

Maximizing first with respect to α we obtain

$$\frac{\partial L}{\partial \alpha} = -1 + \lambda E(U') = 0 \quad \lambda = \frac{1}{E(U')}. \tag{5.33}$$

Maximizing with respect to β we obtain

$$\frac{\partial L}{\partial \beta} = \frac{1}{d} - \frac{2\beta}{d} + \lambda\left[E\left(U'u\right) + E(U')\frac{\beta}{d}\right]. \tag{5.34}$$

Note that $E(U'u) \neq 0$, even though $E(u) = 0$. If $\beta > 0$, then increases in u increase profits and managerial income and cause U' to fall, assuming that the agent has diminishing marginal utility of income. Under this assumption, $\beta > 0$ implies $E(U'u) < 0$.

Using (5.33) to replace λ in (5.34) and setting (5.34) equal to zero, we obtain with a little manipulation

$$\frac{1 - \beta}{d} = -\frac{E(U'u)}{E(U')}. \tag{5.35}$$

As just noted, $\beta > 0$ implies that $E(U'u)$ which is the covariance of U' and u, is negative. $\beta > 0$, therefore, implies that the right-hand side of (5.35) be positive,[15] which implies that $0 < \beta < 1$. The Pareto optimal incentive contract is a *sharing* contract, with the agent getting β fraction of profits ($0 < \beta < 1$), and the principal $(1 - \beta)$ fraction.

Note that if the agent were risk neutral, U' would be a constant, $E(U'u) = 0$, and the Pareto optimal contract would be the optimal incentive contract with $\beta = 1$ and the agent getting all of the residual to induce maximal effort. Conversely, the optimal insurance contract would give the risk neutral principal all of the residual and a fixed compensation to the agent, ($\beta = 0$). With profits dependent on unobserved effort by the agent, and the agent being risk averse, the Pareto optimal principal–agent contract becomes a compromise between the pure incentive and the pure insurance contracts.

Financial contracts

The principal–agent literature focuses on the incentives given to agent–managers by profit sharing contracts. The principal–shareholder writes the contract, and all control implicitly is assumed to remain with her. The financial contracting literature points out, however, that both control *and* profits can be shared between the principal and the agent. Namely, we can think of the contract joining the supplier of capital to a firm and the entrepreneur–manager as having two dimensions, one defining the *control rights* and another the *cash flow rights*. Both might conceivably lie with the capital supplier making the manager a hired employee, or both might lie with the manager making the capital supplier a bond holder. And most importantly, control and cash flow rights might be defined *contingent* on certain events. If, for example, the supplier of capital accepts a share of the profits of a new firm in exchange for financing its start-up, she might stipulate in the contract transferring the funds to the entrepreneur founder, that all control reverts to her, and thus she can dismiss the founder, should the firm not receive FDA approval for the wonder drug being developed.

One of the interesting distinctions emphasized in the financial contracts literature is between "tough" capital suppliers who reserve the right to seize certain assets of the firm in the case of specific contingencies, and soft suppliers who cannot make any specific claims, but can take over control in certain contingencies. The former are, of course, typically suppliers of debt, while the latter are suppliers of equity. By choosing the proper mix of tough and soft suppliers of capital, the optimal degree of constraint may be placed on the managers. One of the contributions of the financial contracts literature is, therefore, to offer a plausible justification for the existence of "optimal" debt/equity ratios.[16]

Managerial compensation

"Money isn't everything." The adage is undoubtedly as true for managers as it is for everyone else. In particular, we noted that managers might pursue growth for the power and prestige that comes with corporate size. Leisure, staff, and other forms of on-the-job consumption are objectives managers might also consume as alternatives to mere pecuniary gains. Managerial discretion may evidence itself in many ways other than in high compensation.

Although money isn't everything, it is something, and in particular it is something that can be fairly easily measured, in contrast say to power and prestige. Thus, not surprisingly, much of the literature which has tested for the effects of managerial discretion has looked for them in the heights of managerial compensation.

The earliest studies of this type typically estimated some variant on the following equation

$$y = a + b\pi + cR + u, \tag{5.36}$$

where y is a measure of managerial compensation, usually the top manager's salary or total compensation, or a small set of top managers, and π and R are profits and sales revenue. In this work, the profits maximization assumption was usually tested against Baumol's sales maximization hypothesis by comparing the coefficients b and c. A strong correlation between compensation and profits was taken to imply profits maximization, a strong correlation with sales to imply sales maximization.[17]

There are several problems with this approach. First, with respect to sales, we have seen that in a hierarchical organization, supervisors generally are paid more than those whom they supervise. The bigger the firm, the more layers there are in the hierarchy and the higher the top manager's salary will be. This size–salary relationship can be expected even for firms whose managers are profit maximizers. To determine whether managers have abused their discretion one must ascertain whether the firm has grown to a bigger size than is optimal for the shareholders, so that managers could rationalize receiving a higher salary.

In a perfectly competitive industry economic profits are zero. Managers must maximize profits for the firm to survive. Thus, some positive profits are necessary for the managers to have any discretion at all, and the higher the profits are the more latitude, ceteris paribus, managers have to pursue their own goals, including collecting a high salary. A positive correlation between managerial income and profitability cannot, therefore, be viewed as evidence that the managers are maximizing company profits.

A growth-maximizing management chooses price so as to maximize the firm's profits. The conflict between growth-maximizing managers and shareholders is *not over the level of profits*, but over their distribution between dividends and retained earnings. Shareholders, who wished to constrain managers from pursuing their own goals would tie managerial compensation to shareholder wealth.

Jensen and Murphy (1990) estimated the relationship between changes in shareholders' wealth and managerial income for a sample of over 1,000 US corporations over the 1974–86 time period. On average, a $1,000 increase in shareholder wealth led to a $3.25 increase in managerial compensation. If we think of this relationship as resulting from a linear principal–agent contract tying managerial income (y) to shareholder wealth (w), ($y = \alpha + \beta w$), then the Jensen–Murphy estimates imply a β for the average firm of 0.00325. The managerial compensation contract is almost a pure insurance contract, that provides little monetary incentive for managers to increase shareholder wealth. Although a few studies have come up with somewhat higher estimates of β, the general tenor of the empirical findings for the United States is that managerial compensation contracts do not provide great incentives for managers to increase shareholder wealth.[18]

One problem that exists in testing for the effect of managerial discretion on compensation comes in trying to measure managerial discretion, since it is likely to depend on the profitability of the firm, its size, the distribution of shareholdings and still other factors. Moreover, each company's management may elect to exercise whatever discretion it has to a different degree. To get around these problems, Mueller and Yun (1997) constructed an index of *exercised managerial discretion*. Since a growth-oriented management invests in projects with returns (r) less than shareholder opportunity costs (i), Mueller and Yun calculated an index of managerial discretion as $D = 1 - (r/i)$, with $(r/i \geq 1) \rightarrow (D = 0)$. They found that managerial compensation rose with D, and that managerial income was greater, the larger the firm was. Since there is no reason for shareholders to reward managers for investing in projects with returns less than the firm's cost of capital, these results imply that shareholders are not writing the managers' contract.[19]

Mueller and Yun tested for the impact of managerial discretion by comparing actual managerial compensation to that predicted by the size of the firm using a simple model of a firm's hierarchy. That model predicts that each supervisors' income is some multiple β of the people she supervises. On the assumption that the βs between each level i and $i - 1$ fall in the range $1.3 \leq \beta_i \leq 1.6$, one can use the firm's employment and predictions about the number of people each supervisor supervises to predict managerial compensation.[20] If the actual compensation of the top managers is much greater than this prediction, then the βs at one or more levels must fall well outside of this range. Since it would be expensive to have inordinately large βs toward the bottom of the hierarchy, one expects if excessive managerial compensation is an outcome of managerial discretion, that a big jump in compensation will occur near the top of the hierarchy. Such a jump was observed by Baker *et al.* (1994) in a detailed case study of a single, medium-sized service company. They observed eight hierarchical levels in the company, with a single person at the 8th level. The average increments (βs) between each level are given in Table 5.1.

The lowest increments are observed between the first and second levels in the hierarchy, and between the second and third levels, where employment is highest and salary increments most costly. All other increments fall roughly in the 1.3–1.6 range suggested by Williamson (1967) *except* for the increment between the 6th and 7th levels. Entry into the second highest level of the hierarchy is accompanied by a doubling of compensation. Although it is possible that there is some

Table 5.1 Employment (N) and average increments in
compensation (β_i) in a firm's hierarchy

Level	N_{1970}	N_{1977}	N_{1984}	β_i
8	1	1	1	1.48
7	2	2	4	2.07
6	9	10	25	1.40
5	22	57	86	1.64
4	212	528	1,003	1.47
3	293	683	1,195	1.23
2	442	789	1,165	1.18
1	439	795	1,253	

Source: Baker *et al.* (1994, pp. 894, 909).

discontinuous leap in managerial productivity or opportunity costs to explain this jump in compensation, it is also precisely the kind of increment one expects if the top managers exercise their discretionary authority by giving themselves high pay. The 7th and 8th levels contain the current CEO and his likely successor, and it is among this small group (between 3 and 5 people in this firm) that the pecuniary rewards of managerial discretion are shared.

Additional evidence linking managerial discretion to managerial compensation exists in other countries. Kato (1997) found that managers of "group" firms in Japan have 20–30 percent lower incomes than managers of independent firms. The shares of group firms are closely held by the other companies in the group, and thus the managers of these companies are more closely monitored than are those of independent companies, whose managements are controlled by outside shareholders as in the United States.

Conyon (1997) observed that the creation of a salary committee of directors to recommend managerial salary increments had a significant impact in constraining these increments. This finding suggests that managerial discretion and compensation can be curbed.

These rewards to managerial discretion can be great. Table 5.2 lists the total pay for the ten highest paid managers in 2001. The highest compensation Mueller and Yun observed over the 1978–90 period in their sample was \$52,661.000, about 50 times the highest salary warranted by the hierarchy model assuming $\beta = 1.6$ between all levels of the hierarchy. In the absence of salary committees or other constraints on managerial discretion, managers can be very generous to themselves. Perhaps, the strongest evidence that managerial compensation is a manifestation of managerial discretion is in the *weak* statistical fit of managerial compensation models to the data. The size of the firm is overwhelmingly the best predictor of managerial compensation, but even it, plus all of the other variables hypothesized to determine compensation, seldom explain more than 10 percent of the variation in managerial pay. Whether the top managers choose to pay themselves \$5 million or \$10 million or some other figure appears to be pretty much up to their own sense of propriety or hubris. The result being, as *The Economist* (June 3, 1995,

Table 5.2 Compensation for 10 Highest Paid CEO's in the United States, 2001

Chief executive	Company	Salary and bonus ($ million)	Long-term compensation ($ million)	Total pay ($ million)
Lawrence Ellison	Oracle	0.0	706.1	706.1
Jozef Straus	JDS Uniphase	0.5	150.3	150.8
Howard Solomon	Forest Laboratories	1.2	147.3	148.5
Richard Fairbank	Capital One Financial	0.0	142.2	142.2
Louis Gerstner	IBM	10.1	117.3	127.4
Charles Wang	Computer Associates Intl.	1.0	118.1	119.1
Richard Fuld Jr.	Lehman Brothers	4.8	100.4	105.2
James McDonald	Scientific-Atlanta	2.1	84.7	86.8
Steve Jobs	Apple Computer	43.5	40.5	84.0
Timothy Koogle	Yahoo	0.2	64.4	64.6

Source: *Business Week*, Special Report: Executive Pay, April 15th, 2002.

pp. 74 –77) noted, that managerial compensation figures are by and large "random numbers."

Conclusions

Technological changes in the nineteenth century required companies to raise vast amounts of capital and transformed corporations from small firms with closely held ownership claims to giant enterprises with dispersed ownership. Although ownership had the incentive and authority to monitor managers in the small firm, in the large enterprise ownership was so dispersed as to dull this incentive. Voice gave way to exit as the means for expressing satisfaction with management policies. Nominally, owners could exercise voice control over managers through "their representatives" on the boards of directors, which had the authority to approve or reject major policy decisions. Practically, outside members of these boards had neither the incentive nor the information to exercise such control. Such was the case from the large corporation's very beginning as is revealed in the following statement of the Board of Directors of the Pennsylvania Railroad in 1874.

> The present form of organisation (part-time directors and full-time officers) makes practical ciphers of the Directors, and this is from no deliberate intention, but from the very necessities of the case. Once a large business had reached a size that required the services of several full-time administrators, the board and the stockholders had only a negative or *veto* power on the government of their enterprise and on the allocation of its resources. They could say no, but they had neither the information or the awareness of the company's situation to propose realistic alternative courses of action.
>
> (Chandler, 1962, p. 313)

Nor are matters any different today, as evidenced in the following remarks of Carl Icahn, corporate gadfly and raider of the 1980s.

> You get there [to a board meeting] early in the morning, and everybody is reading the newspaper. The first thing is that everybody looks at their check, puts it in their pocket, smiles big, and then goes back to reading the newspaper.
>
> The meeting starts, you get the room dark and a few guys go to sleep. Then they put a slide machine up with a lot of numbers that even Einstein wouldn't understand.
>
> The CEO doesn't even do it. He gets some financial guy to show all these numbers. And then everybody is reading the newspaper anyway, or when it is dark they are sleeping.
>
> I was on one board and this went on for a while. I had no inside information being on that board because I couldn't figure out what they were doing. And that is the truth if there ever was truth.
>
> (*Washington Post*, May 19, 1985, p. H3)

That managers have considerable discretion to pursue their own goals there can be no question. What is less clear is what those goals are, and the consequences of their pursuit for the welfare of shareholders and for the welfare of the corporate economy.

We have examined several possible goals of managers that would conflict with shareholders' interests, and the possible constraints on managers' pursuit of these goals. We have also presented evidence indicating that managerial discretion does manifest itself in the arbitrarily large salaries, which managers receive.

Clearly, each extra dollar of potential profits and potential dividends that managers channel into their own pockets comes out of the pockets of shareholders, and thus contributes to the losses imposed on shareholders by the principal–agent problem. Moreover, the heights which managerial incomes sometimes reach offend common notions of propriety and equity.

On the other hand, if the only manifestation of managerial discretion were in the form of higher compensation than is warranted, its existence would have little if any impact on economic efficiency. Higher managerial incomes are essentially transfers from shareholders. To the extent that they lower the returns shareholders earn on equity, they might reduce the flow of funds to the corporate sector and indirectly lower social welfare by reducing corporate investment. But this latter effect is likely to be small, if the exercise of discretion is limited to the highest level managers. If, for example, the top five executives in a large corporation with a $1 billion a year profits, each inflate their incomes by $5 million, the resulting $25 million is but 1/40th of the company's total profits.

More significant social costs may arise if, in pursuing their own objectives, managers alter the size and growth of the firm, or perhaps other dimensions of its operations. Evidence on these matters and their consequences for social welfare are examined in subsequent chapters.

6   Corporate governance

In recent years, considerable attention has been devoted to differences across countries in the institutional environments in which corporations operate, and the consequences of these institutional differences for corporate performance. One branch of this literature has been concerned with corporate governance structures.[1] Under the broad heading of corporate governance are usually included (1) the identity and degree of concentration of ownership, (2) the institutional structure by which owners monitor and control managers by means of boards of directors and the like, and (3) the institutional structure for disciplining and replacing managers as, for example, through proxy contests and/or takeovers. A second branch of the literature focuses upon the broader legal environment in which corporations operate. Within this literature would come laws governing a shareholder's access to various sorts of information about a company, a shareholder's rights to sue the management for certain actions detrimental to the shareholder's interests, and so on.[2] Although corporate governance structures are imbedded within the broader legal system of a country and thus are affected by it, the two sets of institutions are not synonymous, as we shall explain shortly.

One distinction drawn within the corporate governance literature is between "insider" governance systems in which ownership stakes are concentrated and the major stakeholders are directly represented on the boards that monitor managers, and perhaps in management itself, and "outsider" governance systems in which ownership stakes are dispersed, and owners exercise indirect control on management by electing representatives to the monitoring boards, or perhaps by voting on specific proposals of management. The United States and Great Britain are the most important examples of countries with outsider governance systems, and thus this form of governance structure is often called the "Anglo-Saxon" system.

Within the insider category, two rather different structures can be identified. In the first system, which is common in Germany, Austria, Switzerland, and some of the other Continental European countries, and is therefore often called the "Germanic" system, control is typically unidirectional. A family, bank or Company X owns a substantial or controlling interest in a particular Company Y and has representatives on Y's supervisory board. Company Y, in turn, owns a controlling interest in Company Z, which in turn controls Company W, and so on. Companies Y, Z, and W on the other hand, do not own shares in the organizations that stand above them in the corporate pyramid. In this way we can speak of control being unidirectional.

In contrast, in the "Japanese-form" of insider system, several companies are linked together through interlocking directorships, which are backed by cross-holdings of one and another's shares. Within these intertwined groups of firms, there is also typically a bank, which holds shares in several of the companies in the group, and has representatives on their supervisory boards.[3] Within the Japanese or zaibatsu style system, therefore, control is multidirectional with each company able to exercise some control over the companies that control it.

In this chapter, we examine the characteristics of the different types of corporate governance systems that exist around the world, the goals of the different actors in each type of system, and the consequences of each system for company performance.

Ownership and control around the world

Table 6.1 summarizes the key features of the ownership patterns in 39 countries. Column 2 in the table gives the number of firms for which ownership data were available. Any country for which data for five or more firms were available was included in the table. The coverage varies widely from over 3,000 companies in the United States to only five in several countries like Greece and Turkey. The difference between countries with Anglo-Saxon governance systems and countries with non-Anglo-Saxon systems can be discerned in the table, but is less readily apparent than one might expect from the literature. If we take Great Britain, Germany, and France as countries typifying the three major governance systems, then the expected patterns are present. The largest block of shares held by any one person or institution for UK companies averaged 16 percent of all outstanding shares, with a median under 12 percent. The largest blocks in Germany and France, on the other hand, average around 50 percent of outstanding shares. One cannot, however, simply adopt an Anglo-Saxon versus non-Anglo-Saxon dichotomy to divide the countries in the table. The largest blocks in New Zealand average over 45 percent of outstanding shares, in Canada 30 percent or more. Our sample of companies for New Zealand is quite small, of course, but it includes the largest companies in the country. A much larger sampling of New Zealand companies would undoubtedly raise the average largest shareholding.

That this is so can readily be seen in the data for the United States. The ownership data cover more than 3,000 firms, a far larger sampling of US companies than in most published studies. The mean holding of the largest shareholder in this sample is 21.89 percent, the median is 16.83 percent. These figures are not dramatically different from those for the Netherlands (27.13 and 16.00). It is only when one constrains one's attention to the largest 500 US corporations that the mean and median shareholdings resemble those in the United Kingdom and Ireland, the other two Anglo-Saxon countries that best fit the expected pattern.

The Scandinavian countries fall squarely in between the other non-Anglo-Saxon countries and Ireland, the United Kingdom, and the United States. Mean and median largest shareholdings in all four countries lie between 20 and 30 percent except for Denmark, which has a median largest shareholding of only 15 percent.

Columns 6–9 in Table 6.1 present the percentages of companies in the samples for each country that are controlled by families or individuals, the state, non-financial companies, and financial companies (banks, insurance companies, etc.) – where control is defined as one family or institution holding at least 10 percent of the outstanding shares. Column 10 presents the percentage of companies in the residual category, dispersed ownership. One's expectation from the literature is that the fraction of companies with dispersed ownership will be highest in Anglo-Saxon countries, and this expectation is by and large confirmed for the major, developed Anglo-Saxon countries. More than 20 percent of all companies in Australia, Ireland, and Great Britain had no shareholder holding 10 percent or more of a company's shares, and this is true for 80 percent of the 500 largest companies in the United States. In contrast, none of the 30 large Austrian firms in the sample had a largest shareholder with under 10 percent of the outstanding shares and only 2.1 and 3.7 percent of the companies in Germany and France fell into the dispersed category. Dispersed shareholdings are also relatively prevalent in Denmark, Japan, Taiwan, and Korea, however, while in India – a country with a legal system of Anglo-Saxon origin – over 90 percent of the 37 large companies in our sample are controlled by either the state (51.4%) or nonfinancial companies (43.2%), and no firm falls into the dispersed category. In the developing Anglo-Saxon countries, dispersed ownership is no more likely than in French-origin countries and *less likely* than in some other Asian developing countries like Taiwan and Korea.

Large holdings by nonfinancial companies and financial institutions are common in most countries with Ireland, the United Kingdom, and the United States again being the major exceptions. In the case of Continental European countries holdings by nonfinancial companies are often parts of corporate pyramids. Such pyramids also are common in some of the developing countries like Indonesia, Malaysia, and Turkey. In both Europe and the developing countries, holdings by nonfinancial firms also are often holdings by foreign companies.

The reader may be somewhat surprised by the seemingly small fractions of shares held by individuals and families. Here one must recognize that the numbers in Table 6.1 *understate* the extent of family control in countries where pyramidal structures and cross-holdings are common. At the top of a pyramid one typically finds a firm, which is controlled by a person or family. This family then effectively controls *all* of the companies in the pyramid. The ultimate owners of companies in this case are either families or the state.

The situation is somewhat different in Japan with respect to companies that belong to *keiretsu*. A keiretsu consists of a group of firms linked through cross-shareholdings and linked also to a *main bank*. Each company in a keiretsu is effectively owned by the other companies in its group and the affiliated bank. No families own controlling stakes in any of the companies, and individual and family shareholdings tend to be relatively small. This can readily be seen in Table 6.1. Only 5.9 percent of the more than 1,000 Japanese companies in the sample are controlled

Table 6.1 Ownership concentration and identities in 39 countries

1 Country	2 No. of firms	3 Mean largest holder	4 Stand. dev. largest holder	5 Median largest holder	6 Family holdings	7 Financial holdings	8 Non-financial holdings	9 State holdings	10 Dispersed
Antilles (Netherl.)	5	30.45	14.71	32.46	20.0	20.0	60.0	0.0	0.0
Argentina	8	40.18	14.89	41.34	12.5	25.0	50.0	12.5	0.0
Australia	114	24.83	19.34	17.07	30.7	17.5	30.7	0.0	21.1
Austria	30	59.37	21.72	54.50	6.7	23.3	53.3	16.7	0.0
Belgium	41	44.54	21.03	43.00	9.8	34.1	53.7	0.0	2.4
Bermuda	12	49.86	25.28	50.68	25.0	25.0	50.0	0.0	0.0
Brazil	25	58.64	22.61	59.40	12.0	12.0	56.0	20.0	0.0
Canada	280	36.99	24.73	29.65	34.6	19.6	40.4	3.3	2.1
Cayman Islands	5	33.27	18.87	39.30	0.0	0.0	100.0	0.0	0.0
Chile	9	35.22	24.66	30.15	11.1	44.4	33.3	0.1	11.1
Denmark	40	23.13	20.42	15.00	25.0	12.5	25.0	2.5	35.0
Finland	34	26.90	19.80	20.70	5.9	17.6	38.2	23.6	14.7
France	187	48.88	24.32	50.00	25.1	17.6	51.3	2.3	3.7
Germany	240	54.01	24.73	51.72	26.7	15.4	48.8	7.0	2.1
Great Britain	687	16.00	13.29	11.78	17.9	37.0	15.1	1.8	28.2
Greece	5	52.44	21.73	51.00	0.0	0.0	80.0	20.0	0.0
Hong Kong	43	38.61	15.52	35.55	14.0	34.9	51.2	0.0	0.0
India	37	45.07	13.83	39.90	2.7	2.7	43.2	51.4	0.0
Indonesia	41	50.00	18.14	51.00	34.1	9.8	48.8	7.3	0.0
Ireland	24	17.62	13.37	12.20	29.2	20.8	16.7	8.3	25.0

Israel	14	31.18	19.45	24.50	28.6	14.3	50.0	0.0	7.1
Italy	57	45.24	18.59	47.52	3.5	40.4	47.4	3.4	5.3
Japan	1,036	15.08	13.30	8.85	5.9	6.6	58.1	0.2	29.2
Malaysia	158	34.97	16.46	32.77	38.0	10.1	48.1	1.9	1.9
Mexico	8	47.42	11.76	50.78	50.0	0.0	50.0	0.0	0.0
Netherlands	66	27.13	25.02	16.00	6.1	13.6	43.9	6.1	30.3
New Zealand	18	45.01	14.93	49.82	0.0	55.6	44.4	0.0	0.0
Norway	42	29.92	16.95	26.92	16.7	23.8	47.6	7.1	4.8
Portugal	10	42.48	19.21	51.35	0.0	20.0	30.0	50.0	0.0
Singapore	97	38.45	19.47	33.95	27.8	28.9	43.3	0.0	0.0
South Africa	25	42.15	17.10	44.75	24.0	24.0	48.0	4.0	0.0
South Korea	16	19.10	17.60	12.84	25.0	6.3	25.0	12.4	31.3
Spain	59	37.76	25.85	29.10	1.7	23.7	57.6	8.5	8.5
Sweden	54	28.33	16.23	25.00	16.7	38.9	33.3	3.7	7.4
Switzerland	66	45.63	27.73	48.00	33.3	10.6	42.4	4.6	9.1
Taiwan	11	15.75	19.50	5.41	18.2	9.1	9.1	9.1	54.5
Thailand	81	34.53	13.15	35.63	7.4	56.8	32.1	3.7	0.0
Turkey	5	41.49	19.30	37.12	20.0	40.0	40.0	0.0	0.0
United States	3,070	21.89	15.52	16.83	47.3	25.9	14.6	0.9	11.3
United States (largest)	500	13.50	12.94	10.32	3.42	9.2	6.58	0.47	80.33

Source: See appendix to GMY (2002b).

by families, as opposed to the roughly 65 percent that are held either by banks, other financial institutions, and nonfinancial companies. Thus, companies that are parts of Japanese keiretsu represent the extreme form of managerial-controlled firm, since the only effective control that can be brought to bear on them is from the managers of the other firms in the keiretsu.

Table 6.1 reveals that a variety of forms of corporate control exist around the world. Our main interest in this chapter is to discover what differences these different forms of control make for the performance of companies in different corporate governance systems. Before examining this question, however, we need to consider the motivation of the various actors appearing in each system.

The goals of corporate actors

Dispersed ownership

The easiest of the ownership groups to analyze is that where ownership is dispersed. With ownership highly dispersed no single shareholder, be she a person or an institution, can directly control management by exercising her voting rights. Although it is possible that a shareholder identifies with the company and obtains psychic income from seeing the company grow or attempt to improve the environment or contribute to a particular charity, no one would buy shares in a company to achieve these goals, if she knew that she would be able to acquire only a small fraction of the company's shares. An isolated shareholder, who is one of millions, would recognize that she would be unable to affect the company's policies, and thus would rationally disassociate herself from them. The only rational motive for an individual or institution purchasing shares of a company, whose shares are widely dispersed, is to obtain a claim on the income stream that the company produces.[4] The primary goal of owners of shares in a company with widely dispersed shareholdings is to have the company's managers maximize the value of their shares.

Outside individuals of families with large blocks of shares

On first consideration, it might seem that the primary goal of an individual shareholder with a substantial stake in a company would also be to have the company's managers maximize the value of these shares. This was indeed the assumption made by numerous authors in studies of the effects of "the separation of ownership from control."[5] These studies compared profitability and other measures of company performance, and predicted higher profits for firms with concentrated ownership, on the grounds that managers were less free to pursue their own goals when an outsider holds a substantial fraction of the company's shares.

The reason why someone who owns shares in a company would want to see their value maximized is obvious and applies, *ceteris paribus*, to all categories of owners. But for many categories, other motives may play a role. When an individual or a family owns a large fraction of a company's shares, they are quite likely members of the family that founded the company. The company may even still carry their name, and the family may identify strongly with it. Like the entrepreneur who first started the company, their first concern may be that it survives (and their name along with it). They may even be willing to sacrifice some of the company's value to see it remain in its initial line of business, and survive as an independent entity.

Insider owners

When a manager owns a large fraction of a company's shares, he typically has either founded it, or is a direct decedent of its founder. Owner–entrepreneurs are common in young, small enterprises. These firms usually do not issue common shares, or if they do, the shares are held by a small number of individuals, some of whom are themselves relatives of the owner–entrepreneur.

The standard textbook model of the firm assumes that it is led by an owner–entrepreneur who maximizes the firm's profits, or perhaps the present discounted value of these profits. Not all observers of the owner–entrepreneur-led firm have made this assumption, however. Chapter 4 contains a long passage from Schumpeter's (1934, pp. 93–4) classic description of the innovative firm written almost a century ago in which he likens the entrepreneur to a medieval knight seeking to found "a private kingdom" or a "dynasty." Over 50 years ago, Scitovsky (1943) demonstrated that even the familiar profits-maximization assumption, if single mindedly pursued, implied that the owner–entrepreneur is a rather unusual fellow ever ready to take on a fair gamble, a workaholic, who never consumes additional leisure, no matter how wealthy he becomes.[6] Another astute observer of capitalism, Knight (1965, p. 319), saw the businessman as motivated to "produce wealth to be used in producing more wealth with no view to any use beyond the increase of wealth itself."

If these descriptions are at all accurate, it would seem that they ought also to apply to the motives of managers of large corporations, when they own large fractions of their company's shares. When placed alongside the actual behavior of the Krupps, Fords, Gateses, and Maritoes of the industrial world, these descriptions of managerial motivation do not seem like exaggerations. The entrepreneurial founders of the industrial giants in Germany, the United States, and Japan have been empire builders of extraordinary talent and drive. Empire building and empire maintenance must be considered as possible motives of both owner–entrepreneurs in privately held companies, and managers with large ownership stakes in publicly held companies.[7]

The worker as owner

The contractual relationship between a worker and a company typically takes the form of a *service contract*. The worker agrees to undertake certain tasks for specific compensation. She possesses no ownership stake in the company. The goals of the worker, as modeled by economists, are to maximize a utility function whose arguments include income, leisure, and perhaps certain job attributes, like risk of injury.

The claim has been frequently made, more often by non-economists than by economists, that companies would perform better, if the entire workforce shared in their ownership, and/or in their management.[8] This argument has several dimensions, including, for example, the non-economic argument that in a democratic society, workers, like citizens, should be able to control the most important institutions affecting their lives. On a more narrowly economic basis one can make the same efficiency argument for worker-owned firms being more efficient at producing profits as one makes for manager- or entrepreneur-owned firms. The workers are more likely to maximize the profits of the firm, if they receive a share of these profits. Beyond simply their pecuniary interests in the firm, workers as owners might be expected to oppose reductions in the size of the workforce, place extra weight on working conditions and job safety, and so on. Although such goals are obviously likely to reduce the profits of a firm, whether they reduce its *efficiency* or not, depends on one's definition of efficiency and in particular on the weight one places on the workers' welfare.

The literature on worker-ownership and worker-management has been characterized by an unusually strong ideological undertone, with left-oriented economists strongly advocating this form of corporate governance structure, and right-oriented economists strongly opposing any interference with what was commonly thought to be the ideal corporate governance structure, namely one in which control rested entirely with managers, and ownership was separated from the day-to-day operations of the firm, while playing a crucial monitoring role over managers. In recent years, however, many firms have attempted to boost employee productivity and morale by offering partial compensation packages that include shares in the company. This widespread and *voluntarily* chosen strategy of managements has raised the respectability of share-ownership schemes within the mainstream of the economics profession.

Institutional portfolio holders

Upon first consideration it would seem that the objectives of the managers of institutional portfolios should be obvious – to maximize the values of their portfolios. Even if we assume that this is the goal of portfolio managers, and we shall argue shortly that this does not appear to be the case, there are two strategies that they can follow when pursuing this goal. In the terminology of Hirschman (1970), portfolio managers can either employ an *exit* strategy of selling shares in any company in their portfolio, when this company does not perform well, or they can employ *voice* to change the policies of a poorly performing company or, in extreme cases, to help change its management. Over 40 years ago, Berle (1960) argued that portfolio managers possessed "power without property," which they could use to discipline managers and to mitigate the problems caused by a "separation of ownership from control." He lamented, however, that at least as of that time, portfolio managers were not making use of the power and their control over large numbers of share votes, but were merely reacting as individual shareholders and selling out when they were dissatisfied with managers. Portfolio managers have continued to follow this strategy until fairly recently, when they have finally begun to intervene occasionally to block a management's decision, as say in a takeover, or to help remove a management.

The separation of ownership from control gives corporate managers the discretion to pursue their own goals at their shareholders' expense, because no individual shareholder or small group of shareholders owns enough shares to threaten the management. But portfolio managers are also *managers*, and the owners of funds they manage typically are also large in number and lacking in much power to control the portfolio managers. What prevents portfolio managers from pursuing their own personal goals, and if they do, what are these goals?

That institutions engaged in the handling of portfolios of securities do suffer from agency problems is revealed by the fact that the market value of some mutual funds is less than the aggregate value of the securities in them. Just as the assets of some corporations are worth more when sold separately than when retained together under a particular management team (Bhagat *et al.*, 1990), the aggregate values of the securities in some institutional portfolios exceed the market value of the institutional portfolios. In both cases, the management team can be said to have a *negative* value added. It would seem to follow that these managers are either not attempting to maximize the value of the assets that they control, or are doing a rather poor job of it.

If portfolio managers are not maximizing the value of the assets that they control, what are they maximizing? One possibility is job security. Finance theory teaches us that the prices of securities at any point in time reflect the market's unbiased evaluation of the future earnings and risks associated with each security. These prices thus reflect the market's expectations regarding not only the performance of any single company relative to all others, but also of the economy as a whole. Unless someone has different and better information than everyone else – as some insiders might have about their own company – or one person is better than others at evaluating commonly available information, there is no reason to buy or sell a given company to improve the risk adjusted earnings from that investment. Of course, securities must be bought and sold as funds flow into and out of the portfolio, and adjustments between bonds, securities, cash, and the like must from time to time be made. But except for those with inside information, or those with above average abilities to evaluate generally available information, one would expect from finance theory relatively little trading in securities, given that each trade has a small transaction cost. This is of course not what we observe! Trading on the stock exchanges in London and New York in any year is many times the number of shares listed on these exchanges, and it is the institutional traders who drive this high volume of trading. Why do they do so much trading? One explanation, consistent with the job security motive, is that they want to appear to be doing something to increase the value of their portfolios. A portfolio manager who made only modest adjustments in his portfolio over time might be accused of loafing on the job, of not earning his salary. By buying and selling in great quantities, even if it does not increase the value of the portfolio, a portfolio manager at least gives the impression that he is *trying* to increase the value of the portfolio.[9]

Additional evidence consistent with the job security hypothesis is provided by the large swings in stock market prices that occur, swings that tend to be far larger than warranted by subsequent movements in securities' earnings (Shiller, 1981, 1984). These large swings are caused by the "herd-like" behavior of portfolio managers who all seem to enter the market when the general expectation is that it will rise, and leave it when "market expectations" are that it will fall. A portfolio manager who stayed out of the market, when most other portfolio managers were going in, would risk staying out of the market when it rose *and "everyone" thought it was going to rise*. This kind of behavior is much more likely to reflect badly on the manager's competence, and thus to threaten his job, than if he goes into the market when everyone else does, and the market falls. In the latter situation, he can at least offer the defense that "everyone thought it was going to rise."

We conclude that it is reasonable to assume that portfolio managers, like every-one else, maximize their own utilities. With respect to their trading activity, maximizing their own utility is likely to lead portfolio managers to trade too often and at the wrong times. What utility-maximizing portfolio managers do with respect to voting the shares under their control is less obvious. Do they not vote them to avoid the effort and likely conflict that challenging incumbent company managers bring? Do they not vote them out of a sense of solidarity with other man-agers who are merely exercising the discretion that they have due to the separation of ownership from control? Or do they intervene in the affairs of the companies in their portfolio whenever such interventions are likely to increase the value of the shares they hold, since such behavior is in their shareholders' interests and thus indirectly in their own? Without answers to these questions it is not possible to appraise the role institutional investors can and do play in corporate governance.

Other firms

Although the top managers in a corporation may have considerable discretion to pursue other goals, middle managers typically have much less discretion – in large part because the top managers are monitoring them. Managerial discretion arises not only from the absence of close scrutiny by the owners, but also from the authority that managers have to allocate the funds of the company to advance their own interests. If middle managers reallocate corporate funds to benefit themselves, there are less funds for the top managers to allocate to satisfy their goals. The personal goals of middle and top managers conflict, and because top managers have authority over middle managers, they have a personal interest in monitoring middle managers and preventing them from dissipating the resources of the company and thereby limiting the top management's ability to utilize these funds to its own advantage (Williamson, 1975).

Similar considerations apply, when one firm owns a controlling interest in another. If Company *A* owns a controlling interest in Company *B*, then *A*'s managers will want to see *B*'s managers maximize *B*'s profits and pay the value-maximizing amount out as dividends, as this gives them the maximum resources to pursue their own goals. Thus, upon first consideration it seems reasonable to expect the usual principal–agent problems that arise from the separation of ownership and control to be minimal with respect to any company effectively owned by another company.

Upon further consideration, however, there are several reasons to expect companies under the control of other firms to exhibit *worse* performance than independent firms. First, in a long pyramidal chain, where *A* owns *B*, *B* owns *C*, and so on, if the managers of *A* are only able to monitor *B* effectively, then company managers far down in the chain may enjoy sufficient discretion due to "control loss" to pursue their own goals (Williamson, 1967; Franks and Mayer, 2001). Second, if the managers at the top of the pyramid are empire builders, they may wish to see all parts of the pyramid growing rapidly. Third, the firm at the top of the pyramid may introduce policies to benefit it at the expense of companies it controls, so that the latter *appear* to be performing poorly, even if they are not. One such policy would be for Company *C* in the pyramid to sell its product at a loss to *A*, thereby transforming the potential profits of *C* into actual profits for *A*.

Taking all of these things into account, it is not possible a priori to predict whether companies controlled by other companies behave more or less like profit maximizers.

Banks

Banks often hold seats on the boards of directors of companies for which they are a substantial creditor, or in which they have large equity holdings. (Recently, the United States has joined other countries in allowing banks to own and vote the shares of commercial companies.) In the latter case, they can also exercise control directly by voting the shares, of course. When banks control other companies, what is it that they maximize when they are exercising control?

One possibility is obviously their own profits. A commercial bank that maximized its profits would wish to see all of its loans repaid, and that any firms in which it owned shares maximized profits and paid out the optimal amounts in dividends. By pursuing these goals a bank might distort the policies of the companies that borrow from it or whose shares the bank owns. For example, if a bank had made substantial loans to a company, but held none of its equity, it would favor more conservative policies in terms of investment and R&D than those that might maximize the combined value of the company's debt and equity, since the bank would only have an interest in seeing the company pay interest and principal on its loans. The converse would be true for a bank that had substantial equity holdings in a company, but was not its creditor. Thus, even when a bank's managers maximize its market value, they may not pursue policies which maximize the market values of the companies that they control.

Banks are typically corporations with professional managers and as such may also suffer from agency problems. If a bank's managers are empire-builders, they might encourage empire-building by the companies it controls in the form of mergers, since the bigger the companies it controls are, the more they are likely to borrow from their bank. Where banks supply advice and other assistance on mergers and collect fees for these services, they have an additional reason to encourage companies that they control to merge, even when the mergers are not in the best interests of the companies making them. We conclude, that the goals of bank managers who exercise control over commercial companies may not always coincide with the goal of maximizing the market value of these companies.

The state

In a democratic country, the state does not have an unwavering set of goals which it pursues. Indeed, to the extent that "the state" has any goals at all, they are the goals of the government, and these will change in response to both changes in citizen preferences, and to changes in the party composition of the government. Any company owned or controlled by the state might be expected, therefore, to pursue policies that enhance the interests of the parties constituting the government.

Among these interests could certainly be obtaining revenue to be used elsewhere in the budget to win votes. Thus, having state-owned companies maximize profits cannot be ruled out as a motive. But, it seems unlikely that state-owned companies are formed to provide revenue for the state, since more revenue could be obtained by taxing all privately owned companies a small amount than by creating one or a handful of new, state-owned firms. If companies are not formed to provide revenue for the state, it is unlikely that they adopt this objective after they are formed. We need to search for other goals for state-owned firms.

Perhaps, the most obvious goal other than revenue for the state to own a firm is to protect consumers from being exploited by the firm in a "natural monopoly" situation. The goal of the state in this case should be the maximization of consumers' surplus. State ownership of utility companies, railroads, postal services, and the like can be explained in this way.

A third objective behind the state's ownership of companies is to provide a good in the "national interest." State-owned airlines, armaments manufacturers, and the like would fall into this category. The argument here seems to be that national pride or national security requires that the state operate the airline, tank manufacturer, petroleum company, etc.

A fourth objective behind the state's ownership of companies is to protect the workers from "exploitation." This was, of course, ostensibly the rationale behind communism, and many governments with socialist leanings have nationalized various companies that have been left to function as private firms in other countries. Roe (1999) has recently argued that the left-of-center orientation of Western European governments relative to that of the United States helps explain the relatively poor performance of its corporate sector. European governments put pressure on corporations to maintain employment levels and thus effectively these companies behave like growth maximizers, investing more than they should to sustain the firm and protect jobs. Roe makes his argument in reference to European firms in the private sector, but it applies even more so for companies under state control.

In addition to these different, ostensible goals for state ownership, the possibility again exists that the managers of the state-owned companies have the discretion to pursue their own goals. A state-owned company is typically assigned to some ministry, say transportation for the state's airline, which has the responsibility for monitoring it. The long-run nature of this relationship, however, creates the danger that the ministry becomes "captured" by the state company.[10] The ministry is in turn monitored by the parliament, which in turn is monitored by the citizens who discipline it at each election. Thus, in a democracy, the citizens can be regarded as the ultimate owners of state companies. If managers of private firms have considerable discretion to pursue their own goals, because of the difficulties shareholders have monitoring and disciplining them, then it is likely that managers of state firms have *enormous* discretion to pursue their own goals, because of the difficulties citizens have monitoring and disciplining them.

Professional managers

The goals of the professional manager were discussed in the previous chapter. Suffice it here to say that they do not necessarily coincide with those of the outside owners of the firm.

The impact of managerial entrenchment

The impact of managerial ownership concentration

Following the appearance of the models of Baumol (1959), Marris (1964), and Williamson (1964) postulating that managers pursue their own goals at the shareholders' expense, numerous articles appeared that purported to test these hypotheses. These tests typically consisted of regressions of profits or sales on a measure of ownership concentration like the fraction of shares held by the largest shareholder. Since the managerial discretion problem was assumed to arise because shareholdings were widely dispersed, the early studies assumed that performance, usually measured as profitability, would improve as ownership concentration increased. Most studies confirmed this prediction.[11]

The bulk of the early studies testing for a relationship between ownership concentration and performance did not distinguish among types of owners. All shareholders were assumed to desire that the firm's managers maximize profits or shareholder wealth, and greater ownership concentration would lead to a greater fulfilment of that goal. McEachern (1975) was the first to point out that concentrated shareholdings in the hands of a company's managers might actually *worsen* the performance of the company as far as the shareholders are concerned, since larger shareholdings for managers would tend to protect them from the disciplinary effects of proxy contests and takeovers. McEachern presented evidence that firms with dominant shareholders as managers retained and reinvested significantly more than firms with large stakeholders outside of the firm.[12]

In a much cited paper Morck, Shleifer, and Vishny (1988a) (hereafter MSV) presented evidence of managerial entrenchment using Tobin's q as a measure of company performance, and shareholdings of the board of directors as an explanatory variable. They found that q rises from around 0.72 when the board holds no shares to a bit above 1.0, when it holds 5 percent of the shares. At this point the effects of managerial entrenchment appear to set in and q falls as directors' shareholdings increase. When the board holds 25 percent of the outstanding shares, predicted q has fallen back to only 0.7. Beyond a board holding of 25 percent, managerial and shareholder interests appear to become more aligned and q starts to rise, although it does not obtain a value of 1.0 again until an ownership concentration of 65 percent.

Several studies have examined the relationship between various measures of corporate performance and ownership concentration since MSV's article appeared. Four of these, Cho (1998), Short and Keasey (1999), Cosh *et al.* (2000), and Gugler, Mueller, and Yurtoglu (2002b) (hereafter GMY) come up with the same sort of nonlinear relationship between performance and ownership concentration as MSV did. McConnell and Servaes (1990, 1995) observe only the first part of the curve – an inverted parabola – in their US data, as do Thomsen and Pedersen (2000) in data for European corporations.[13]

The turning points observed by MSV were at ownership concentration levels much lower than the 22 and 68 percent observed by GMY, and the 40–50 percent range at which McConnell and Servaes record corporate performance peaking. One explanation for this difference is that the MSV sample of 371 Fortune 500 companies contains on average much larger firms than do the McConnell and Servaes (over 1,000) and GMY (over 3,000) samples (Kole, 1995). Managers of small companies probably must hold larger fractions of their company's shares before they can feel safe from the threat of a takeover or proxy contest.

Several authors have questioned the MSV results on the grounds that ownership concentration may not be an exogenous variable (Kole, 1995, 1996; Loderer and Martin, 1997; and Cho, 1998). This possibility was first emphasized by Demsetz (1983). He argued that for firms in industries in which agency problems could potentially significantly lower a firm's market value, ownership would remain concentrated to mitigate the agency problems. In industries in which the performance of managers could be easily judged, on the other hand, as say a regulated industry, the advantages of diversifying shareholdings would dominate monitoring advantages, and ownership would be unconcentrated. Demsetz thus hypothesized that there would be *no* relationship between insider ownership concentration and company performance, a hypothesis for which he and Kenneth Lehn subsequently presented some empirical support.[14] Kole (1995, 1996), Loderer and Martin (1997), Cho (1998), and Bøhren and Ødegaard (2001) all present evidence suggesting that directors' or insiders' ownership holdings do not causally determine company performance, once the simultaneous nature of the relationship is taken into account.

The criticism that ownership concentration might be endogenous is certainly valid with respect to those studies that have used Tobin's q or some other measure of overall company performance, like the returns on total assets. The possible endogeneity of ownership *cannot* account for the evidence of the effects of managerial entrenchment reported by GMY, however, for they use an estimate of a *marginal q*, which is equivalent to the ratio of the returns on investment to company costs of capital. Although it might be reasonable to assume that insider shareholdings vary across firms as a function of the height of investment opportunities, the riskiness of investment, and so on, the returns *realized* on investment depend on the investments actually made and these are the result of the decisions of the managers at the time they are made. GMY's estimates imply that company returns on investment are less than their costs of capital from roughly the point where managers own 20 percent of a company's shares, and fall until an ownership concentration of 68 percent is reached. The fact that the returns on investment fall short of the costs of capital implies over (poor) investments and thus the exercise of discretion on the part of managers. Managers must be viewed as deciding on the nature and amounts of investment, the nature of investments cannot be assumed to determine the identity of owners or managers. Since the returns on investment follow from the nature of the investments made, these too must be regarded as endogenous. The GMY results imply the existence and growing importance of managerial discretion as managerial shareholdings increase from 22 to 68 percent of outstanding shares.

The impact of managerial entrenchment via cross-shareholdings

In many countries instances may be found where one company, say Company A, owns shares in Companies B and C, B owns shares in A and C and C owns shares in A and B. The existence of such *cross-shareholdings* can lead to a particular form of managerial entrenchment in so far as the managers of a given firm in the group are monitored and controlled to a large extent by other managers who they themselves control. Using data on cross-holdings for European companies, GMY find that the ratio of returns on investment to company costs of capital are significantly lower when cross-shareholdings are present. Yurtoglu (2000) reports similar negative performance effects from cross-shareholdings among Turkish companies.

The special case of the Japanese keiretsu

In the Japanese keiretsu both cross-shareholdings among the different firms in the corporate group and cross-holdings between the group-firms and an affiliated bank are present. One set of studies argues that the combination of an interlocked set of firms tied to a group bank leads to better monitoring of all firms in the keiretsu, the exchange of other sorts of valuable information, and thereby to better performance (Gilson and Roe, 1993; Berglöf and Perotti, 1994). As noted above, however, the addition of a bank to the group might actually aggravate agency problems as, for example, by shielding the group firms from the discipline of external capital markets. So far the weight of the evidence seems to be that companies which are parts of Japanese keiretsu perform worse than other Japanese firms with respect to exports, investment performance, productivity, and profitability (Caves and Uekusa, 1976; Nakatani, 1984; Kester, 1986; Lichtenberg and Pushner, 1994; Hundley and Jacobsen, 1998; Weinstein and Yafeh, 1998; Sakuma, 2001; and GMY, 2002b).

The impact of ownership identity

The evidence cited in the previous section indicates that ownership structures can influence corporate performance in a negative way, when they help to entrench managers and allow them to pursue their own goals. Implicitly, this literature would seem to imply that corporate performance would be improved by ownership structures that improved the monitoring of managers by those having an interest in good performance. In this section, we review the literature that has tested to see whether the identity of the major shareholders in a company matters. Somewhat surprisingly perhaps, it appears that it usually does not matter.

Institutional owners (pension funds, mutual funds, etc.)

The prediction that large stakes held by pension funds and other institutions primarily seeking high returns on their investments should be associated with superior corporate performance is fairly easy to rationalize and receives the most empirical support. McConnell and Servaes (1990) find Tobin's q and institutional holdings to be positively related in US data. Nickell *et al.* (1997) find productivity growth and institutional holdings to be positively related in UK data, while Cosh *et al.* (1998) observe a slightly better post-performance for UK acquirers with large institutional holdings. Thomsen and Pedersen (2000) find Tobin's q and profitability to be positively related to institutional holdings in a sample of 435 large European companies.

Banks

The claim that banks improve the performance of companies in which they own large blocks of shares is most frequently made for German banks. Boehmer (2001) reviews the large literature on the influence of German banks on corporate performance and finds as much evidence against this hypothesis as there is for it. GMY (2002b) also find little evidence of significantly better performance for firms controlled by banks and other financial institutions in their large cross-national study. Lichtenberg and Pushner (1994), on the other hand, do find that the performance of Japanese companies improves with the fraction of shares held by financial institutions.

Families

As discussed in the previous section, the recent literature has largely focused on the effects of insider ownership on company performance. Insider-controlled firms fall into the category of family-controlled firms, of course, but it can also be the case that individuals or families own controlling stakes in companies and are *not* involved in the day-to-day management of the company. These persons will often have seats on the boards of directors, and thus in studies like that of MSV are treated as insiders. Their interests may, in fact, be quite different from those of the active managers. Unfortunately, very few studies have estimated the effects of individual shareholdings by managers and separately by individuals who are not managers. When I made this distinction, I found that company profitability declined as managerial shareholdings increased, but that the fraction of outstanding shares concentrated in the hands of persons who were not managers had no significant effect on profitability (Mueller, 1986a, ch. 7). Jacquemin and Ghellinck (1980) failed to observe a significant difference in profitability between family-controlled and non-family-controlled firms in France, as was also true for Górriz and Fumás (1996) in Spain. GMY found that in countries with English-origin legal systems family-controlled firms have significantly higher ratios of returns on investment to costs of capital than do firms that are not family controlled. In no other country group was there a significant difference between the performance of family-controlled firms and all other firms. The belief that family-controlled firms perform better than other companies has received little empirical support to date.

The state

A vast literature exists in the public choice field reasoning why and demonstrating that publicly owned firms perform worse than private firms.[15] Many of these studies compare firms in a particular industry, like electricity production, which traditionally has been thought of as a "natural monopoly" and thus reserved for the state. Our interest here is more in the impact of state ownership in industries in which little or no natural monopoly elements exist. Boardman and Vining (1989) find that among the 500 largest non-US corporations, profitability is significantly lower for partially or fully state-controlled companies. Gugler (1998, 2001b) also finds significantly lower returns on total capital for state-controlled companies in Austria. GMY's results for the three Germanic countries in Europe – Austria, Germany, and Switzerland – corroborate Gugler's findings. State-controlled firms in these countries have returns on investment that average only 37 percent of their costs of capital, a lower ratio than for any other ownership category in any other country group in their study. GMY also found, however, that state-controlled companies in countries with French-origin legal systems had significantly *higher* ratios of returns on investment to costs of capital than did other ownership categories in this set of countries.

Thus, the results for state-controlled firms are not totally out of line with those for other ownership categories. Although state-control in most instances has either no effect on company performance or tends to worsen it, in at least one set of countries there is evidence that the state can actually do a better job of monitoring managers than do the other ownership groups.

The impact of boards of directors

In all countries, there exists some form of supervisory board that is supposed to approve major decisions of the firm like mergers, the replacement of senior managers and the like. In some countries like Japan this board is dominated by senior executives of the firm, and plays no monitoring role with respect to management (Sakuma, 2001, p. 143). Even in countries like the United States, however, where directors from outside of the management circle often make up a majority of the board of directors, they often have neither the information nor the incentive to actively monitor the company's operations. Nor is this phenomenon new, as the previously quoted statement from the Board of Directors of the Pennsylvania Railroad, issued in the late nineteenth century, reveals. "The present form of organization (part-time directors and full-time officers) makes practical ciphers of the Directors, and this is from no deliberate intention, but from the very necessities of the case."[16]

One does not expect ciphers to have much impact on the day-to-day operations of companies, and this expectation seems to be fulfilled. In one of the largest and most recent studies of the impact of board composition on operating performance, Bhagat and Black (2000) could find no relationship in a sample of 934 large US companies between the profitability of a company and the fraction of its board that was independent of management. Similar findings for the United States have been reported in several studies (e.g. Baysinger and Butler, 1985; Hermalin and Weisbach, 1991) with some studies even suggesting the possibility of a *negative* association between the fraction of the board which is independent of management and various measures of company performance like Tobin's q (Agrawal and Knoeber, 1996; Yermack, 1996; Klein, 1998). Evidence that board composition has a measurable positive impact on company performance is also lacking in studies from outside of the United States (Gugler, 2001c, p. 211).[17]

Things are somewhat different in times of crisis or when major decisions affecting the future of the company must be made, like the instigation of a takeover bid. On such occasions, clear conflicts of interest can arise between the interests of managers and those of shareholders, as for example, whether the top managers should be replaced. Companies with larger fractions of outside directors or with committee structures that prevent managers from blocking such decisions are more likely to undertake actions in these situations that go against the managers' interests, although even here there is not much evidence that these actions measurably improve the performance of the companies.[18]

The importance of legal systems

Each country's legal institutions differ from those of other countries with respect to the protections that they offer to shareholders. In some countries, for example, shareholders can demand access to the names and address of all other shareholders for the purpose of calling a special meeting of the shareholders, in other countries they cannot. In some countries managers must publish their shareholdings and their compensation packages, in others they do not have to do so. Provisions like these obviously strengthen the shareholders' hand *vis-à-vis* the management's, and help to align shareholder and managerial interests.

La Porta, Lopez-De-Silanes, Shleifer, and Vishny (1997, 1998) (hereafter LLSV) have examined the content and historical development of legal institutions in different countries to determine which ones best align shareholder and managerial interests. They have concluded that the common law systems found in the Anglo-Saxon countries and former British colonies offer outside and minority shareholders greater protection against managerial abuse of their position than do civil law systems. Within the civil law systems LLSV distinguish French, German, and Scandinavian systems, with the French system, according to LLSV (1997, p. 1132), offering the shareholder the least protection among the three civil law systems, and the Scandinavian system providing the most protection.

In Table 6.2 we list a large group of countries according to the LLSV legal classifications.[19] When one considers the list of English-origin countries (Australia, Canada, . . . , and the United States), one is tempted to conclude that common law systems and Anglo-Saxon-outsider corporate governance systems go together, as do insider corporate governance and civil law systems. To some extent this is true, and the historical development of the institutions regarding corporate governance and the legal rights of owners are certainly intertwined, but there is not a one-to-one correspondence between them. de Jong (1997), for example, has divided European countries into Anglo-Saxon, Germanic, and Mediterranian systems according to differences in their corporate governance structures. This division would seem to correspond to the distinction between English, German, and French civil law systems drawn by LLSV. But, de Jong places the Netherlands in the Germanic corporate governance category, while LLSV place it in the French-origin civil law category. Thus, we conclude, that corporate governance and civil law systems are indeed two different, although related, institutional environments in which corporations find themselves, and that each might have a somewhat independent impact on corporate performance. We have already discussed the literature relating ownership structures to corporate performance, we turn now to an examination of the impacts of legal institutions.

Legal systems and the size of external capital markets

The more confidence an individual has that a company's management will invest its capital wisely and pay sufficient dividends to yield attractive returns for the shareholders, the more willing the individual will be to become one of those shareholders. Thus, the demand schedule for corporate shares in a country should be further to the right, the greater is the protection offered by a country's legal system to shareholders. *Ceteris paribus* this should lead to larger markets for corporate securities in countries with legal institutions that protect shareholders against managerial exploitation.

Columns 2–4 in Table 6.2 present evidence taken from LLSV (1997) consistent with this prediction. Column 2 measures the size of the external capital market as

Table 6.2 Differences across countries in legal systems and various economic statistics

1 Country	2 External capital/GNP	3 Domestic firms/Pop	4 IPOs/ Pop	5 GDP growth	6 $q_m = r/i$	7 n
Australia	0.49	63.55	—	3.06	0.94	346
Bermuda	—	—	—	—	0.91	215
Canada	0.39	40.86	4.93	3.36	1.16	1,478
Cayman Islands	—	—	—	—	0.58	42
Great Britain	1.00	35.68	2.01	2.27	0.85	1,331
Hong Kong	1.18	88.16	5.16	7.57	0.78	127
India	0.31	7.79	1.24	4.34	0.80	246
Ireland	0.27	20.00	0.75	4.25	1.10	63
Israel	0.25	127.60	1.80	4.39	1.27	56
Kenya	—	2.24	—	4.79	—	—
Malaysia	1.48	25.15	2.89	6.90	0.86	381
New Zealand	0.28	69.00	0.66	1.67	0.86	66
Nigeria	0.27	1.68	—	3.43	—	—
Pakistan	0.18	5.88	—	5.50	0.40	46
Singapore	1.18	80.00	5.67	1.68	0.97	208
South Africa	1.45	16.00	0.05	7.48	1.07	118
Sri Lanka	0.11	11.94	0.11	4.04	—	—
Thailand	0.56	6.70	0.56	7.70	0.64	243
United States	0.58	30.11	3.11	2.74	1.05	8,591
English-origin average	0.60	35.45	2.23	4.30	1.02	—
Denmark	0.21	50.40	1.80	2.09	0.65	101
Finland	0.25	13.00	0.60	2.40	0.96	79
Norway	0.22	33.00	4.50	3.43	1.04	103
Sweden	0.51	12.66	1.66	1.79	0.65	156
Scandinavian average	0.30	27.26	2.14	2.42	0.78	—
Austria	0.06	13.87	0.25	2.74	0.71	82
Germany	0.13	5.14	0.08	2.60	0.57	425
Switzerland	0.62	33.85	—	1.18	0.64	160
European Germanic-origin average	0.27	17.62	0.16	2.17	0.64	—
Japan	0.62	17.78	0.26	4.13	0.86	2,219
South Korea	0.44	15.88	0.02	9.52	0.70	82
Taiwan	0.88	14.22	0.00	11.56	1.26	126
Asian-Germanic-origin average	0.65	15.96	0.09	8.40	0.94	—
Germanic-origin average	0.46	16.79	0.12	5.29	0.74	—
Argentina	0.07	4.58	0.20	1.40	0.78	24
Belgium	0.17	15.50	0.30	2.46	0.51	79
Brazil	0.18	3.48	0.00	3.95	0.25	133
Chile	0.80	19.92	0.35	3.35	1.24	73
Columbia	0.14	3.13	0.05	4.38	0.43	15

(*continued*)

Table 6.2 (Continued)

1 Country	2 External capital/GNP	3 Domestic firms/Pop	4 IPOs/ Pop	5 GDP growth	6 $q_m = r/i$	7 n
Ecuador	—	13.18	0.09	4.55	—	—
Egypt	0.08	3.48	—	6.13	—	—
France	0.23	8.05	0.17	2.54	0.57	495
Greece	0.07	21.60	0.30	2.46	0.54	49
Indonesia	0.15	1.15	0.10	6.38	0.84	132
Italy	0.08	3.91	0.31	2.82	0.64	150
Jordan	—	23.75	—	1.20	—	—
Luxembourg	—	—	—	—	0.70	12
Mexico	0.22	2.28	0.03	3.07	0.50	81
Netherlands	0.52	21.13	0.66	2.55	0.69	174
Netherl. Antilles	—	—	—	—	1.19	19
Panama	—	—	—	—	1.25	4
Peru	0.40	9.47	0.13	2.82	0.11	20
Phillippines	0.10	2.90	0.27	0.30	1.00	83
Portugal	0.08	19.50	0.50	3.52	0.46	49
Spain	0.17	9.71	0.07	3.27	0.54	117
Turkey	0.18	2.93	0.05	5.05	0.52	29
Uruguay	—	7.00	0.00	1.96	—	—
Venezuela	0.08	4.28	0.00	2.65	0.58	10
French-origin average	0.21	10.00	0.19	3.18	0.59	—

Sources: Columns 2–5, LLSV (1997, table II); columns 6 and 7, Gugler *et al.* (2002b, table 2).

the ratio of stock market capitalization in a country to its GDP in 1994. According to the LLSV evaluation of legal systems we should expect the relative sizes of external capital markets in the four country groups to be English > Scandinavian > Germanic > French. This ranking appears, if we restrict our attention to the three European countries with Germanic legal systems. The average for the six Germanic-origin countries is higher than for the Scandinavian countries when the three Asian countries with Germanic-origin legal systems are included. Clearly, legal institutions are not the only determinants of the size of the external capital market.

Column 3 measures the size of the external capital market as the ratio of the number of domestic firms listed in a country to its population in millions in 1994. Here, the numbers correspond to the predicted ranking exactly, and there are no discernable differences between European and Asian countries in the Germanic-origin group.

Column 4 measures the size of the external capital market as the ratio of initial public offerings of equity in a country (IPOs) to its its population in millions for the one-year period beginning in July of 1995. The English-origin and Scandinavian-legal-system countries both have slightly more than two IPOs for every one million inhabitants, a figure which is more than ten times larger than the number of IPOs in the Germanic- and French-origin countries. Thus, all three sets of comparisons do seem to suggest that English-origin legal systems lead to the largest external capital markets and French- and German-origin systems to the smallest markets with the Scandinavian countries generally coming closest to the English-origin group. LLSV (1997) use regression analysis to control for several other possible determinants of the size of external capital markets. This analysis confirms the picture painted in Table 6.2 regarding the relationship between legal systems and the size of external capital markets.

In addition to the work of LLSV, two additional studies, which emphasize the importance of legal institutions as determinants of the size of a country's external capital markets must be mentioned. Modigliani and Perotti (1997) develop a model in which legal protections for minority shareholders influence the size of a country's equity market, and present some evidence consistent with their model. Demirgüç-Kunt and Maksimovic (1998) present evidence linking the *efficiency* of a country's legal system to the size of its external capital markets, where efficiency is measured using several indexes of the ease with which suppliers of credit can write and enforce debt contracts.

Legal systems, the size of external capital markets, and economic growth

One obvious consequence of having thin external capital markets is that firms with attractive investment opportunities may have difficulties raising the funds required for them to invest optimally. Rajan and Zingales (1998) present evidence that this is the case. Industries that require large amounts of capital, like drugs and pharmaceuticals develop relatively more rapidly in countries with larger external capital markets. More generally, Levine and Zervos (1998) have established a positive link between the size of a country's equity market and its rate of economic growth.

If legal institutions affect the size of a country's external capital markets, and the size of a country's external capital markets affects its growth rate, then there should be a relationship between the characteristics of a country's legal system and its rate of economic growth. Column 5 of Table 6.2 suggests that such a relationship exists, once one takes into account the significant differences between the European and Asian members of the Germanic-origin group. The three Asian, Germanic-origin countries have the highest average growth rates in GDP per capita over the 1970–93 period. They are followed in order by the English-origin, Scandinavian, French-origin, and last the three European countries with Germanic legal systems. French-origin and, at least within Europe, German-origin countries have the slowest growth rates, English-origin and Scandinavian countries the fastest growth rates.

Mahoney (2001) has confirmed the importance of legal institutions in explaining country growth rates using growth equations that control for other variables as for example initial level of GNP. Mahoney restricts his attention to the common-law civil-law distinction. Holding other variables constant, countries with civil-law legal institutions grew more slowly over the 1960–92 period than did countries with common-law systems. Mahoney offers an alternative explanation for this phenomenon from that presented by LLSV, however. He argues that in common-law systems there is a greater respect for individual rights, and greater legal protections against arbitrary state actions to redistribute income and wealth. Thus, according to Mahoney, it is the protections common-law systems give to individual citizens against the expropriations of property by the state that explains their better economic performance, not the protections common-law systems give to shareholders against expropriations of their wealth by company managers. Neither explanation rules out the other.

Legal systems and the returns on investment

LLSV emphasize the differences among legal systems in the constraints that they place on managers, Paul Mahoney emphasizes their differences with respect to the constraints placed on the state. As further evidence in support of their position, LLSV (2000) have presented evidence that dividend payments are on average higher in countries with English-origin legal systems. Differences in views concerning the desirability of paying dividends lie at the heart of the conflict between managers and shareholders, and thus LLSV's findings with respect to dividend payment differences across legal systems is fairly strong evidence that legal institutions affect the relative positions of shareholders and managers as well, perhaps, as the position of the citizen *vis-à-vis* the state.[20]

Although disagreements over dividend payments lie at the heart of the conflict between managers and shareholders over the use of company cash flows, they are an imperfect signal of whether managers are maximizing shareholder wealth or not. For a company with attractive investment opportunities, the optimal dividend payout ratio from the point of view of a shareholder can be zero. GMY's (2002b) test for the effects of legal systems on managers' investment decisions more accurately measures the quality of these decisions. They estimate a marginal q, the ratio of a company's returns on investment, r, to its cost of capital, i, $q_m = r/i$. Any management that maximizes its shareholders' wealth invests in only those projects having an $r \geq i$, and thus has a $q_m \geq 1$ for its total investment. A $q_m < 1$ is evidence of overinvestment or at least poor investment decisions on the part of managers. Of course, for firms with identical investment opportunities and cash flows, q_m and dividend payouts will be inversely related and either can serve as a measure of the extent of agency problems with respect to investment. Marginal q is superior to dividend payout statistics, however, in so far as it allows for differences in investment opportunities and cash flows across firms.[21]

Column 6 in Table 6.2 presents GMY's estimates of q_m by country and country group for the period 1985 through 2000. In many of the developing countries data were available for only a few firms and for the last few years of the sample period. In column 7, the number of firms used to calculate q_m is given. When this number is small, the estimates are not very reliable. As with the figures in columns 2–5, the estimates of q_m follow the pattern implied by LLSV's ranking of legal systems in terms of shareholder protections. The estimate of q_m for the pooled sample of English-origin countries is 1.02, for the pooled sample of French-origin countries it is only 0.59. Where each dollar invested in an English-origin country produces $1.02 worth of assets, each dollar invested in a French-origin country creates only 59 cents worth of assets. Once again the four Scandinavian and six Germanic countries fall in between these two extremes. Once again a dramatic difference between the three Asian countries with legal systems of Germanic origin and their three European counterparts can be observed. The average of the q_ms for the three Asian countries is 0.94, for the three European countries it is only 0.64, barely above that for the French-origin countries. These differences in investment performance between the Asian and European members of the Germanic-origin group may be due to differences within their legal systems that have emerged over time, or they may reflect differences in investment opportunities between Asia and Europe. These differences in investment opportunities may be reflected in the dramatic differences in growth rates reported in column 5.

As noted above, the sample sizes for each country in the GMY study differ widely, with the sample for the United States being particularly large. The good results for the English-origin countries are not simply a reflection of good investment performance by US companies, however. An examination of the individual country estimates reveals that 8 of the 16 estimated q_ms for the English-origin countries are either greater than 1.0 or insignificantly different from it, the same can be said for only 6 of the 20 q_ms for the French-origin countries.[22]

Conclusions

Adam Smith (1776, p. 700) was probably not the first, but certainly was the most famous economist to point out the potential for a conflict of interests between hired managers and shareholders in joint-stock companies.[23] Concern about managerial behavior heightened after the publication of *The Modern Corporation and Private Property* in 1932 and the revelations of managerial malfeasance that occurred in the aftermath of the Great Crash of 1929. A large fraction of the economics profession regarded Berle and Means as cranks, however, and continued to analyze corporate behavior as if no conflict of interest between managers and shareholders existed for decades after the publication of their book. Indeed, a conference held at the University of Chicago on the 50th anniversary of its publication was still more of an effort to bury the book rather than to recognize its achievement.[24] The development of principal–agency theory by economists with impeccable neoclassical economics credentials and an ever growing amount of empirical evidence to support this theory has led to the general acceptance of both the existence and importance of principal–agent problems in "the modern corporation."

Both Adam Smith and Berle and Means saw the problem of managerial discretion arising because managers held few shares in their company, and in the case of Berle and Means, because the remaining shares were widely dispersed. This image of the modern corporation came to dominate the managerial-discretion/principal–agent literature. By implication, no managerial-discretion problems were thought to exist when shareholdings were concentrated in someone's – anyone's – hands. During the 1970s and 1980s, the US and UK economies did not seem to be performing as well as many European and Asian economies, and in particular corporations in these Anglo-Saxon countries appeared to be underperforming relative to leading companies across both the Atlantic and the Pacific oceans. Many begin to believe that the US corporate governance system was inferior to those existing in at least some parts of Europe and Japan (e.g. Roe, 1993a; Charkham, 1994).

The weak performance of both the German and Japanese economies over the past decade and in both absolute and comparative terms the strong performance of both the US and UK economies has led to some second thoughts on this matter. As Shleifer and Vishny (1997) point out, no country's economy could achieve the levels that the United States, the United Kingdom, and Germany have achieved, if their institutional structures and in particular their corporate governance systems did not both supply capital to firms with attractive investment opportunities and to some extent deny capital from those who would invest it poorly. All corporate governance systems in the advanced countries of the world must be judged as successes on an absolute basis. Although all corporate governance systems in advanced countries are obviously doing reasonably well, some appear to be doing better than others, and most recently the best preforming systems appear to be in the Anglo-Saxon countries.

The literature on managerial-discretion and principal–agent problems evolved with the supposedly archetypical Anglo-Saxon corporation in mind. Managers might use their discretion to pursue growth, and when they did it was the helpless and hapless individual holding a few hundred shares who suffered. An examination of companies in other countries reveals, however, that empire-building occurs everywhere. Indeed, the vast pyramidal corporate structures that one observes in countries like Italy and Turkey suggests that the families controlling these giant structures may be even more willing to sacrifice wealth to preserve their empires than are their Anglo-Saxon counterparts, and minority shareholders in these companies are *even more hapless* than their Anglo-Saxon counterparts.[25]

This chapter has reviewed the hypotheses and evidence about corporate governance structures. On the one hand, we have seen that the differences across countries are to some extent less dramatic than the literature might lead one to expect. Concentrated shareholdings in companies outside of the largest 500 are the rule not the exception in the United States, and are characteristic of the very largest companies in such Anglo-Saxon countries like Canada. Nevertheless, we did find several significant differences across countries in both patterns of ownership structure and economic performance. Many of these differences appear to be related to the type of legal system a country has. In countries where shareholders rights are better protected, more equity is issued, capital markets are better developed, new firms find it easier to raise capital, investment performance is better, and so too is economic growth.

These relationships are summarized in Figure 6.1. Although there has been considerable discussion in the corporate governance literature about which variables are endogenous and which exogenous, the one variable that must clearly be assumed to be exogenous is country legal systems, for these originated decades ago

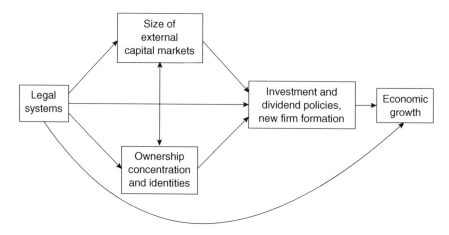

Figure 6.1 Legal systems, ownership structure and economic performance.

and in many cases centuries ago. These legal systems determine both a country's ownership structure and the size of its external capital market. The latter in turn along with the legal institutions determine the quantity and quality of its corporate investments, new firm start-ups and the like. Economic growth follows from these investments with a country's legal system possibly having a separate effect through its relationship to the amount of political rent seeking and transfers that occur in a country.

7 Investment

When John Maynard Keynes developed macroeconomic theory to explain why unemployment could exist in an equilibrium, one of his conditions for that equilibrium was that planned aggregate investment must equal planned aggregate savings. The central role investment played in the *General Theory* led to the study of investment becoming a topic largely confined to macroeconomics. This has changed in more recent years, but even today it is rare to find a chapter on capital investment in micro-oriented industrial organization texts, even though other investment decisions, like advertising, R&D, and mergers are featured there. This neglect of investment is unfortunate for two reasons. First, because plant and equipment purchases, advertising, R&D, and mergers are all forms of investment, whatever theory explains one should in principle explain the others. Understanding the determinants of plant and equipment purchases may help in understanding purchases of plant and equipment embodied in ongoing firms (mergers), and the purchase of the intangible assets created by advertising and R&D. Second, knowledge of the determinants and effects of all forms of investment can help sort out the various hypotheses about managerial motivation and discretion discussed in the previous two chapters.

In this chapter, therefore, we take up some of the hypotheses that have been put forward to explain plant and equipment purchases, the empirical support for these hypotheses, and empirical evidence on the returns on investment. Because a potentially important determinant of investment is the firm's cost of capital, we shall also explore its determinants as put forward in modern finance theory. We shall also take up the dividends payment decision of the firm, because of its close relationship to investment. We begin, however, with the determinants of capital equipment purchases.

The basic investment decision

Assume that the firm's production function contains as arguments only the capital stock, K, and the quantity of labor, L, so that $Q = f(K, L)$. The firm's profits can then be written as

$$\pi = PQ - iK - wL = Pf(K, L) - iK - wL, \tag{7.1}$$

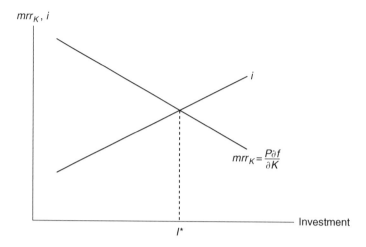

Figure 7.1 The basic investment decision.

where P is the price of the output, i is the firm's cost of capital, and w is labor's wage. Each of these prices might in turn be assumed to be functions of other variables. Maximizing equation (7.1) with respect to K, we obtain

$$\frac{\partial \pi}{\partial K} = \frac{P \partial f(K, L)}{\partial K} - i = 0, \qquad \frac{P \partial f(K, L)}{\partial K} = i. \tag{7.2}$$

The firm maximizes profits by equating the marginal return on its capital to its cost of capital. If we measure additions to capital stock, investment, along the horizontal axis, and the marginal returns (mrr_K) and cost of capital along the vertical axis, then the firm's investment decision can be depicted as in Figure 7.1. I^*, the optimal investment, is a function of those factors that affect the firm's returns on capital, and its cost of capital. Logically, both blades of this investment scissors should be important. But, some theories of investment have concentrated on only one set of factors.

The accelerator theory

One of the first theories of investment to come out of the macroeconomic revolution launched by Keynes's *General Theory* was the accelerator theory. It is extremely simple in its micro-foundations, and focuses only on the marginal returns side of the investment scissors.

Let $f(K, L)$ be a linear homogeneous production function, and i and w be constant. The firm's output expansion path is then a straight line, with its output being a constant proportion of its capital stock,

$$Q = (1/b)K. \tag{7.3}$$

Equation (7.3) defines the amount of capital the firm needs to produce any level of output. If demand conditions are such that its optimal output in time t is Q_t, then its *desired* capital stock in period t can be written as

$$K_t^D = bQ_t. \tag{7.4}$$

The purchase and installation of capital equipment takes time, and thus it is reasonable to assume that a firm can adjust its capital stock only partially toward its desired level. If a represents this adjustment factor, $0 < a < 1$, then the change in capital stock in any period, that is to say investment, is proportional to the difference between existing and desired capital stock.

$$I_t = K_t - K_{t-1} = a(K_t^D - K_{t-1}). \tag{7.5}$$

Using equation (7.4) to replace the desired capital we obtain the basic accelerator equation.[1]

$$I_t = abQ_t - aK_{t-1}. \tag{7.6}$$

The key determinant of investment in the accelerator model is the firm's output, or sales.

Although sales is a *flow* variable, the rigid link between sales (output) and capital stock assumed in (7.3) makes the accelerator model a form of stock adjustment model. The first term on the right-hand side of equation (7.6) measures the firm's demand for capital stock, the second term measures the supply of that stock. In the accelerator theory investment is essentially modelled as an excess demand equation for capital stock.

Cash flow models

The basic hypothesis

The basic assumption behind cash flow models is that managers have a desired *flow* of investment rather than a desired capital stock. Once again we make the assumption that a firm can only go a partial way toward its desired investment flow in any period, so that the change in flows of investment between periods t and $t-1$ is given by

$$I_t - I_{t-1} = a(I_t^D - I_{t-1}), \tag{7.7}$$

with again $0 < a < 1$. The key assumption in cash flow models is that the desired flow of investment in period t is proportional to some measure of cash flow, F_t

$$I_t^D = bF_t. \tag{7.8}$$

Substituting (7.8) into (7.7) and adding I_{t-1} to both sides of the equation yields the basic cash flow investment equation

$$I_t = abF_t + (1-a)I_{t-1}. \tag{7.9}$$

Today's investment is a function of cash flow and lagged investment.

When estimating equation (7.9) two measures of cash flow have generally been used, profits plus depreciation, or profits plus depreciation less dividends. Use of the second measure implicitly assumes that dividends are a higher priority use of cash flow than investment and are thus decided first. This assumption in turn raises the question of what determines dividends. We shall return to this issue later in the chapter.

Where the simple accelerator model stresses only the demand for capital side of the investment decision, the simple cash flow model stresses only the cost of capital side. The difference between the two is depicted with the help of Figure 7.2. On the left-hand-side, part (a), the firm is assumed to have a constant cost of capital across all sources of funds. If F measures the level of its cash flows before dividends are paid, then a firm with a marginal return schedule mrr_{K1} would invest I_1 and pay $F - I_1$ out as dividends. Shifts in its marginal returns schedule, as say to mrr_{K2}, have a big impact on its level of investment. Shifts in F have no impact.

All cash flow models of investment assume that the firm's cost of capital rises for some reason when it has to resort to outside sources of finance. In the extreme we might assume that the firm can raise no outside capital. A firm with internal cash flows of F_1 and mrr_{K1} as in Figure 7.2b would then be constrained to undertake only F_1 in investment. A shift in its marginal returns schedule to mrr_{K2} would leave its investment unchanged at F_1. On the other hand, if its marginal returns schedule were mrr_{K2} and its cash flow was to increase to F_2, its investment would increase from F_1 to F_2.

It is apparent from this discussion that cash flow can be expected to be an important determinant of investment, if the firm's cost of capital rises significantly

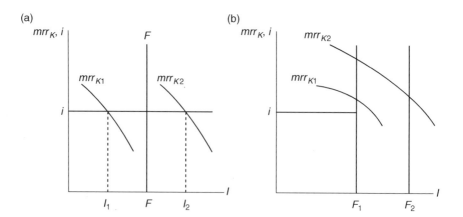

Figure 7.2 Cash flow and investment.

when it has to resort to external sources for funds. We discuss three explanations that have been given for why such a rise in the cost of capital might be expected as the firm enters the external capital market.

Transaction costs

James Duesenberry (1958) argued that external capital was more costly than internal capital because of the *transaction costs* of raising capital externally. Bonds or common shares must be printed, investment bank fees must be paid, advertisements must be placed in newspapers, and so on. Each of these transactions has costs associated with it that are not present when investment is entirely financed out of internal fund flows.

The costs of external finance are often assumed to differ between debt and equity issues leading to a *hierarchy of finance* as illustrated in Figure 7.3. A firm with the marginal returns schedule mrr_{K1} issues no new debt or equity, and finances all of its investment, I_1, out of internal cash flow. A firm with the marginal returns schedule mrr_{K2} invests I_2, which is made up of its entire cash flow and a new debt issue equal to $I_2 - F$. On its debt issue it must pay a higher cost of capital, d, than that implicit on its internal cash flows, i. A firm with the marginal returns schedule mrr_{K3} invests I_3, which is made up of its entire cash flow, a new debt issue equal to its *debt capacity*, $D - F$, and a new equity issue, $I_3 - D$. On this new equity it pays a still higher cost of capital, e.

Asymmetric information

Myers and Majluf (1984) have argued that external capital may be effectively more expensive than internal capital, because of the existence of asymmetric information. When managers know the true value of a company's capital stock and investment opportunities and the capital market does not, it can happen that the

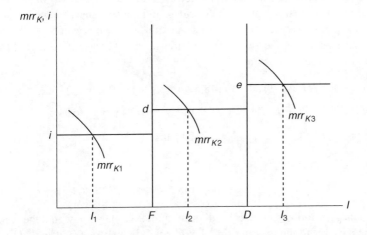

Figure 7.3 The hierarchy of company finance.

Table 7.1 Payoffs from investing 100 in the presence of asymmetric information

	State 1	State 2
Net returns on investment	25	12
Value of assets in place	200	60
(Value of firm with $I = 0$)		
Value of firm when $I = 100$	325	172

capital market *undervalues* the company's common shares. This underevaluation can in turn lead the firm's managers to forgo an investment with positive returns, if the firm lacks the internal fund flows to finance the investment, because to finance it through a new equity issue would harm the existing shareholders.

We illustrate this possibility with an example taken from Myers and Majluf (1984). Let there be two possible states of the world, States 1 and 2, each occurring with an equal probability. The firm's managers contemplate an investment of 100. If State 1 occurs, this investment will return the 100 invested plus 25, if State 2 occurs, the investment returns the 100 plus 12. The value of the firm's assets in place, and thus the value of the firm if it does not undertake the investment, is 200 in State 1, and 60 in State 2. With the investment, the respective values in States 1 and 2 will of course be 325 (200 + 100 + 25), and 172 (60 + 100 + 12). The possibilities are depicted in Table 7.1.

At the time the managers would undertake the investment, the market is uncertain as to whether State 1 or State 2 will occur. The value of the shares of the existing (old) shareholders at this time should the managers undertake the investment, P', is thus the expected value of the assets in place and the net returns to the investment, $P' = 0.5(200 + 25) + 0.5(60 + 12) = 148.5$. The value of the shares of the new shareholders at this point in time is, of course, the value of the equity issued to finance the investment, $E = 100$. Thus, the old shareholders' shares will be worth $P'/(P' + E)$ fraction of whatever value the firm is eventually worth once the market learns what the true state of the world is, and the new shareholders' shares will be worth $E/(P' + E)$ fraction of whatever value the firm is eventually worth. Should State 1 come up, the value of the shares of the old and new shareholders will therefore eventually become

$$V_{OLD_1} = (P'/(P' + E))V_1 = (148.5/(148.5 + 100))325 = 194.2,$$
$$V_{NEW_1} = (E/(P' + E))V_1 = (100/(148.5 + 100))325 = 130.8.$$

If State 2 comes up, these respective values become

$$V_{OLD_2} = (P'/(P' + E))V_2 = (148.5/(148.5 + 100))172 = 102.8,$$
$$V_{NEW_2} = (E/(P' + E))V_2 = (100/(148.5 + 100))172 = 69.2.$$

If the managers know that State 1 will occur, however, they know that the value of the firm's shares to the existing shareholders will be worth 200, if they do not undertake the investment. Since the old shareholders' share of the value of the firm in State 1, when it does undertake the investment is only 194.2, the managers would actually make the old shareholders worse off by undertaking the investment even though the investment itself promises positive net returns. This surprising result comes about because to finance the investment, the managers must issue new shares at a price that is less than their true value, given that State 1 is going to occur. If the firm had a 100 in cash flow, it could of course finance the investment without harming the existing shareholders. Thus, arises the link between investment and cash flow, and the implicit rise in the firm's cost of capital when resort is made to the equity market in the presence of asymmetric information.

This example illustrates that the existence of asymmetric information, in the sense that managers know the true returns to existing and new capital and the market does not, *may* make the managers shy away from issuing new equity, and thus make the financing of investment dependent on the levels of cash flow. This possibility rests on several strong assumptions, however. First of all, the managers must be assumed to be maximizing the wealth of only the old shareholders. If managers weigh the welfare of old and new shareholders equally, then they will issue the equity and undertake the investment under both states of the world, since the two groups of shareholders together benefit from the investment being undertaken. Second, one must assume that the firm is unable to issue debt to finance the investment. If it could issue debt of 100 at a cost of less than 12 under both states of the world, the old shareholders would receive all of the excess returns and would gain from the investment. The firm must also be assumed not to be paying dividends, for if it were, the old shareholders would be better off if the managers cut the dividends and used the funds to finance the investment.

Managerial discretion

In the Marris' growth model discussed in Chapter 5, managers wish to expand the growth rate of their company beyond the level which maximizes shareholder wealth, while maintaining the company's share price at a sufficiently high level to avoid a takeover by outsiders who will dismiss the managers. The managers' utility function can thus be written as a function of the growth rate of the firm, g, and the probability of its being taken over, p, $U = U(g, p)$, with $\partial U/\partial g > 0$, and $\partial U/\partial p < 0$. The probability of takeover increases as the share price falls. The market value of the firm's equity is the present discounted value of its dividend payments,

$$E_t = P_{St} N_{St} = \sum_{j=0}^{\infty} \frac{\text{Div}_{t+j}}{(1+i)^j} \tag{7.10}$$

where E_t is the market value of outstanding equity, P_{St} and N_{St} are the price of a common share and the number of shares outstanding, Div_{t+j} is the dividends payment in year $t+j$, and i is the firm's cost of capital. Thus, share price rises *ceteris paribus* with dividends. If we assume that all cash flows go either to dividends or investment, $F_t \equiv I_t + \text{Div}_t$, then the firm's share price falls as investment increases, and the probability of takeover rises as investment increases, $p = p(I)$, $p'(I) > 0$.

Of course, today's investment increases tomorrow's profit, and thus may increase tomorrow's dividends thereby having a positive impact on today's share price. For this reason the Latin words *ceteris paribus* – other things held equal – were inserted in the previous paragraph. A growth-seeking management invests more than the amount that maximizes shareholder wealth, and thus for it the marginal impact of investment on share price is negative. (This proposition is proved in the section on "The Irrelevance debt and dividends" of this chapter.) The marginal impact of investment on growth is positive, $g'(I) > 0$. A growth-oriented management's utility-maximizing level of investment thus satisfies the following condition

$$\frac{\partial U}{\partial g} g'(I) + \frac{\partial U}{\partial p} p'(I) = 0, \tag{7.11}$$

or

$$\frac{\partial U}{\partial g} g'(I) = -\frac{\partial U}{\partial p} p'(I). \tag{7.12}$$

The investment decision of a growth-oriented management is depicted in Figure 7.4. If it equated the marginal return on investment to its costs of capital, it would invest I^*, the value of the firm's shares would be maximized, and the probability of takeover to replace the management because of its investment choices would be zero. As the managers push investment beyond I^*, the probability of takeover increases. A utility-maximizing management invests to the point

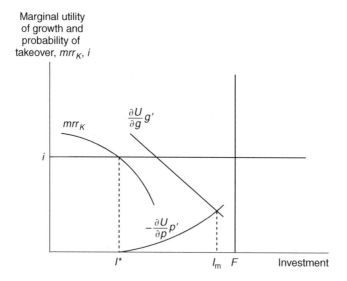

Figure 7.4 Managerial discretion and investment.

where the marginal increase in utility from the growth caused by an extra unit of investment just equals the marginal *disutility* from the rise in the probability of takeover caused by this investment. Cash flow is favored by a growth-oriented management, because its *implicit* cost is lower than that of external finance. The implicit cost of capital for the managerial-discretion firm rises as managers resort to outside capital, because they must pay the full cost of this capital when it is obtained by issuing debt, or because they must increase the probability of takeover still further by placing still more shares in the hands of outsiders.

The neoclassical theory of investment

The neoclassical theory emphasizes the importance of the neoclassical cost of capital in determining the level of a firm's investment. Consider again equation (7.2)

$$\frac{P \partial f(K, L)}{\partial K} = i. \tag{7.2'}$$

The profit-maximizing firm equates the marginal return on capital to its (neoclassical) cost of capital. Assume now that the firm has a Cobb–Douglas production function

$$f(K, L) = A K^\alpha L^\beta. \tag{7.13}$$

Its marginal product of capital can then be written as

$$\frac{\partial f(K, L)}{\partial K} = \alpha A K^{\alpha-1} L^\beta = \frac{K}{K} \alpha A K^{\alpha-1} L^\beta = \frac{\alpha A K^\alpha L^\beta}{K} = \frac{\alpha Q}{K}. \tag{7.14}$$

Substituting from (7.14) into (7.2') we obtain

$$\frac{\alpha P Q}{K} = i, \tag{7.15}$$

from which we derive an expression for the firm's desired capital stock, K^D

$$K^D = \frac{\alpha P Q}{i}. \tag{7.16}$$

From here we can proceed as under the accelerator theory to replace K^D in equation (7.5) with the expression in (7.16) to obtain

$$I_t = a\alpha \frac{P_t Q_t}{i_t} - a K_{t-1}. \tag{7.17}$$

As is evident from comparing equations (7.6) and (7.17), the neoclassical theory incorporates the accelerator model by making investment a function of output and lagged capital stock. It differs from the accelerator model, however, by also making investment depend on product price, and most importantly, on the firm-specific cost of capital. A crucial question in estimating an equation to test the neoclassical model of investment is how one measures a firm's cost of capital. We take up this issue in the section on "The neoclassical cost of capital and the Modigliani and Miller theorems," but before that we describe one more set of investment theories.

Expectations theories of investment

The accelerator and neoclassical theories both make today's investment a function of today's output. A firm invests not to produce *today's* output, however, but *tomorrow's*. Obviously, a firm with a current output of one billion units is more likely to have an output next year of around a billion units, than is a firm with a current output of one hundred units. But today's output will be an inaccurate predictor of future outputs to the extent that firm growth rates differ.

Considerations such as these led Grunfeld (1960) to propose that investment should depend on a variable that captures expected future growth in the demand for capital. He proposed the firm's current market value, a variable that varies across firms both because of scale differences, and because of differences in market expectations regarding future growth rates. Thus the Grunfeld model might be written as one in which $K^D = bM$, where M is the market value of the firm.

Most recent theories that use the market value of the firm to explain investment incorporate it into Tobin's q. Assume again that capital and labor are the only factors of production. The market value of the firm is the present value of the payments to capital,

$$M = \frac{PQ - wL}{i}. \tag{7.18}$$

If we further assume that the firm has a production function that exhibits constant returns to scale, then total output is exhausted if each factor is paid its marginal physical product[2]

$$Q = \frac{\partial f(K, L)}{\partial K} K + \frac{\partial f(K, L)}{\partial L} L. \tag{7.19}$$

Substituting from (7.19) into (7.18), and assuming that labor receives the value of its marginal product, $w = P\partial Q/\partial L$, yields

$$M = \frac{P(\partial Q/\partial K)K}{i}. \tag{7.20}$$

Assuming further that the production function is not only linear homogeneous, but also Cobb–Douglas ($Q = AK^\alpha L^{1-\alpha}$), allows us to use (7.14) to obtain

$$\frac{\partial Q}{\partial K} = \alpha \frac{Q}{K}. \tag{7.14'}$$

Plugging (7.14') into (7.20) gives

$$M = \frac{\alpha PQ}{i}. \tag{7.21}$$

Tobin's q is defined as the market value of the firm divided by the replacement cost of its capital

$$q = \frac{M}{K}.$$ (7.22)

Combining equations (7.22) and (7.21) we obtain

$$q = \frac{\alpha P Q}{i K}.$$ (7.23)

Under the neoclassical theory's assumptions, we have

$$K^D = \alpha P Q / i.$$ (7.16′)

Combining (7.16′) and (7.23) we obtain

$$q = \frac{K^D}{K}, \quad K^D = q K.$$ (7.24)

Adding time subscripts and substituting into equation (7.5) yields the basic Tobin's q investment equation

$$I_t = a q K_{t-1} - a K_{t-1}.$$ (7.25)

Note that the q-theory of investment incorporates the basic assumptions and conditions of the neoclassical model. Under these assumptions, differences in q across firms reflect differences in desired capital stocks relative to actual capital stocks and thus should explain differences in investment, without actually having to measure the costs of capital of individual firms.

Both the q-theory of investment and the neoclassical theory make rather strong assumptions about the functioning of the capital market, and its effects on investment decisions. These assumptions can be justified by appeal to modern finance theory. Given the importance of this theory to the investment decision, we shall take a brief detour in the following two sections to examine some of the basic propositions of this theory. Readers familiar with modern finance theory, or not interested in learning about it, can skip there two sections without losing the thread of the argument.

The neoclassical cost of capital and the Modigliani and Miller theorems

The irrelevance of debt and dividends

If managers maximize the wealth of their shareholders, then they should invest in only those projects that promise returns at least as great as those the shareholders can obtain by investing in other firms of comparable risk. This alternative return, the opportunity costs of the shareholders, is the neoclassical cost of capital. Modigliani and Miller (1958, 1961) (hereafter M&M) showed that this opportunity cost is the appropriate measure of the firm's cost of capital, *regardless of whether the firm uses internal fund flows, or new debt, or new equity* to finance the investment. In a series of remarkably novel theorems, they also proved that under certain conditions the market value of the firm is independent of its capital structure (the debt/equity ratio), and dividend policy. The originality and significance of their efforts was subsequently recognized in their receipt of Nobel prizes.

The Modigliani–Miller theorems abstract from considerations of transaction costs, taxes, and the like. They also assume that both firms and individuals can issue riskless (default free) debt. The importance of this assumption will become apparent as we run through the proofs.

Each firm is engaged in a business involving certain risks – shifts in demand, changes in technology, labor unrest, and so on. Let us assume that companies with similar risks can be grouped into *risk classes*, groups of firms with identical risks. Let j be a firm in the jth risk class with earnings of π_j per share, which are expected to remain constant indefinitely. If P_j is the price of a common share of firm j, then its cost of capital is

Definition. *The cost of capital, i_j, of a firm in the jth risk class is*

$$i_j = \frac{\pi_j}{P_j}.$$

Note that P_j is the present value of the constant earnings stream π_j from now to infinity ($P_j = \pi_j / i_j$). Firms in the jth risk class will have different share prices depending on their earnings and the number of shares that they have outstanding, but all will have the *same ratio* of share price to earnings. This ratio, P_j / π_j, is the price of a unit of earnings for a firm in the jth risk class.

Prior to M&M it had been commonly assumed that firms had optimal debt/equity ratios, and that a firm's cost of capital would increase dramatically, if it exceeded its optimal debt/equity ratio. M&M proved that under the assumptions given above, this was not the case.

Theorem 1. The cost of capital of a firm in the jth risk class is $i_j = \pi_j / P_j$, and is independent of the firm's capital structure.

Let E_j be the value of the common stock of company j,
P_j be the price of a share of the common stock of company j,
N_j be the number of shares of common stock of company j outstanding,
D_j be the total debt of company j, and
r be the risk free interest payable on all debt.

By definition the value of company j, V_j, is the sum of the market values of its debt and common equity,

$$V_j \equiv E_j + D_j.$$

We wish to prove that $V_j = \Pi_j / i_j$, where Π_j is the total earnings of the firm, and that V_j is independent of the proportions between E_j and D_j. Let U and L be two firms in the jth risk class with

$$\Pi_U = \Pi_L = \Pi.$$

Let U be unlevered, and L be levered

$$V_U = E_U, \quad V_L = E_L + D_L.$$

Suppose an investor wishes to earn a gross return of $\alpha \Pi$. There are two different routes that the investor can take to achieve this end.

Action	Investment	Earnings
1 Buy α fraction of U's shares	$\alpha E_U = \alpha V_U$	$\alpha \Pi$
2 Buy α fraction of L's shares	$\alpha E_L = \alpha(V_L - D_L)$	$\alpha \Pi - \alpha r D_L$
Buy αD_L	αD_L	$\alpha r D_L$
Combined effects action 2	αV_L	$\alpha \Pi$

Both routes lead to the same earnings, $\alpha \Pi$. By assumption both firms are in the same risk class, and thus the choice of routes should be independent of risk considerations. If $V_L < V_U$, the second route to obtaining these earnings is cheaper than the first, and all investors will choose to follow the second route. The price of L's shares rises, and the price of U's falls until $V_L = V_U$, and the two routes are equally attractive. If $V_L > V_U$, the second route to obtaining these earnings is more expensive than the first, and all investors choose the first route. The price of L's shares falls, and the price of U's rises until $V_L = V_U$. Given that the two firms have the same earnings and are in the same risk class, their market values must be the same independent of their capital structure.

As mentioned above, prior to M&M's path-breaking work, it was generally believed that shareholders would have to be offered a substantial premium to hold a company's shares once its debt equity ratio had passed some critical value, that is the return on a company's common shares, k, rose dramatically after some D/E ratio as depicted in Figure 7.5a. Under the M&M assumptions, however, k rises linearly with D/E.

Theorem 2. The rate of return on common shares of firms in a given risk class is a linear function of their leverage.

The return on equity is (we drop the j subscripts for simplicity)

$$k = \frac{\Pi - rD}{E}. \tag{7.26}$$

By Theorem 1

$$V = \frac{\Pi}{i}. \tag{7.27}$$

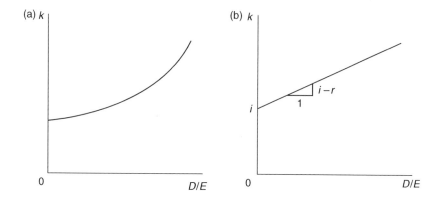

Figure 7.5 Relationship between returns on equity and leverage. (a) with critical D/E and
(b) under Modigliani–Miller assumptions.

Thus,

$$\Pi = iV = i(E + D), \tag{7.28}$$

and

$$k = \frac{i(E + D) - rD}{E} = i + (i - r)\frac{D}{E}. \tag{7.29}$$

Firms with no debt outstanding must promise their shareholders a return of i in
line with the risks inherent in the firm's basic operations. As the firm's debt/equity
ratio expands it must promise shareholders an additional premium of $(i - r)$ to
compensate them for the additional, leverage risk that they bear (see Figure 7.5b).
This risk is the danger that the firm will not make its normal dividend payments
to equity holders, because of the extent of its fixed interest commitments.

The reason that shareholders do not demand increasingly high premia to offset
the extra leverage firms incur is because they are able to offset these risks themselves by buying debt. If the firm issues more or less debt than the shareholder
thinks is optimal, she simply "corrects" the firm's decision by selling or buying
the appropriate amount of debt herself. We now see the importance of the assumption that individuals can both buy and sell riskless (default free) debt. Although
the ability to create "homemade leverage" was an important assumption in the
first proofs of the key Modigliani–Miller theorems, we shall show in the next
section that Theorem 1 can be proved without resorting to this assumption. Before
demonstrating this, however, we prove two more theorems that have important
implications in the industrial organization field.

Theorem 3. If the managers maximize the wealth of their shareholders, the shareholders are indifferent as to whether an additional sum of funds F is reinvested in
the firm, or paid out as dividends.

Let the firm's assets in place promise a return of π in perpetuity. Assume for simplicity, that the firm has no debt outstanding. The wealth of the firm's shareholders thus equals the value of the firm

$$w_0 = E_0 = \frac{\pi}{i}. \tag{7.30}$$

Let the managers of the firm now discover that they have F in funds that they did not know they had. If these are paid out as dividends, the wealth of the shareholders is

$$w_1 = E_0 + F. \tag{7.31}$$

Assume alternatively that F is invested at a return of m, and that the return on the assets in place is unaffected by this investment. Then the wealth of the shareholders from following this second route is

$$w_2 = \frac{\pi}{i} + \frac{mF}{i} = E_0 + \frac{m}{i}F. \tag{7.32}$$

Then

$$(w_1 \gtreqless w_2) \longleftrightarrow (m \gtreqless i). \tag{7.33}$$

Whether the shareholders are better off from the management's paying F out as dividends or reinvesting the funds, depends on whether the return on that investment, m, is less than or greater than the firm's cost of capital. If the firm's management is maximizing shareholder wealth, however, it will be investing to the point where $m = i$, and the shareholders are indifferent as to whether the extra funds are invested or paid out as dividends. This theorem illustrates what we saw in Chapter 5, that conflict between managers and shareholders over investment and dividend policy rests crucially on the extent of a firm's investment opportunities.

To explain why some firms appear to earn lower returns on their shares than their shareholders' opportunity costs without abandoning the assumption of shareholder-wealth maximization, it is sometimes argued that mangers make these investments because capital gains are generally taxed more lightly than dividends. Even when dividends are more heavily taxed than capital gains, however, investments with returns less than shareholder opportunity costs are not warranted. Capital gains equivalent to a dividends payment can be given to shareholders by using the funds to repurchase the firm's shares. This point is demonstrated in the following theorem.

Theorem 4. Shareholders are indifferent as to whether an additional sum of funds F is used to repurchase the firm's shares, or paid out as dividends.

Let the firm's assets in place promise a return of π in perpetuity, with again no debt outstanding. The wealth of the firm's shareholders equals as before

$$w_0 = E_0 = P_0 N_0 = \frac{\pi}{i}, \tag{7.34}$$

where P_0 and N_0 are the initial price of a share and the initial number of shares outstanding. The managers again discover that they have F in funds that they did not know that they had. If these funds are paid as dividends, the wealth of the shareholders is

$$w_1 = E_0 + F. \tag{7.35}$$

Assume alternatively that the managers use F to repurchase some of the outstanding shares. As soon as they announce this action, the price of the company's shares rises to P_1 at which M shares are purchased.

$$F = P_1 M. \tag{7.36}$$

Subsequent to this action the firm's earnings and market value equal their initial values

$$w_2 = w_0 = \frac{\pi}{i} = P_0 N_0 = P_1 (N_0 - M). \tag{7.37}$$

Using (7.36) to replace M in (7.37) and rearranging yields

$$\frac{F}{N_0} = P_1 - P_0. \tag{7.38}$$

The left-hand-side of (7.38) is the per share dividend payment, if the funds are paid out as dividends. The right-hand-side of (7.38) is the per share capital gain accruing to all shareholders, both those who immediately sell their shares and those who do not. Shareholders receive the identical increase in wealth regardless of whether the funds are paid out as dividends, or used to repurchase shares, but in the latter case the increase in wealth occurs as a capital gain.

An alternative demonstration of the irrelevance of capital structure

As we noted earlier, the original M&M proofs of the irrelevance of capital structure rely on the assumption that both individuals and companies can issue defaultless debt. The irrelevance of debt theorem can be proved without relying on homemade leverage and defaultless bonds, if we assume perfectly competitive markets exist for every type of company shares and bonds. The key assumptions underlying the proof are as follows:[3]

Assumption 1. Perfect Capital Market and No Transaction Costs. There are no transaction costs from issuing and buying debt and equity. There are no transaction costs from bankruptcy. There are no taxes.

Assumption 2. Given Investment Strategies. Firms face a set of investment opportunities that are independent of how the investments are financed.

Assumption 3. Perfect Substitutes. There are perfect substitutes for all securities.

Assumption 4. Shareholder Wealth Maximization. The managers maximize the value of the firm ($V = E + D$).

Theorem 5. Given Assumptions 1–4 and a general equilibrium in the capital market, then

(a) *V* is unaffected by changes in the firm's financing decisions,
(b) the financing decisions are of no consequence to the shareholders, and
(c) the capital market is perfectly competitive.

The logic underlying the theorem runs as follows: Assumption 2 makes present and future profits depend only on the amount of investment undertaken, not upon how it is financed. Assumption 3 ties these profits to *V*. Assumption 4 fixes *V* at its maximum.

If a firm faced downward sloping demand schedules for its common shares and bonds, it might be possible for it to raise its market value by altering its capital structure. Its market value would increase, for example, if it issued debt and used the funds to reduce the amount of its equity outstanding, if the demand for its debt was more elastic than the demand for its equity. But Assumption 3 states that there are perfect substitutes for both its common shares and its debt, that is, there are infinitely many companies offering shares and debt with identical risk and return characteristics. If a firm contracts the amount of equity it has outstanding, it cannot raise its price, because other companies whose equity has identical characteristics will simply expand their offerings to offset the firm's action. An expansion of equity will be offset by the contraction of other firms. The firm's financing decisions do not matter, because each of its actions is offset by the actions of the other firms operating in the capital market.

The capital asset pricing model (CAPM)

The basic relationships

If the marginal utility of income of a person declines as her income increases she is said to be *risk averse*.[4] A risk averse person will prefer a certain $100 to a gamble that pays $200 with probability 0.5, and nothing with probability of 0.5. More generally, given a choice between two income streams which promise the same mean return, a risk averse individual always prefers the income stream with the smallest variance.

Considerations such as these led early researchers to measure the riskiness of a company by the variance of its profits or by the variance of the returns on its shares. William Sharpe (1964), another Nobel Prize winner in economics, pointed out, however, that for those individuals who hold portfolios of stocks, it is the variance of the returns on the *portfolio* that is of primary concern, not the variance of an individual company's returns. The relevant measure of risk for a company is related to the contribution that company's equity makes to the variance of the portfolio.

To see what is involved, consider a portfolio, a combination *C*, formed by combining shares in companies *A* and *B*. Let R_A and R_B be the expected returns on the shares of *A* and *B*. Then if the combination is made up of α fraction of *A* and $(1 - \alpha)$ of B, the expected returns on the combination are

$$R_C = \alpha R_A + (1 - \alpha) R_B. \tag{7.39}$$

The variance in the returns on the combination is then

$$\sigma_{R_C}^2 = \alpha^2 \sigma_{R_A}^2 + (1 - \alpha)^2 \sigma_{R_B}^2 + 2r_{AB}\alpha(1 - \alpha)\sigma_{R_A}\sigma_{R_B}, \tag{7.40}$$

where σ_{Ri} is the standard deviation of the returns on i $(i = A, B, C)$, and r_{AB} is the simple correlation between the returns on the securities of A and B. If $r_{AB} = 1$, the returns on the two securities are perfectly correlated, and (7.40) becomes

$$\sigma_{R_C}^2 = \alpha^2 \sigma_{R_A}^2 + 2\alpha(1 - \alpha)\sigma_{R_A}\sigma_{R_B} + (1 - \alpha)^2 \sigma_{R_B}^2 = (\alpha\sigma_{R_A} + (1 - \alpha)\sigma_{R_B})^2, \tag{7.41}$$

from which we obtain

$$\sigma_{R_C} = \alpha\sigma_{R_A} + (1 - \alpha)\sigma_{R_B}. \tag{7.42}$$

When the returns on two securities are perfectly correlated, both the mean return on a combination of the two and the standard deviation of the combination are simple linear combinations of the individual company returns and standard deviations. When $r_{AB} < 1$, $\sigma_{RC} < \alpha\sigma_{RA} + (1 - \alpha)\sigma_{RB}$, and the combination promises a lower risk than the simple linear combination of the standard deviations of the two securities would imply. The relationship is illustrated in Figure 7.6. The straight line joining points A and B depicts all of the risk and return options for different combinations of A and B, when their returns are perfectly correlated. As the correlation between their returns falls below 1.0, this line sags downward offering lower levels of risk for a given expected return in the combination.

If we were to consider next all of the possible portfolios that we could form with all of the securities traded, they would form an opportunity set that is bowled out to the right and downward due to the lack of perfect correlation between the various

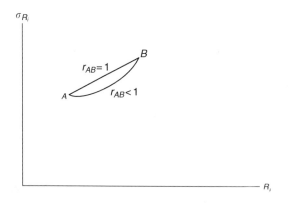

Figure 7.6 Risk/return options for combinations of two securities.

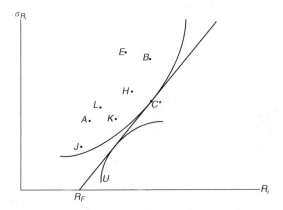

Figure 7.7 Risk/return options for all possible combinations.

securities. Such an opportunity set is shown in Figure 7.7. Now assume that there exists a riskless asset, F say a government treasury bill, promising a return of R_F at zero risk. An investor can then form combinations consisting of the risk free asset and bundles of securities. The various possibilities are given along the line from R_F through C^*. Since investors get positive utility from R and disutility from σ, their indifference curves are concave downward to the right as illustrated by the curve U. Investors are able to reach the highest levels of utility by choosing different combinations of the risk-free asset at the combination C^*. But this implies that all investors hold the same combination C^*, only in different proportions with F. What then becomes of a security like say J, with return and risk characteristics that do not lead to its being part of the combination C^*? *Nobody* holds J. But then J's price falls, and its returns rise until it becomes sufficiently attractive to be included in the portfolio that everyone holds. The opportunity set of combinations collapses along the line from R_F as shown in Figure 7.8. This combination, in which all securities are represented, is called the *market portfolio*.

Suppose, at different points in time, say each month, we were to measure the return on the market portfolio, R_g, and on a individual company, R_i. If we then plotted the one against the other, we would expect to find a positive relationship. When the return on the market portfolio is high, the return on an individual company's shares is high. A possible scatter of points is depicted in Figure 7.9. If we then fit a straight line to that set of points, we could write it as

$$R_i = \alpha_i + \beta_i R_g. \tag{7.43}$$

To calculate β_i we would need the covariance of the returns of security i with those of the market portfolio, $\text{Cov}(R_i, R_g)$, and the variance of the return on the market portfolio, $\text{Var}(R_g)$, $\beta_i = \text{Cov}(R_i, R_g)/\text{Var}(R_g)$. If we were then to plot the returns of different firms against their individual βs, we would also find a linear relationship, with the intercept of the equation being R_F and the slope of the line

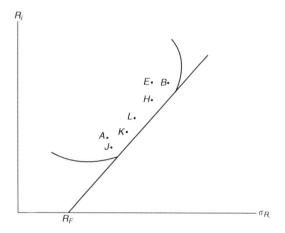

Figure 7.8 The risk/return options when the capital market is in equilibrium.

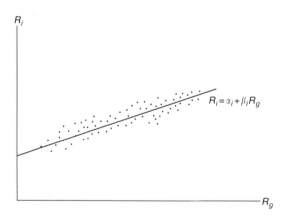

Figure 7.9 The relationship between R_i and R_g.

being $(R_g - R_F)$.

$$R_i = R_F + (R_g - R_F)\beta_i. \tag{7.44}$$

Equations (7.43) and (7.44) constitute the fundamental relationships of the CAPM. With individuals holding portfolios of shares, the risk from including company i in a portfolio is measured by the β_i of that firm's returns against the returns on the portfolio. Thus, the CAPM shifts attention away from the variance of a firm's returns to the covariance of these returns with those of the portfolio being held. Much of the CAPM literature assumes that individuals hold the market portfolio, and thus measures firm βs against that portfolio. We shall show in the next section, however, that the basic CAPM equations hold for any mean/variance efficient portfolio. After demonstrating this point, we discuss its implications.

Derivation of CAPM equation

The fundamental theorems that make up the CAPM were originally derived under the assumptions that investors had *homogeneous expectations* with respect to the risks and returns of every security, that is to say *identical* expectations, and that each investor held all shares in the market portfolio. It was subsequently proved, however, that the basic linear relationships presented above hold not only for the market portfolio, but for all mean/variance efficient portfolios. We follow Levy's (1983) proof.

Let R_i be the returns on shares of company i, and R_F the risk-free asset's returns, as before. An investor forms a portfolio $C(x_1, x_2, \ldots, x_i, \ldots, x_n)$, where x_i is the fraction of company i's shares in the portfolio. To find a mean/variance efficient portfolio, we minimize its variance holding the mean return on the portfolio (R_M) constant. Let S_{ii} be the variance in the returns on company i's shares, and S_{ij} the covariance between the returns of companies i and j. The variance of the portfolio can then be written as

$$S^2 = \sum_{i=1}^{n} \sum_{j=1}^{n} x_i x_j S_{ij}, \tag{7.45}$$

and our task is to find x_i to minimize

$$C(x_1, x_2, \ldots, x_i, \ldots) = \sum_i \sum_j x_i x_j S_{ij} + 2\lambda \left[R_M - \sum_i x_i R_i - \left(1 - \sum_i x_i \right) R_F \right]. \tag{7.46}$$

The expression in square brackets looks a bit cumbersome, but does equal zero as required under the Lagrangian procedure since

$$R_M = \sum_i x_i R_i, \quad \sum_i x_i = 1. \tag{7.47}$$

Minimizing (7.46) with respect to x_i and setting equal to zero gives us

$$\frac{\partial C}{\partial x_i} = 2 \sum_j x_j S_{ij} + 2\lambda (R_F - R_i) = 0. \tag{7.48}$$

Multiplying (7.48) by x_i and summing over all n securities in the portfolio gives

$$2 \sum_i \sum_j x_i x_j S_{ij} + 2\lambda \sum_i x_i (R_F - R_i) = 0, \tag{7.49}$$

or

$$2S^2 + 2\lambda (R_F - R_M) = 0, \tag{7.50}$$

from which

$$S^2 = \lambda(R_M - R_F). \tag{7.51}$$

Using (7.51) to replace λ in (7.49) gives

$$2\sum_i \sum_j x_i x_j S_{ij} + \frac{2S^2}{R_M - R_F} \sum_i x_i (R_F - R_i) = 0. \tag{7.52}$$

Cancelling the 2s and rearranging (7.52) produces

$$R_i - R_F = (R_M - R_F)\frac{\sum_i x_i S_{ij}}{\sum_i \sum_j x_i x_j S_{ij}}. \tag{7.53}$$

Now $\sum x_i S_{ij}$ is the covariance of the returns on security i with those of the portfolio. $\sum\sum x_i x_j S_{ij}$ is the variance of the returns on the portfolio. Thus, the fraction on the right-hand-side of (7.53) is the β_i one obtains from regressing R_i on the returns of the portfolio. Making this substitution and shifting R_F to the right-hand-side of (7.53) yields

$$R_i = R_F + (R_M - R_F)\beta_i, \tag{7.54}$$

which is identical to (7.44) except that the mean of the portfolio C, R_M, replaces the mean return on the market portfolio R_g. All mean/variance efficient portfolios, including the market portfolio under the homogeneous expectations assumption, satisfy equation (7.54).

Further insight into the logic of the portfolio choice can be obtained by reconsidering (7.48). The first term can be separated into the variance in the return on i's shares and something closely resembling a covariance term (ignoring the 2 which cancels out)

$$\sum_j x_i S_{ij} = x_i S_{ii} + \sum_{j\neq i} x_j S_{ij}. \tag{7.55}$$

Using (7.55) we can then solve for x_i in (7.48) to obtain

$$x_i = \frac{\lambda(R_i - R_F)}{S_{ii}} - \frac{\sum_{j\neq i} x_i S_{ij}}{S_{ii}}. \tag{7.56}$$

The first term on the right-hand-side of (7.56) can be thought as the *profit motive* for holding i's shares. The bigger the return on i's shares relative to the risk-free return and relative to the variance on its returns, the larger the fraction of i that it is optimal to have in the portfolio. The second term on the right-hand-side of (7.56) can be thought of as the *diversification motive* for holding i. The smaller the covariance of i's returns are with other members of the portfolio, the greater the proportion of i that should be in the portfolio.

In minimizing (7.46) we placed no constraints on the sign of the x_i. Equation (7.56) implies that the optimal fraction of i's shares in a portfolio could be negative, if its returns were relatively low compared with their covariance with the returns of other stocks in the portfolio. When one uses data on realized returns, variances, and covariances, the implied optimal x_i are often negative. Portfolios in which some companies' shares are held short outperform those in which all shares are held long.

Although it is possible for individuals to sell some companies' shares short, *the market*, which consists of all traders, cannot do so, because there is no one outside of the market who can hold the shares long. The net holdings of all shares must be positive, the market holds all shares long. But this suggests that the market portfolio might be mean/variance dominated by portfolios in which some firms are held short, and others are excluded. And so it is (see, Levy, 1983).

These findings illustrate the strength of the homogeneous expectations assumption that underlies the basic CAPM and the argument that it is mean/variance efficient. If all shareholders had the same expectations, all would solve the identical set of equations to determine their optimal portfolios. If x_i was negative for one investor, it would be negative for all. The price of i's shares would have to fall to induce individuals to hold them, and it would fall until the return on i's shares was large enough to compensate for their covariance with the other companies' shares, and all outstanding shares were optimally held.

In the real world, however, all individuals do not have the same expectations about the performance of each company's shares. For whatever reason, some people are more optimistic about i's future returns than others. The optimists hold i, the pessimists do not. Optimal portfolios do not contain all shares traded in the market.

This conclusion has an important implication for how we need to measure a firm's cost of capital. If the homogeneous expectations assumption of the CAPM were valid, and all individuals either did or should hold the market portfolio, a firm's cost of capital could be estimated using its β with the market portfolio, and equation (7.44). But with shareholders holding smaller and differing portfolios, this is no longer valid. As individuals hold smaller portfolios, the variance of a company's returns begins to become important again (Levy, 1983). We shall, therefore, wish to consider both β-type measures of risk and variance related measures when measuring firms' costs of capital.

Empirical investigations of the determinants of investment

The evidence

Most empirical studies of investment, like other empirical work in economics, estimate a single model or hypothesis about the determinants of investment, and usually conclude that the data are consistent with the hypothesized relationship.

All of the models of investment discussed in this chapter have found empirical support in the literature.

Much more rare are empirical studies that compare two or more hypotheses about the determinants of investment. One of the first, and most ambitious of these, was by Jorgenson and Siebert (1968). They sought to compare the performance of the accelerator, cash flow, expectations and neoclassical models of investment. They did so by estimating equations that differed only in the definition of the desired capital stock, K_t^D, and the lag structure allowed. The assumptions made with respect to the desired capital stock were as follows:

Accelerator theory: $K_t^D = \alpha X_t$

Cash flow (liquidity) theory: $K_t^D = \alpha F_t$

Expectations theory: $K_t^D = \alpha M_t$

Neoclassical theory: $K_t^D = \alpha P_t X_t / c$

where X is output, F is cash flow after dividends, M is the market value of the firm, P is price, and c is the neoclassical cost of capital à la M&M (current profits divided by the market value of the firm) adjusted for changes in prices of investment goods, depreciation, and the tax treatment of profits and depreciation. Jorgenson and Siebert ranked the performance of the four models as follows:

Neoclassical > Accelerator $\approx$ Expectations > Cash Flow

Jorgenson and Siebert drew their conclusions from time-series estimates of investment equations for 15 large US companies. Although this technique allows the estimated lag structure to differ across firms, it imposes the same lag structure over time. One might expect that a firm's ability to adjust its capital stock to its desired level would be easier when this level is close to the existing capital stock, as it would be under the accelerator model in a recession, than when it is far away, and thus that different lag structures hold at different points in time. Cross-section estimates of investment equations allow for different lag structures at different points in time, but at the cost of imposing the same lag structure on all firms. Elliott (1973) reestimated the four Jorgenson/Siebert models both cross-sectionally and with time series data, and expanded the sample to 184 companies. Elliott's rankings of the models were

Cross-section: Cash Flow > Accelerator > Neoclassical > Expectations

Time Series: Cash Flow > Accelerator > Expectations > Neoclassical

Grabowski and Mueller (1972) (hereafter G&M) compared the performance of a neoclassical model against that of a cash flow model motivated by the managerial discretion-growth hypothesis (hereafter MDH). They specified equations for capital investment, R&D and dividends, and were the first to emphasize the importance of the dividends equation in testing the MDH against the neoclassical model. In the neoclassical world of M&M *there is no dividends equation*. Dividends are a pure residual after investment has been decided. If the firm's marginal returns on investment schedule is mrr_{K1} in Figure 7.2a, the firm invests I_1 and pays $(F - I_1)$ in dividends. If the firm's marginal returns on investment schedule is mrr_{K2}, the firm invests I_2, pays zero dividends, and raises $(I_2 - F)$ externally. The neoclassical firm's management determines the optimal level of investment, and dividends or external finance requirements fall out as residuals.

Under the MDH managers push investment beyond the point that maximizes shareholder wealth, and increases in investment lower share price and raise the probability of takeover. Dividends raise share price and reduce the threat of takeover. G&M concluded that the MDH outperformed the neoclassical model based on its overall fit to the data, the particularly good fit of the dividends equation in the MDH, and the strong performance of cash flow in both the investment and R&D equations of the MDH in comparison with the weak performance of both measures of the neoclassical cost of capital employed.[5] Gugler (2002) has also presented evidence in support of the MDH using G&M's model and data for Austrian companies.

Additional evidence in support of the MDH has recently been presented by Lamont (1997) using data for petroleum companies. He observed a significant decrease in investment in non-petroleum activities by these companies following a sudden drop in their cash flows in 1986. It appeared that the petroleum firms regard investment in non-petroleum operations as a discretionary investment which they only undertook when their cash flows were high.[6]

Several recent studies of cash flow and investment account for cash flow's importance by appeal to the asymmetric information hypothesis (hereafter AIH). Tests of the AIH are predicated on identifying companies for which (a) managers know the investment opportunities of the firm but the market does not, and (b) the companies' internal funds and debt capacity are insufficient to finance the profitable investments.

Fazzari *et al.* (1988) were the first to test the AIH. They based their test solely on the financial constraint part of the hypothesis. A sample of 422 US corporations was divided into low, medium, and high retention ratio subsamples, and used to estimate cash flow/investment equations that also included Tobin's q to capture differences in investment opportunities. They estimated positive coefficients on cash flow for all three subsamples that increased in size as the level of retentions rose, and interpreted this finding as supportive of the AIH. Another study supporting the AIH that used dividends to identify cash-constrained companies was by Hubbard *et al.* (1995).

Devereux and Schiantarelli (1990) tried to identify both financial constraints and information asymmetries in their study of 720 UK corporations by dividing their sample by size, growth, and age. Some support for the AIH was found. For example, cash flow had a (slightly) higher coefficient in the small, young firm subsample than in the small, old firm subsample, as one expects if the market learns to evaluate firm investment opportunities with time.[7]

A particularly imaginative strategy for identifying companies with possible asymmetric information problems was adopted by Hoshi *et al.* (1991). They divided their sample of 146 Japanese corporations into independent and group firms, with the former having dispersed outside ownership, and the latter being parts of groups of companies with much cross-holding of one another's shares. Hoshi *et al.* hypothesize that group firms are not subject to asymmetric information problems when financing their investments, because of the access to information other members have. Consistent with this hypothesis, they find that cash flow has a positive and significant coefficient only in the investment equation for the independent companies. Similar evidence has been provided for small firms in the United States (Petersen and Rajan, 1994), and for Italy (Schiantarelli and Sembenelli, 2000).

Although many of the results of these studies are consistent with the hypothesis that managers are maximizing shareholder wealth but face financial constraints and information asymmetries, many are also consistent with other hypotheses that link investment to cash flows, like the MDH. The samples used in these studies consist of companies with common shares traded on the major exchanges. These firms are often quite large, and mature, not the kind of companies for which one anticipates great market uncertainties as to the quality of investment opportunities. When information asymmetries and financial constraints are not present, neoclassical theory does not simply predict a smaller, positive coefficient on cash flows – the criterion these studies use – but a *zero* coefficient. The cost differentials between internal and external finance implied by the estimates often are much larger than those obtained by direct measurement (Chirinko, 1993, p. 1903; 1994). Such large apparent differentials might also be measured, if managers used internal funds to finance investments with much lower marginal returns than their shareholders' opportunity costs. In this context, one of the findings of Devereux and Schiantarelli (1990) is particularly relevant. Their estimated coefficient on cash flow for the largest firms in their sample (0.41) is almost double that for the smallest and medium-sized companies (0.23). This difference contradicts the AIH, but not the MDH.

Devereux and Schiantarelli's findings suggest that their sample may contain firms that fit both the AIH and MDH. The large coefficient on cash flow for small/young firms supports the AIH, the large coefficient for large firms the MDH. One difficulty with these tests is that *not all* small or young firms necessarily are cash constrained, and not all large firms are necessarily overinvesting their cash flows. When firms do underinvest because they are cash constrained, the returns on their investment will exceed their costs of capital. Conversely, companies that overinvest have returns on investment that are less than their costs of capital. Kathuria and Mueller (1995) and Gugler *et al.* (2002a) have used this fact to test the AIH and MDH by breaking their samples according to estimates of the ratios of returns on investment to company costs of capital. Both studies find support for both the AIH and MDH hypotheses.[8]

Discussion

A profit-maximizing management equates the marginal returns on its firm's investments to its cost of capital. Models of investment differ in the weight that they give to these components of the investment decision, and in the way that they go about measuring them. On the marginal returns side, quantity variables like output as implied by the accelerator theory seem to outperform both price variables and expectations variables like Tobin's q (Chirinko, 1993). On the cost of capital side, cash flow outperforms the various measures of the neoclassical cost of capital that have been tried. The best equation for explaining investment at the firm level probably combines accelerator and cash flow variables.

Of particular relevance to the theory of the firm is whether cash flow's significant impact on investment is due to informational asymmetries and financial constraints facing managers who seek to maximize shareholder wealth, or to the attractiveness of internal cash flows to managers who maximize their own goals by overinvesting. The existing literature provides evidence consistent with both hypotheses. Asymmetric information problems and financial constraints are particularly important for small, young firms with attractive investment opportunities, the kind of Schumpeterian firms which we encountered in Chapter 4. Managerial discretion problems are particularly acute for large mature companies with limited investment opportunities. Both hypotheses account for the behavior of different groups of firms. Both can account for the behavior of a single firm, but at different points in its life cycle.

Although these two hypotheses are similar in the emphasis they place on cash flow explaining investment, they differ dramatically in their premises and in their policy implications. Under the AIH, managers wish to maximize shareholder wealth, have investment opportunities with returns greater than their shareholders' opportunity costs, but do not have enough internal funds to finance them. Thus, they cannot undertake the investments, because they cannot reveal to their shareholders just how attractive these investment opportunities are and raise the funds externally. Under the MDH, managers have more than enough funds to maximize shareholder wealth, invest in projects with lower returns than their shareholders' opportunity costs, and if anything want to keep their shareholders from learning what the returns on these investments are. The government should be undertaking policies that supply cash to businesses that fit the AIH, while at the same time forcing firms that fit the MDH to payout greater fractions of their cash flows. In short, policies are needed to transfer capital from the companies with too much cash and too much managerial discretion to those with too little.

Rates of return on investment

The rate of return of an investment I_0 made at time $t = 0$, is that rate r, which equates the present value of the flow of cash generated by the investment, F_t, to the investment

$$I_0 = \sum_{j=0}^{\infty} \frac{F_{t+j}}{(1+r)^j}. \tag{7.57}$$

If one made a single investment, say purchasing shares in a company, at time 0 and sold them at $t = n$, one could calculate the return on that investment by inserting the dividends received at each point in time, and including the funds received at t_n in F_{t+n}. But a firm is an ongoing organization. Only rarely is it sold in its entirety. Some of its investments today, like R&D to develop new products, may generate funds far into the future. Its profits today in turn are the result of many investments at different times in the past. How then can one allocate a firm's profits to the investments that caused them to come up with a measure of the returns on these investments? To do so, some assumptions have to be made about the time patterns of the flows generated by investment, and how they are realized by the firm. Several different sets of assumptions have been used to obtain estimates of returns on investment. We describe three, and the results that have been obtained with them.

The Baumol, Heim, Malkiel, and Quandt (BHMQ) approach

Let I_t be invested in year t at a return of r and generate a stream of cash, F_{t+d} in perpetuity, commencing d periods after the investment. Assume that today's capital stock generates today's profits in perpetuity. Then the difference between today's profits and observed profits in $t + d$ will be due to I_t.

$$\Delta \pi_{t+d} = r I_t. \tag{7.58}$$

If the investment I_{t+1} also earns a return of r, then the difference between profits in year $t + d + 1$ and today's profits will be due to the investments in t and $t + 1$.

$$\Delta \pi_{t+d+1} = \pi_{t+d+1} - \pi_t = r(I_{t+1} + I_t). \tag{7.59}$$

Continuing on we have after $k + 1$ periods

$$\Delta \pi_{t+d+k} = r \sum_{j=0}^{k} I_{t+j}. \tag{7.60}$$

Adding all of these equation gives

$$\sum_{j=0}^{k} \Delta \pi_{t+d+j} = r \sum_{j=0}^{k} I_{t+j}. \tag{7.61}$$

This addition should smooth out the ups and downs of profits caused by business cycle factors to give an estimate of the average return on investment over the $k + 1$ periods. BHMQ (1970) experimented with different values of k and d and produced a range of estimates of returns on investment for large US corporations in the 1970s.

BHMQ used as measures of a firm's investments the different sources of funds from which investments are financed – retained cash flows, changes in debt, and changes in outstanding equity – and estimated separate returns on each. Their estimated returns on new equity issues fell in the range from 14.5 to 20.8 percent, similar or slightly higher than estimates of the returns on the market portfolio of equities during this period. (Fisher and Lorie, 1964, report returns on common shares in the range from 13 to 18 percent in the 1950s.) The estimated returns on ploughed back cash flows ranged only from 3.0 to 4.6 percent, much lower than the returns on equity and shareholder opportunity costs. The estimated returns on debt fell between these other two sets of estimates (4.2 to 14 percent). The BHMQ results seemed to support the idea of a hierarchy of investment funds with debt being cheaper than equity, and internal cash flows cheaper than debt. They also supported the MDH in that the returns on reinvested cash flows were not only lower than those on new debt and equity, but were also substantially below shareholder opportunity costs.

The BHMQ study precipitated several follow-up works. Some supported their findings, some were highly critical of their approach and results.[9] In one of these, Friend and Husic (1973) (F&H) criticized BHMQ for including large numbers of firms that issue no equity or debt in their samples when they estimated returns on these sources of funds. When F&H restricted their sample to firms that did issue debt and equity, the estimated returns on ploughback were both much higher, and insignificantly different from the returns on new debt and equity. In response, BHMQ (1973) presented estimates of returns for those firms that issued *no new debt or equity*. They were even lower than their previous estimates, indeed, often negative.

The picture that emerged from the BHMQ/F&H exchange was that two sorts of firms exist, one resorts to the external capital market and earns returns on its investments equal to or greater than its shareholders' opportunity costs, the other relies only on internal funds to finance its investments and earns much lower returns. These results are also consistent with a life-cycle view of the firm, if younger firms are more dependent on the external capital market to finance their investments than mature firms are.

G&M (1975) tested this life-cycle interpretation of the BHMQ findings by separating firms into samples of mature and non-mature companies. Their estimated returns for mature firms fell in the range from 9.2 to 12.5 percent, not as low as some of the estimates of BHMQ, but lower than shareholder opportunity costs at this time, and substantially lower than G&M's estimates of returns on investment for non-mature companies (13.7–26.3 percent).

The Shinnar, Dressler, Feng, and Avidan (SDFA) approach

BHMQ assumed a uniform flow of funds F_t commencing d periods after the investment was made, and checked the sensitivity of their results to different choices for d. SDFA (1989) experimented with both different values of d and different patterns of F_t, and assumed that the flow of funds generated by investment ceased after n periods, with n also being a parameter that might vary. SDFA assumed four possible patterns of cash flows from an investment (see Figure 7.10). Given

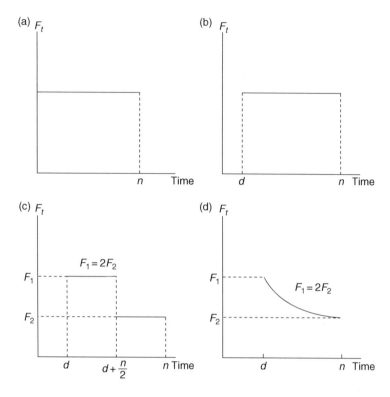

Figure 7.10 Possible patterns to cash flows (F_t) from investment.

these assumptions about the patterns of returns to investment, SDFA used data on firm investments and cash flows to allocate observed cash flows to previous investments to calculate rs using equation (7.57). These calculations were made under the assumptions that F_t could follow each of the four patterns in Figure 7.10, with $d = 2$, and n set equal to 10, 15, 20, 25, and 30. Had the range of estimates been very large, one would have to conclude that we cannot estimate the returns on investment for a firm without knowing precisely the pattern of cash flows it generates. But the range of estimates was for the most part fairly narrow. Table 7.2 presents the midpoints of the ranges of estimates SDFA obtained for a sample of 38 of the largest US corporations for three different time intervals, with the length of the range in parentheses. Two things stand out from these estimates: a pronounced downward trend exists for most companies, and many of the estimated returns, particularly for the 1975–84 period, are below shareholder opportunity costs.[10]

The Mueller and Reardon (M&R) approach

The difficulty one faces when measuring the returns on a company's investments is to determine the pattern of cash flows the investments generate. The M&R

Table 7.2 Estimated returns on investment (*r*) by SDFA approach for 38 large US corporations

Company name	Time period, *r*					
	1955–64		1965–74		1975–84	
Exxon	8.1	(1.6)	6.9	(1.8)	5.6	(0.6)
Monsanto	10.0	(1.4)	5.75	(0.9)	3.3	(0.8)
Bethlehem Steel	6.45	(2.7)	3.1	(2.4)	−8.5	(10.0)
International Paper	10.95	(2.5)	6.65	(1.3)	4.85	(1.9)
IBM	14.0	(1.0)	13.3	(1.6)	6.4	(1.4)
General Motors	12.55	(3.3)	9.5	(2.8)	5.0	(2.2)
Alcoa	4.4	(2.2)	4.75	(1.3)	3.35	(1.1)
Allid Chemical	7.35	(1.1)	4.55	(1.3)	2.7	(1.6)
American Can	7.25	(1.5)	3.2	(1.8)	2.45	(1.9)
American Cyanamid	9.15	(2.1)	7.05	(3.3)	3.7	(1.0)
Amoco	4.55	(0.7)	5.9	(1.4)	7.0	(1.0)
AT&T	5.55	(2.7)	5.6	(1.0)	2.5	(2.4)
Boeing	14.2	(4.2)	8.05	(4.1)	8.15	(6.7)
Champion	7.05	(1.3)	5.75	(1.3)	3.3	(2.8)
Con Edison	6.8	(1.6)	3.4	(2.2)	2.55	(2.7)
Olin	5.65	(5.5)	1.6	(2.6)	0.1	(0.8)
Procter & Gamble	10.5	(2.8)	9.35	(3.3)	7.05	(1.3)
U.S. Shell	7.25	(1.3)	4.95	(0.7)	4.9	(1.0)
Texaco	8.95	(0.9)	7.3	(2.0)	4.0	(2.2)
Union Carbide	10.2	(2.6)	5.0	(1.2)	1.0	(2.2)
US Steel (USX)	4.95	(1.1)	2.3	(1.6)	−1.2	(2.0)
Westinghouse	5.1	(0.6)	5.9	(1.2)	5.45	(3.9)
Corning Glass	17.55	(1.9)	8.9	(6.4)	4.05	(1.5)
Dow Chemicals	8.4	(2.0)	9.6	(2.4)	6.3	(1.8)
Dupont	12.85	(4.9)	7.7	(2.4)	4.4	(0.6)
Firestone	7.3	(2.6)	5.45	(0.9)	−2.6	(5.4)
General Electric	11.4	(4.4)	12.15	(6.7)	9.7	(5.2)
General Foods	10.35	(4.1)	7.9	(2.4)	5.55	(1.7)
Goodyear	6.65	(1.7)	6.55	(0.9)	2.6	(1.2)
Illinois Glass	10.2	(3.6)	7.35	(1.7)	2.5	(2.0)
Mobil	5.7	(1.2)	7.9	(2.6)	7.7	(1.4)
Ford	15.65	(5.9)	8.65	(2.1)	2.2	(0.8)
International Harvester (Navister)	6.95	(2.3)	6.25	(1.7)	−13.55	(7.9)
Johnson & Johnson	8.8	(1.8)	13.05	(2.1)	9.35	(0.7)
Kodak	15.5	(4.2)	15.9	(2.6)	7.5	(2.2)
Merck	17.9	(3.8)	23.2	(5.0)	11.15	(2.5)
NCR	12.65	(2.5)	7.75	(3.3)	5.0	(2.8)
3M	20.55	(3.5)	16.1	(3.2)	8.45	(1.9)

approach relies on an efficient capital market to correctly determine what this pattern will be.

The present value of an investment I_t made at time t is

$$PV_t = \sum_{j=1}^{\infty} \frac{F_{t+j}}{(1 + i_t)^j},$$ (7.62)

where i_t is the firm's discount rate (neoclassical cost of capital) in t, and F_t is the cash flow generated by the investment in year t. This identical present value would be generated by the same I_t, assuming that it earned a constant r_t in perpetuity, where r_t satisfies the following equation

$$PV_t = \frac{r_t I_t}{i_t}. \tag{7.63}$$

The market value of the firm, M_t, at the end of period t satisfies the following identity

$$M_t \equiv M_{t-1} + PV_t - \delta_t M_{t-1} + \mu_t, \tag{7.64}$$

where δ_t is the depreciation in the firm's total assets (market value), if the firm were to invest zero, and μ_t is the error that the market makes when evaluating M_t. Subsequent values of M_t are defined by the analogous identity. Repeated use of (7.64) to eliminate the lagged values of M yields

$$M_{t+n} = M_{t-1} + \sum_{j=0}^{n} PV_{t+j} - \sum_{j=0}^{n} \delta_{t+j} M_{t+j-1} + \sum_{j=0}^{n} \mu_{t+j}. \tag{7.65}$$

Letting $q_{m_t} = r_t/i_t$, we can construct a weighted average of the q_{m_t}s using the I_ts as weights

$$q_m = \frac{\sum_{j=0}^{n} q_{m_{t+j}} I_{t+j}}{\sum_{j=0}^{n} I_{t+j}}. \tag{7.66}$$

Dividing all terms in (7.65) by $\sum I_{t+j}$, using (7.63) to replace the PV_{t+j} terms, and rearranging yields

$$q_m = \frac{M_{t+n} - M_{t-1}}{\sum_{j=0}^{n} I_{t+j}} + \frac{\sum_{j=0}^{n} \delta_{t+j} M_{t+j-1}}{\sum_{j=0}^{n} I_{t+j}} - \frac{\sum_{j=0}^{n} \mu_{t+j}}{\sum_{j=0}^{n} I_{t+j}}. \tag{7.67}$$

The ratio of r to i is called q_m to indicate that it is essentially a *marginal* Tobin's q. Tobin's q equals the ratio of the firm's market value to its total assets, q_m equals the ratio of the *change* in the firm's market value to the change in its total assets (investment) that caused it. Tobin's q thus equals the ratio of the firm's returns on its total assets to its cost of capital, while q_m equals the ratio of its returns on investment to its cost of capital.

The assumption of capital market efficiency implies that the capital market makes an unbiased evaluation of the market value of the firm in every period. The expected values of all μ_{t+j} are zero, and the ratio of their sum to the summation of all investments should approximate zero for large ns. The third term to the right of the equal sign in (7.67) can be ignored for large ns. Ignoring the middle term on the right, we see that (7.67) has a very intuitive interpretation. If a firm invests in projects with returns equal to its cost of capital (and thus $q_m = 1$), then each dollar invested should increase the market value of the firm by a dollar. The middle term to the right of the equal sign adjusts for the depreciation in the firm's existing assets. If a dollar's investment offsets a dollar of depreciation, the return on this investment also equals the firm's cost of capital.

A firm's market value represents the market's evaluation of *all* of its assets – physical capital, intangible capital from R&D, intangible capital from advertising, and goodwill capital. Accordingly, an equally comprehensive definition of investment is needed to calculate a firm's q_m using (7.67). M&R (1993) defined investment as

$$I = \text{After tax profits} + \text{depreciation} - \text{dividends} + \text{changes in debt}$$
$$+ \text{changes in equity} + \text{R\&D} + \text{Advertising}. \qquad (7.68)$$

Using this definition of investment, and assuming a constant depreciation rate δ of 10 percent, they calculated q_ms for 699 companies over the period from the end of 1969 to the end of 1988. Approximately four out of five firms had a return on investment less than their cost of capital ($q_m < 1$). Half of the 699 companies had a return on their investment of less than 71 percent of their costs of capital.

Table 7.3 gives the main components of the formula for computing q_m, the calculated q_m, SDFA's midpoint estimate of r, and the implied i from the relationship $q_m = r/i$ for 23 companies from the SDFA study for which M&R report figures. The SDFA calculations are for but 10 of the 19 years in the M&R data, and SDFA attribute all profits to capital investment, while M&R include mergers and investments in intangible capital in their measure of investment, so one does not expect the two sets of figures to line up perfectly. But the match is fairly close, and the implied costs of capital in most cases fall in or near the range of 6–11 percent which seem reasonable.[11]

The M&R findings, like those of BHMQ and SDFA, suggest that many large firms invest in projects with much lower returns than their shareholders' opportunity costs. This conclusion has important implications for the theory of the firm to which we have already alluded, and important implications regarding the overall efficiency of the corporate sector. The aggregate investments of the 699 companies in the M&R sample over the 19-year period amounted to $3.67 trillion. If we assume that the present value of this investment was equal to the present value of the investment of the firm with the median q_m, then the cumulated investments of these 699 companies created assets worth $1.06 trillion less than would have been created if each firm's investments brought a return equal to its cost of capital.

Differences in q_m across country legal systems and sources of funds

Both BHMQ and M&R estimated separate returns on investments out of different sources of finance. As discussed earlier in this chapter, BHMQ's estimates followed the pattern expected from the "hierarchy of finance" literature, namely $r_{CF} < r_D < r_E$, where CF, D, and E represent cash flows, new debt, and new equity. M&R, on the other hand, observed the highest returns from investments out of new debt,

Table 7.3 Estimated ratios of returns on investment to firm costs of capital (q_m) by M&R approach for 23 large US corporations

Company name	M_{1969}[a]	M_{1988}[a]	$M_{88} - M_{69}$[a]	$\sum INV$[a]	M&R q_m[b] (1969–88)	SDFA r[c] (1975–84)	Implied i[d]
Exxon	44,081.3	5,6219.9	12,137.7	11,3870.3	0.862	5.6	6.5
International Paper	5,722.5	6,336.5	614.0	13,155.8	0.766	4.85	6.3
IBM	114,398.6	72,031.1	−42,367.4	16,5499.3	0.604	6.4	10.6
General Motors	66,919.1	13,2921.8	77,002.7	2,97,572.0	0.481	5.0	10.4
Alcoa	6,071.6	5,643.1	−428.5	14,453.9	0.567	3.35	5.9
Amoco	11,581.0	22,261.4	10,680.4	56,588.2	0.775	7.0	9.0
Procter & Gamble	12,504.3	15,434.0	2,929.7	37,311.6	0.746	7.05	9.5
U.S. Shell	17,555.0	30,808.9	13,254.0	92,393.7	0.551	4.9	8.9
Texaco	25,957.9	17,309.1	−8648.8	55,723.5	0.456	4.0	8.8
Union Carbide	8,449.3	5,204.3	−3245.0	20,273.0	0.505	1.0	2.0
US Steel (USX)	8,308.8	13,764.0	5,455.2	53,819.6	0.403	−1.2	−3.0
Westinghouse	7,826.5	13,812.8	5,986.3	23,660.9	0.745	5.45	7.3
Dow Chemical	8,410.2	16,983.1	8,572.9	36,991.3	0.861	6.3	7.3
Du Pont	14,333.6	22,461.7	8,128.0	66,531.5	0.567	4.4	7.8
General Electric	21,542.2	86,051.7	64,509.4	1,16,836.7	0.971	9.7	10.0
Goodyear	8,341.1	5,540.0	−2801.1	18,643.2	0.368	2.6	7.1
Mobil	15,160.2	21,989.5	6,829.4	61,026.5	0.683	7.7	11.3
Ford	14,057.7	82,647.6	68,589.9	1,69,904.0	0.551	2.2	4.0
Johnson & Johnson	9,079.2	13,452.0	4,372.8	20,332.9	1.131	9.35	8.3
Kodak	36,417.9	20,628.9	−15,789.0	47,325.8	0.587	7.5	12.8
Merck	11,123.3	19,881.1	8757.8	14,390.4	1.972	11.15	5.7
NCR	5,956.8	3,991.8	−1965.0	13,024.0	0.325	5.0	7.4
3M	16,907.1	12,391.6	−4,515.5	22,239.1	0.899	8.45	9.4

Notes
a Millions of 1982 dollars.
b Calculated using equation (7.66) assuming $\delta = 0.10$.
c Midpoint of range of estimates as given in Table 7.2.
d Calculated from $q_m = r/i$ using q_m and r values from two previous columns.

$q_{mD} = 0.92$, $q_{mE} = 0.65$, and $q_{mCF} = 0.56$ where q_{mD} is the estimated q_m for investments out of new debt issues, etc. Only investments financed out of newly issued debt came close to earning returns equal to company costs of capital in the M&R study.

In their cross-national comparison of returns on investment, Mueller and Yurtoglu (2000) also estimated separate q_ms on investments out of different sources of finance. When observations were aggregated across country legal systems, Mueller and Yurtoglu observed the same sort of pattern as BHMQ did. The q_{mCF}s < 1.0 for all four country-legal systems, with $q_{mE} > q_{mD}$ for three of the four groups and nearly equal to it in the fourth group. All estimated q_ms on new debt and equity were equal to or greater than one.[12] In the Mueller and Yurtoglu study, external capital markets appeared to play a disciplining role, forcing managers to earn returns on their investments out of externally raised funds equal to or greater than their costs of capital.

Subsequent work by Gugler *et al.* (2002b) (GMY) has shown that this interpretation gives too much credit to the discipline of external capital markets. Table 7.4 presents some of their findings. Separate results are presented for each of the four groups of legal systems. The first row in each country group presents the results for the full samples for each group. Looking first at the column of median q_ms, we see that the same pattern exists as discussed in the previous chapter. The median q_m is highest for the English origin countries, and they are the only group of countries with a median above 1.0. The lowest median is for the French-origin countries. Fifty-five percent of the English companies have a q_m greater than one, while this is true for only around 40 percent of the companies in the other three groups.

Turning next to the estimated q_ms by sources of funds for the full samples, we see the hierarchy of returns observed by BHMQ, q_{mCF}s < q_{mD}s < q_{mE}s, for both the English- and German-origin samples. The reverse pattern is observed in Scandinavia, however, and it is new debt issues that earn the highest returns in the French-origin countries.

Additional insight into what is going on emerges when the q_ms are estimated for firms having returns on their total investment equal to or greater than their costs of capital ($q_{mI} \geq 1$), and $q_{mI} < 1$. The q_ms on all three sources of finance are ≥ 1.0 for all four country groups, when $q_{mI} \geq 1$. All three q_ms are less than one, on the other hand, for firms with $q_{mI} < 1.0$. For companies with $q_{mI} < 1.0$, GMY observed the same hierarchy in q_ms as M&R did – investments financed out of new debt earn the highest returns. Although these returns on new debt all fall short of company costs of capital, the q_{mD}s are generally much higher than either the q_{mE}s or q_{mCF}s across each of the different country groups.

How do we explain these disparate findings? The easiest one to explain is why new debt and not new equity has the highest returns, when the returns on both fall short of company costs of capital. The contractual obligations between managers and debt holders are far more explicit and easier to enforce for debt than for equity. When the debt is issued by a bank, the bank can refuse to make the loan if it is not confident of being repaid. Loans are often secured by specific assets of the

Table 7.4 Estimates of q_m by legal system and source of funds

Legal system	Sample	No. (%) of firms	Median q_m	CF_t/M_{t-1}	$\Delta Debt_t/M_{t-1}$	$\Delta Equity_t/M_{t-1}$
English	All	11,311	1.09	0.86	1.09	1.37
				0.00	0.00	0.00
	$q_{mI} \geq 1$	55	1.74	1.48	1.35	1.99
				0.00	0.00	0.00
	$q_{mI} < 1$	45	0.51	0.36	0.77	0.63
				0.00	0.00	0.00
Scandinavian	All	350	0.85	1.31	1.08	0.55
				0.04	0.22	0.00
	$q_{mI} \geq 1$	42	1.56	2.29	1.42	1.37
				0.00	0.00	0.00
	$q_{mI} < 1$	58	0.55	0.71	0.86	0.21
				0.03	0.00	0.00
German	All	2,476	0.84	0.70	0.98	1.09
				0.00	0.13	0.13
	$q_{mI} \geq 1$	39	1.45	1.57	1.27	1.59
				0.00	0.00	0.00
	$q_{mI} < 1$	61	0.55	0.47	0.83	0.55
				0.00	0.00	0.00
French	All	1,433	0.78	0.64	1.02	0.52
				0.00	0.50	0.00
	$q_{mI} \geq 1$	38	1.67	1.39	1.41	1.10
				0.00	0.00	0.27
	$q_{mI} < 1$	62	0.46	0.46	0.84	0.37
				0.00	0.00	0.00
Transition	All	78	0.76	0.39	1.25	1.29
				0.00	0.04	0.34
Africa	All	17	0.71	0.45	0.90	1.05
				0.00	0.32	0.78
China	All	48	0.60	0.28	1.14	−0.46
				0.00	0.29	0.00

Source: Gugler *et al.* (2002b, table 7).

Notes
Numbers under coefficients are the probability that the coefficient is significantly different from 1.0; two-tailed test.

firm. Defaults on interest payments can lead to a firm's lenders foreclosing on it. All of these considerations suggest that a management will make sure that its investments generate sufficient funds, or almost sufficient funds, to pay the interest on its debts.

The explanation for some studies' estimating returns on equity greater than returns on debt and others the reverse, harkens back to the initial exchange between BHMQ and F&H. In any economy some firms are earning returns on their investments that exceed their costs of capital, others the reverse. If firms with attractive investment opportunities often issue equity to finance their investments, then cross-sectional estimates of returns on equity will be dominated by the returns of these companies with good investment opportunities. The GMY results in Table 7.4 clearly demonstrate that in any country both types of firms exist, and the companies earning high returns on their total investments are often earning returns on new equity far in excess of their costs of capital. Companies that are overinvesting, on the other hand, earn low returns on both reinvested cash flows and new equity issues. New and old shareholders alike suffer from the investment policies of these firms. M&R's results for their full sample resemble GMY's results for companies with q_ms on total investment less than one, because four out of five firms in the M&R sample had q_ms on total investment that were less than one. Mueller and Yurtoglu's results resemble BHMQ's, because by the late 1980s and 1990s a greater fraction of US companies had q_{mI}s ≥ 1.

Conclusions

The amounts firms invest are important determinants of the growth and productivity of an economy, and consequently models of the determinants of investment have received much attention. Many of the models are macroeconomic in their origins and have been estimated with macroeconomic data. This macro-perspective has led to much interest in the effects of tax and other government policies on investment, and at the econometric level in accurately predicting the timing of investments, the lags between policy changes and investment changes, and the like. These issues have been ignored in this chapter.

From an industrial economics perspective, the most interesting questions concern the different determinants of investment predicted by different theories of the firm, and questions concerning investment performance. We have found that the simple view of the firm as choosing a level of investment that equates its marginal return to its cost of capital does not receive much empirical support. Agency problems, informational asymmetries and perhaps still other factors lead managers to place more weight on the levels of their internal fund flows, when deciding how much to invest, than the simple view of the investment decision implies. Estimates of the realized returns on investment suggest that managers often pay little heed to their shareholders' interests when deciding how much to invest.

In the next chapter, we take up another type of investment decision – the corporate merger. We shall see that the approach to this investment decision has been quite different from that of investment in capital equipment. Once again, however, we shall find that different theories of the firm make quite different predictions about the nature and consequences of merger activity.

8 The determinants of mergers

Figure 8.1 records the number of mergers occurring in each year for the United States over the last century. In recent years this number dwarfs those from the end of the nineteenth century, just as the size of the US economy dwarfs the US economy of a century ago. Relative to the size of the economy, the first great merger wave was roughly comparable in scope to that of the late 1980s (*The Economist*, April 27, 1991, p. 11). The wave in the late 1990s was unprecedented, however, in terms of the number of mergers, their size, and their international character.

If one ignores the upward trend in the number of mergers, two remaining features of merger activity stand out immediately. First, and most obviously, mergers come in waves. In the late 1890s, 1920s, 1960s, and 1980s the numbers of mergers

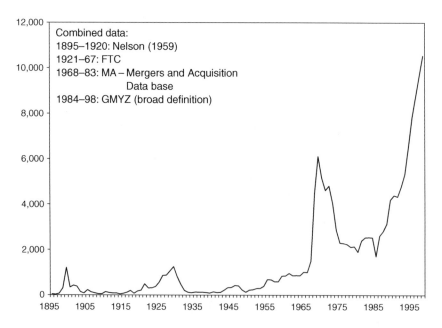

Figure 8.1 Numbers of US mergers, 1895–1998.

far exceeded their levels in the early years of the following decades. The same appears to be true for the wave of the late 1990s. Second, all these waves have tended to be correlated with stock market prices and economic activity. The Great Crash in stock market prices on Wall Street was accompanied by a great crash in merger activity. Careful econometric work has established that stock prices tend either slightly to lead or coincide with the number of mergers.[1] A similar pattern of merger activity and relationship to stock prices has been observed for the United Kingdom.[2]

The Nobel laureate George Stigler (1950) once referred to the first great merger wave in the United States as the wave that created monopolies. One motivation for these mergers may have been to avoid prosecution under the Sherman Act, passed in 1890 (Bittlingmayer, 1985). This law prohibited cartels and in several cases members of a cartel simply combined to form a single firm. No such anti-cartel law was introduced in the United Kingdom at this time, however, and yet this country also saw a wave of mergers at the end of the nineteenth and during the early twentieth century (Chandler, 1990, pp. 286–91). Whatever their motivation these mergers certainly did increase concentration levels in many industries, and transformed the structures of the American and British economies.

Up until 1950 in the United States, and 1989 in the European Community, no law existed that could effectively prevent horizontal mergers that fell short of creating a (near) monopoly. Prior to these dates most mergers were horizontal. The Celler–Kefauver Amendment passed in 1950 closed a gaping loophole in the 1914 Clayton Act, and made both horizontal and vertical mergers that might "substantially lessen competition" difficult to complete. The consequence was not, as can be seen in Figure 8.1, to bring merger activity to an end, but rather to divert it into mergers that were not vulnerable to attack under the antitrust laws – diversification mergers, that is, mergers between firms that neither operate in the same industry nor in industries that are vertically linked in the production chain. Such mergers are typically called *conglomerate mergers*, with the connotation being that they create a conglomeration of economic activities. These mergers have also transformed the structure of economic activity. The General Foods Corporation, an early conglomerate, was formed through acquisitions of firms like Maxwell House Coffee, Jello, Birdseye, and Post Cereals, pioneering brands and market leaders in their industries. In the late 1980s, both General Foods and Kraft Foods were acquired by Philip Morris. Today, this one-time specialist in cigarette manufacturing has joined conglomerates Lever Brothers and Nestles to become one of the largest, diversified food and consumer products companies in the world, all as a result of mergers.

What explains these and other mergers, and what are their economic consequences? These are the questions that will concern us in the present and following chapters. We begin by examining a number of hypotheses that have been put forward to explain why mergers occur. When considering each of these, the pattern of merger activity presented in Figure 8.1 should be kept in mind. Any *general* theory of mergers must be consistent with their occurring in waves, which in turn are correlated with stock market upswings.

Market power increases

If managers maximize the profits of their companies, then a merger must be expected to increase the profits of the participating firms, and thus must be expected either to increase revenues or reduce costs. Revenues should increase following an increase in the merging firms' market power, costs will fall if the merger increases the efficiency of the merging firms. Market power and efficiency increases are the two most obvious motives for mergers. The way in which each can come about differs somewhat for each type of merger.

Horizontal mergers

It is obvious that a merger, which replaced twenty competitors in an industry with a monopoly, would be likely to increase the price and profits of the single remaining firm. More generally, a horizontal merger that falls short of creating a monopoly can lead to higher prices in an oligopolistic industry simply by reducing the number of firms in it. This can occur, for example, if the firms are Cournot quantity setters. In a symmetric Cournot equilibrium, with a homogeneous product and all firms having the same, constant unit costs c, the following relationship holds

$$L = \frac{p - c}{p} = \frac{H}{\varepsilon}, \tag{8.1}$$

where H is the Herfindahl index of concentration, and ε is the industry demand elasticity. Since a horizontal merger always increases H, it also increases the industry price–cost margin and profits, if the industry is in a Cournot equilibrium before the merger and reaches a Cournot equilibrium again afterward. Nevertheless, in such a Cournot world horizontal mergers are generally *not profitable for the merging firms* (Salant et al., 1983). When all firms have identical unit costs, equation (8.1) implies that they are all of the same size. If the industry is in a Cournot equilibrium before and after the merger, equation (8.1) must hold before and afterward. Since the immediate effect of the merger is to make the merged firm twice as big as its competitors, it needs to shrink following the merger to return to the same, new size of its rivals. Except when the merger creates a monopoly, the loss of profits to the merging firms from having to shrink to rejoin the symmetric Cournot equilibrium more than offsets the gain in profits from the increase in price cost margin caused by the increase in H (see next section).

This somewhat surprising result depends heavily on the assumptions that the firms are quantity setters, and that they are in a symmetric Cournot equilibrium both before and after the merger. With Cournot quantity setting, reaction curves are negatively sloped. A horizontal merger produces perfect collusion between the merging firms and leads them to reduce their output, but the gain to them from this is, in part, offset by the reaction of their competitors to increase their outputs. With positive sloped reaction curves, as under price setting behavior, rivals will follow the price increase of the merging firms with their own price increase, and all firms in the industry profit from the merger (see Deneckere and Davidson, 1985).

The assumption that merging firms shed assets to return to the same size of their rivals is also implausible. When it is relaxed, a horizontal merger may also prove to be profitable for the merging firms (Perry and Porter, 1985).

Horizontal mergers with Cournot equilibria

Consider first the case of Cournot quantity setters in symmetric equilibrium. Let the demand schedule for the homogeneous product be linear and of the form

$$p = 1 - \sum_{j=1}^{n} x_j. \tag{8.2}$$

As with Cournot's original example of mineral water, let us assume that each firm's marginal costs are constant and equal to zero, $c = 0$. Firm i seeks to maximize its profits

$$\max \pi_i = \left(1 - \sum x_j\right) x_i, \tag{8.3}$$

which leads to values for firm i's output and profits of

$$x_i = \frac{1}{n+1}, \quad \pi_i = \frac{1}{(n+1)^2}. \tag{8.4}$$

For a merger between two firms to be profitable, the profits of one firm in a symmetric equilibrium with $n - 1$ firms must exceed twice the profits of two firms in an n-firm equilibrium

$$\frac{1}{n^2} > \frac{2}{(n+1)^2}. \tag{8.5}$$

This inequality is satisfied for $n = 2$, but not for $n \geq 3$. A merger between a pair of duopolists is profitable, but a merger between two firms in an industry with three or more sellers is not profitable under the conditions assumed in this example including that of a symmetric Cournot equilibrium.

Vertical mergers

Vertical acquisitions can increase the merging firms' market power by increasing barriers to entry at one or more links in the vertical production chain (Comanor, 1967). To make aluminum ingots one needs bauxite, to sell it one needs fabricators willing to buy. If the aluminum industry is fully vertically integrated, then a firm wishing to enter at any one stage will have to either buy inputs from one of its competitors or sell its output to one if its competitors, or both. For example, a firm which wished to enter into aluminum refining in the United States prior to the Second World War would have found that all known bauxite deposits were owned by its main competitor ALCOA. Should ALCOA have decided to sell the new entrant bauxite at a price that was far above ALCOA's costs of mining the bauxite, it might have prevented the firm from entering the industry even if its process for refining aluminum was as or even more efficient than ALCOA's. By charging a very high price for bauxite to the potential entrant, ALCOA would have *foreclosed* the bauxite market to the entrant and thus created an entry barrier. The potential for vertical acquisitions to facilitate market foreclosure is their most serious possible anti-competitive effect.

Conglomerate mergers

Tacit collusion is often thought to evolve when the same firms compete against one another over time. In such multi-period, supergame situations, firms cooperate with their rivals in maintaining high prices, because the present discounted loss in profits over all future periods exceeds today's gain from cheating. A similar sort of tacit collusion may emerge when the same firms confront one another in several markets *at the same point in time*. If a given group of firms come into contact with one another in *m* markets, then a firm contemplating cheating on its rivals in one of these markets must weigh the loss from retaliation by its rivals if it is caught, not only in this market but potentially across all *m* markets.

Scott (1982, 1993) has found that adding an interaction term between concentration and an index of *multimarket contact* to a standard structure–performance equation significantly increases its explanatory power. An increase in concentration leads to a greater increase in profits in a market in which the sellers also face one another in other markets than when such multimarket contact is not present. Such gains from multimarket contact can also be the cause of *purposeful diversification*. A firm wishing to diversify purchases a company in a market in which several of its current competitors already operate. Scott reports that such purposeful diversification characterized the merger patterns of the large US firms in the 1950s and 1960s.

Efficiency increases

Horizontal mergers

In any industry with significant scale economies as depicted in Figure 8.2, a horizontal merger can reduce the average costs of the merging firms by increasing their scale of operation. If the decline in average costs tapers off as scale increases, as in Figure 8.2, the expected cost reductions from horizontal mergers are greater for pairs of small firms like *A* and *B* than they are for big firms like *D* and *E*. We thus expect that if scale economies are the driving force behind horizontal mergers, they most frequently occur between the smaller firms in an industry. This prediction was tested with data on mergers in the 1960s and 1970s for seven countries (Mueller, 1980a). In Belgium, the Federal Republic of Germany, the United States, and the United Kingdom merging pairs of companies were significantly *bigger* than randomly selected nonmerging companies. In

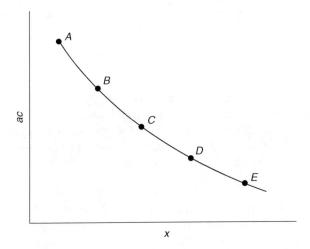

Figure 8.2 Industry with significant scale-economy.

France, the Netherlands, and Sweden merging pairs were insignificantly different in size from randomly selected nonmerging companies. Thus, in none of the seven countries was the prediction that merging firms tend to be smaller than average borne out.[3]

Vertical mergers

Vertical acquisitions can sometimes reduce costs by eliminating steps in the production process. For example, if steel ingots are made by one firm and sold to another to make steel wire, the ingots must be first cooled and shipped, and then reheated and drawn to make the wire. In a vertically integrated firm the hot steel can be immediately drawn into wire.

A vertical merger can also reduce *transaction costs*. Imagine that a steel smelter locates near an iron ore mine to reduce transportation costs. Both firms possess assets dedicated to supplying or buying from the other firm. This *asset specificity* essentially places the two firms in a bilateral monopoly situation. Each may try to exploit this situation by laying claim to a greater fraction of the profits generated by their joint production. A merger between the two companies eliminates the bargaining between them and thereby economizes on transaction costs.

Conglomerate mergers

Economies of scope arise when the production of two different products by the same firm leads to lower production costs for one or both products. An example of such economies might be the warehousing and delivery of products to particular retailers. Although there may be no economies in a single firm's producing both coffee and dog food, because they are both sold in supermarkets they can be stored and shipped together, and a firm that sells them both may economize on these costs. The presence of economies of scope is a possible justification for conglomerate mergers.

Discussion

Although each of the hypotheses about market power or efficiency increases discussed so far is a plausible explanation for why a merger might occur, none of them seems likely to generate the wave pattern of mergers observed in the introduction to this chapter. Competitive pressures and thus the incentive to cut costs seem likely to be strongest in a recession when demand is weak and many firms have excess capacity. Mergers that reduce costs would seem likely to follow a *counter-cyclical* pattern, therefore, if they showed any pattern at all.

Similarly, one expects the pressure to cut price and steal customers from one's rivals to be greatest in a recession when demand is weak and excess capacity exists. Mergers to eliminate competitors are going to be most attractive when these competitors are stealing one's customers, and thus again should follow a counter-cyclical pattern. The strong correlation between merger activity and stock market prices does not seem likely to be generated by mergers that are motivated simply to cut costs or raise market power.

Speculative motives

Students of the early waves often spoke of "promoters' profits" as a cause for mergers. During these waves men like J.P. Morgan often approached corporate managers and suggested a possible merger. They amassed large fortunes from the fees they charged for their advice and the various services they rendered to finance and facilitate the mergers. Underwriters of the securities floated in the great merger that created the United States Steel Corporation in 1901, earned fees of $57.5 million – over $1 billion in today's dollars (*The Economist*, April 27, 1991, p. 11). Perhaps, the most famous promoter of mergers in recent years is Michael Milken, the inventor of the junk bond, whose fees for brokerage services in one year amounted to some $500 million.

The notion that promoters' profits could drive a merger wave seems at first implausible without the mergers also generating profits for the merging firms themselves, since the mergers cannot go through without the managers of the firms involved expecting some gains too. Thus, this hypothesis would seem to require one of the other hypotheses that predicts gains for the merging firms. But as we shall see in the next chapter, the evidence suggests that mergers *do not* generate profits for the merging firms, and this evidence is therefore consistent with the promoters' profits hypothesis. Moreover, the kind of speculative environment that can generate truly large promoters' profits is only to be found during stock market booms. The initial offering of US Steel's shares was at $38 a share, and it soon rose to $55 a share in the booming stock market in which it was floated. Two years later after the stock market fell, US Steel's shares were selling for $9 a share. Our third hypothesis as to why mergers occur is consistent with their wave pattern.

The adaptive (failing firm) hypothesis

Dewey (1961, p. 257) once characterized "most mergers [as] merely a civilized alternative to bankruptcy." McGowan (1965) put forward a similar, *adaptive theory* to account for why small firms are typically the targets in mergers, and why the much more competitive US and UK economies had far more mergers in the 1950s than the less competitive Austrian and French economies.

If *most* mergers were to rescue firms from impending bankruptcies, one would not expect to observe the wave pattern in Figure 8.1. Why would these rescue operations reach a feverish pace in the late 1920s, and then come to a screeching halt when many firms were entering into bankruptcy? Bankruptcies were also much more prevalent in the 1970s than in the late 1960s and 1980s, yet the pattern of merger activity was the reverse.

Although avoiding impending bankruptcy is an unlikely explanation for most mergers, it undoubtedly explains some. More generally, some mergers are part of a Darwinian process in which poorer than average performing firms disappear, even though the acquired firms are not facing immediate bankruptcy (see next section).

Micro level evidence in support of the adaptive theory is mixed. Most studies of mergers in the United States have found that acquired firms have the same average profit rates as similar non-acquired companies, and also the same as the firms that acquire them (Boyle, 1970; Conn, 1973, 1976; Stevens, 1973; Melicher and Rush, 1974; Mueller, 1980b; Harris *et al.*, 1982). In the case of the conglomerate mergers of the 1960s, it was the *acquiring* companies that had the below average profits and also lower profits than the firms they acquired (Weston and Mansinghka, 1971; Melicher and Rush, 1974). Ravenscraft and Scherer (1987, ch. 3) found that a sample of acquired companies, including many small, privately held firms, had profit rates *significantly higher* than their lines of business.[4] They did, however, find that targets of hostile takeovers earned somewhat lower profits, offering some support for the market-for-corporate-control hypothesis of the next section. Morck *et al.* (1988b), on the other hand, found no significant difference between the Tobin's qs of acquired firms and their industries, even when the companies were targets of a hostile takeover.

Companies acquired during the 1960s and 1970s were found to have significantly lower profit rates than non-acquired companies matched by size and industry in Belgium, the Federal, Republic of Germany, France, and the United Kingdom. No significant differences in profit rates between acquired and similar non-acquired firms were found for these periods in Sweden and the Netherlands, and for the 1970–81 period in Australia.[5]

Table 8.1 presents mean profits to asset rations for acquiring and acquired companies from the international comparison study of mergers between 1985 and 1999 by Gugler *et al.* (2002). Targets had lower profits than the acquirers on average

Table 8.1 Mean profit to asset ratios for merging firms in different countries between 1985 and 1999

Country	Number of mergers	Acquirers	Targets
United States	1,967	0.029	0.019
United Kingdom	379	0.066	0.039
Continental Europe	172	0.035	0.033
Japan	16	0.011	0.030
Australia/New Zealand	172	0.024	0.027
Rest of the world	47	0.052	0.013
Total	2,753	0.034	0.023

Source: Gugler *et al.* (2002).

in the United States, United Kingdom, and a residual country category.[6] Targets had higher profits than the acquirers in Japan, and about the same profit rates in Continental Europe and Australia/New Zealand. As is true of the earlier literature, no clear pattern of support for the adaptive theory emerges in the Gugler *et al.* (2002) data. At best the adaptive theory seems consistent with the evidence for *some* mergers in *some* countries at *some* points in time.

The market for corporate control hypothesis

At any point in time t a firm contains a bundle of assets, K_t, that includes not only the physical assets of the firm, but also intangible capital stocks arising from past advertising and R&D. Managers who run the firm in the interests of its owners seek to employ those assets to maximize the market value of the firm, M_t. If $M_t > K_t$, the assets bundled together as a firm are worth more than their sum as measured by K_t. In the absence of entry barriers and the like, when $M_t > K_t$ we expect other entrepreneurs to try and duplicate the activities of the firm so that they can pocket the difference between M_t and K_t. Thus, under perfect competition $M_t = K_t$, and $M_t/K_t = 1$. Marris (1963, 1964) measured K_t as the book value of the firm's assets and called M_t/K_t the *valuation ratio*, V_t. Tobin (1969) measured K_t as the replacement cost of the firm's assets and called M_t/K_t, q_t. In either case perfect competition should drive M_t/K_t toward one *if the managers are maximizing shareholder wealth.* Marris postulated that the managers maximized the growth of the firm, by investing more than the amount that would maximize V_t (see Chapter 5). As V_t falls from its maximum possible value, it becomes more and more attractive for someone to buy the firm and either introduce policies that raise V_t, or simply sell the firm's assets and pocket the difference, when $M_t < K_t$.

In the Marris' model, it is only the managers' pursuit of growth instead of shareholder welfare that leads to V_t falling below its maximum possible value. Manne (1965) noted that V_t might fall short of its maximum potential value for a variety of reasons including the exercise of managerial discretion in other ways than through the pursuit of growth and through mere incompetence. Whatever the cause, Manne argued that buyers in *the market for corporate control* would step in whenever V_t falls short of its maximum value, and thus that this process ensured that corporate assets gravitated into the hands of both the most competent managers and those intent on maximizing shareholder welfare.

Smiley (1976) attempted to measure how effective the market for corporate control is by comparing the actual market values of acquired companies prior to being taken over to a projected value on the assumption that their shares would have performed as other companies' shares were performing over the same period. He found that the market values of takeover targets began to fall below their predicted values on average ten years before the takeovers, and that the cumulative declines in market values averaged 50 percent of the predicted values. Smiley's results are consistent with the market-for-corporate-control hypothesis, but suggest considerable slack in this market. Although other studies have found the shares of acquiring firms to be underperforming prior to their takeover (Mandelker, 1974; Ellert, 1976; Langetieg, 1978; Asquith, 1983; Malatesta, 1983), this has by no means been true of all studies (Dodd and Ruback, 1977).

When Marris and Manne first discussed the potential disciplining role of takeovers in the early 1960s, they were comparatively rare events in the United States. Hostile takeovers did not become sufficiently numerous to cause managers to fear losing their jobs until the merger wave of the 1980s, when corporate raiders like Boone Pickens and Carl Icahn became famous by threatening top takeover companies that they felt were underperforming. Although there were some spectacular hostile takeovers of giant firms, the total number of hostile takeovers even during this period was not large (Bhagat *et al.*, 1990). Managers took the threat to their job security sufficiently serious, however, to introduce "golden parachutes" that would reward them generously in the event of their dismissal following a takeover, "poison pills" that triggered legal actions that seriously reduced the value of the firm to any buyer following a takeover, and to lobby – quite successfully – state legislatures to pass laws to protect firms in their states from takeovers (Roe, 1993b).

The economic disturbance hypothesis

At any point in time individual investors may have different expectations regarding the future profits of a particular firm.[7] Associated with each expected profit for firm B, $E(\pi_B)$, there is a price p_B that an individual would be willing to pay for firm B's shares. Figure 8.3a depicts a possible distribution of $E(\pi_B)$s and p_Bs at a particular point in time. The price of B's shares adjusts to the level, p_B^*, at which the area under the curve to the right of p_B^* just equals N_B, the number of shares of B outstanding. All individuals with expectations to the right of p_B^* are holders of B's shares, all other individuals are non-holders.

Now suppose that a group of non-holders suddenly raises its expectations about B's future profits. The distribution of expectations shifts to the dotted line in Figure 8.3b. Some non-holders find that the price of B's shares is far below what they think the shares are worth. They decide to buy not just a few shares of B, but

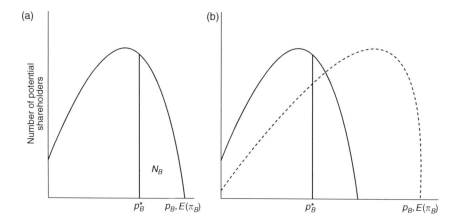

Figure 8.3 A possible distribution of $E(\pi_B)$s and p_Bs at a particular point in time.

the entire firm. If these non-holders are managers of another firm, the transaction takes the form of a merger.

It is reasonable to expect that the kinds of differences in expectations that would lead to mergers under this hypothesis are more likely in periods in which the stock market is experiencing rapid changes in value. Thus, the economic disturbance hypothesis is consistent with increases in merger activity during rapid upswings in stock market values. The hypothesis would also seem to predict intensive merger activity during sudden drops in stock market values. Indeed, since share prices generally fall (crash) faster after a stock market boom has peaked than the speed of their rise to the peak, one should observe even more differences in expectations during stock market declines and thus even more mergers. But merger activity crashes just as fast when a boom ends as does the stock market. Despite this empirical contradiction, the economic disturbance theory does posit at least in part the kind of wave like patterns of merger activity that have been observed.[8]

While Gort's theory focuses on differences in expectations about the value of the acquired firm in a merger, Shleifer and Vishny (2001) have recently developed a model that takes into account the market's valuation of both the buyers and their targets in mergers. In their theory firms make acquisitions by issuing stocks during stock market booms, because their shares are overpriced at this time and this effectively lowers the price of the acquisition. Their theory predicts merger waves during stock market booms, even when there are no synergies from the mergers.[9]

Financial efficiencies

Several hypotheses have been put forward that posit certain financial savings that may arise from mergers. These might be considered special cases of the cost savings discussed in the section on "Efficiency increases," but we think it is useful to treat them separately. We discuss the two most frequently mentioned financial motives for mergers.[10]

Savings on borrowing costs

Yields on the bonds of large firms and the interest rates banks charge them are on average much lower than for small firms. The relationship between a firm's borrowing costs, i, and its size might look something like that drawn in Figure 8.4. If each firm invests up until the point where its marginal return on investment equals its cost of capital, the last investment project undertaken by firm S has a return of r_s, while the last project undertaken by L has a return of r_l. If L and S merge, the additional investments available to S with returns between r_s and r_l can be undertaken with the difference between the returns of these investments and L's cost of capital somehow shared.

Although it is true that such a merger would allow privately beneficial investments to take place, it is not true that these possible gains justify a *merger* between the two companies. Superior to a merger would be for L to *lend* S the needed cash. Suppose, for example, that S has assets of 100 and a market value of 100. Its assets depreciate at a 10 percent rate per annum. The firm must therefore invest 10 each year to maintain K and M at 100. S has an additional 10 in investment projects available on which it could earn a 9 percent return in perpetuity. Its cost of capital on the market, however, is 12 percent. L on the other hand has a cost of capital of 6 percent. If L could make this investment of 10, it would have a present value of 15 to it, and thus a profit of 5 would be made.[11] To make this investment through a merger with S, however, L must acquire not just the 10 in new assets,

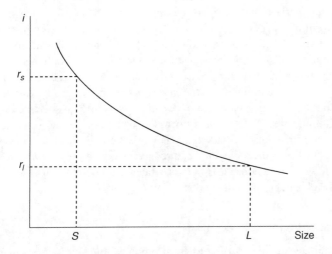

Figure 8.4 The relationship between a firm's borrowing costs i and its size.

but the 100 that already exist. To do so it will generally have to pay a premium over the pre-merger market price of the firm. On average these have ranged from 15 to 20 percent during normal times to over 50 percent during the late 1980s. Even at 15 percent, however, the aggregate payment for the target firm over its pre-merger market price (15) would exceed the gain on the investment. A superior alternative would be for L to lend S the money at an interest rate of say 7.5 percent, which would allow it and the owners of S to share the gains equally.

Riskpooling

As we saw in the previous chapter, the variance in returns on a portfolio of assets is less than a weighted sum of the variances in returns on the individual assets, if the returns on these assets are less than perfectly correlated. A portfolio provides the same average return at lower risk (measured as variance) than the sum of its elements.

A diversified firm can be thought of as a portfolio of assets of the separate lines of business in which the firm is engaged. The variance of its profits should be less than a weighted sum of the profits from the lines of business, and thus a diversified firm in 10 lines of business is less risky than the 10 businesses as stand alone companies would be. Although profit variances do tend to decline with firm size and diversification, this again is not a justification by itself for mergers. As in the previous section, there exist superior alternatives for reducing owners' exposure to risk.

To create a diversified firm with 10 divisions out of 10 separate companies, one firm must acquire 9 others. Each acquisition entails paying the premium of 20 percent or more needed to get the owners to sell. An individual could purchase shares in several companies, however, with brokerage fees of 1 percent or less. Some companies operate in 30 or more industries, and it may be difficult for an individual with limited savings to put together a portfolio of 30 companies.[12] As nearly always, "the market" has provided a solution to this problem for the small investor in the form of a wide range of mutual funds with different earnings/risk profiles, so that the small investor can now achieve the benefits of a diversified portfolio of securities with a single investment. Diversification through mergers is an inefficient way to spread market risks from the point of view of shareholders.

Mergers may be an efficient way for the *managers* of the firm to spread their risks, on the other hand. Stock option and incentive plans often result in a large fraction of both a manager's income and his assets being tied to the fortunes of his firm. If the firm is in a volatile market, a manager's income and wealth may be highly variable. The firm's diversification can reduce this variability for managers and may explain why they choose this merger strategy, even though it is to their shareholders' disadvantage (Amihud and Lev, 1981).

The capital redeployment hypothesis

One of the advantages claimed for the M-form organizational structure is that it allows a diversified firm to set up an internal capital market, and thereby avoids the dangers of the external capital market associated with the lack of appropriability of information. If the advantages of an internal capital are large, it might even warrant creating a diversified firm through mergers to establish one. This hypothesis resembles the capital cost argument of the section on "Savings on borrowing cost," but goes beyond it by positing ongoing potential gains from a central management team's ability to monitor the investment opportunities of each division and shift capital across them (see, Weston, 1970; Williamson, 1970).

The life-cycle-growth-maximization hypothesis

A mature firm in a slow-growing or declining market must follow the path of its market unless it diversifies. Mergers are the quickest way for a firm to grow and diversify and thus are an attractive way for managers with limited time horizons to achieve growth. The life-cycle-growth-maximization hypothesis predicts diversification mergers by mature firms.[13] It predicts essentially the same pattern of mergers as the capital redeployment hypothesis, but does not presume that such mergers generate any capital cost savings or other synergies. Where the capital redeployment hypothesis predicts that the whole is greater than the sum of the parts, the life-cycle hypothesis predicts that mergers occur even when this is not the case.

The constraint on managerial pursuits that harm shareholders is that the share price of the firm falls sufficiently, that the firm is taken over, and they are thrown out. If mergers are purely growth motivated, one expects managers to prefer announcing them in periods when their negative effects on share prices may be offset by other good news. As we shall see in the next chapter, not only do most mergers occur during stock market advances, but acquiring firms tend to substantially *outperform* the market for extended periods prior to their making their acquisitions. A likely reason for this superior stock market performance, is that the company's profits have risen faster than those of other companies. These profits provide acquiring firms with cash to finance the acquisition. Thus, the life-cycle-growth-maximization hypothesis is consistent with the wave pattern observed for mergers. The managers of acquiring firms choose to announce their mergers at times when they are least likely to fear takeover themselves and when their firms enjoy the "excess cash" to finance the mergers.[14]

The life-cycle-growth-maximization hypothesis as an explanation for mergers was first put forward by Mueller (1969). As we saw in Chapter 6, internal cash flows are an important resource for discretionary investments by managers of all sorts. This fact has been stressed by Jensen (1986) in his "free cash flow" hypothesis. Harford (1999) has provided direct evidence in support of the hypothesis that some mergers are driven by managerial objectives. He found for the period 1950–94, that (1) cash rich companies are more likely to undertake acquisitions, (2) their acquisitions are more likely to be diversifying acquisitions, (3) the abnormal share price reaction to bids is negative and lower for bidders who are cash rich, and (4) operating performance deteriorates after mergers by cash rich companies.[15]

The winner's-curse-hubris hypothesis

Suppose that the distribution of expectations for future profits of a given firm B is again as in Figure 8.3a, but now several companies are among the potential holders of B's shares. Each is willing to bid a price up to the value it thinks the shares are worth. The company making the highest bid acquires B, and thus the bidder with the most optimistic prediction about B's future profits acquires it a price somewhere toward the far right of the distribution. With *rational expectations* on the part of all bidders, the expected true value of the firm should be at the *mean* of the distribution. The winning bidder has almost certainly bid too much. He has fallen prey to the *winner's curse*.

The winner's curse is consistent with the evidence presented in the next chapter indicating that acquiring firms' shareholders tend at best to break even on mergers, and more likely lose from them. What is perhaps a puzzle is why anyone would ever enter a bidding contest, when one knows that the "winners" are sure to lose. One explanation would be that the bidders, the managers of the acquiring firm, do not really lose, because they are interested in their firm's growing and are prepared to see it's share price fall to accomplish this goal – the hypothesis of the previous section. A second explanation has been offered by Roll (1986). Managers of acquiring firms suffer from *hubris*, excessive pride and arrogance. They know that the average acquiring firm loses on a merger, but they believe that they are not average. They can beat the odds. They can spot true value in a target firm, where others cannot.

Such arrogant confidence is perhaps more likely to seize managers during a stock market boom, when their firm is doing well. Thus, the hubris' hypothesis would also seem consistent with the wave pattern we have observed.[16]

The eclectic hypothesis

Following a review of different hypotheses about mergers that was almost as long as the one just completed, Steiner (1975, pp. 180–4) once came down in favor of "all of the above." This *eclectic* theory of mergers is most certainly valid, at least in part. It is not very helpful, however, in allowing us to predict the effects of mergers either for the firms involved or for the economy. Nevertheless, it is important to keep it in mind for it reminds us that no single hypothesis about mergers can explain them *all*, and all of the hypotheses discussed here probably can account for *some* mergers.

We can do somewhat better than throw up our hands in frustration even at this juncture, however. We have seen that some of the hypotheses are more compatible with the observed wave pattern of mergers than others. Since large swings in share prices are difficult to reconcile with models of rational investment behavior,[17] it is perhaps not surprising, that the hypotheses, which seem most consistent with the positive correlation between mergers and share price increases, also do not view mergers as simply normal, profit-maximizing investments. The hypotheses that are most consistent with mergers' wave pattern see them driven by interests of promoters in speculative profits, differences in expectations between managers, manager interests in growth, and managerial hubris. As we shall see in the next chapter, these hypotheses are also the ones which are most compatible with the effects of mergers that have been observed. But before closing this chapter, let us briefly examine one effort to test the competing hypotheses about the determinants of mergers directly.

Testing competing hypotheses about the determinants of mergers

Hypotheses about the determinants of mergers can be grouped into three, broad categories. One set postulates that the goal of the managers is to increase the wealth of their shareholders and that some sort of *synergy* will arise if the two merging companies are joined. Examples would be a horizontal merger that increased the market power of the two merging companies, or a vertical merger that reduced transaction costs. With mergers such as these the synergistic gains from the merger arise from the specific characteristics of the two merging firms. It is reasonable to assume, therefore, that both firms share these gains, since each firm's participation in the merger is required for there to be any gains at all. One reasonable assumption might be that the two firms share the gains equally. A weaker assumption would be simply that the shareholders of both firms benefit from the merger.

Under the market-for-corporate-control hypothesis *all* of the gains from the merger are tied to the target firm. In principle, *any* other firm could buy the target and replace its managers and obtain the wealth increase from this action. Due to this, some authors have postulated that a bidding for the target takes place once one firm has identified that a particular firm is badly managed.[18] If this bidding continues until the target's share price rises by enough to reflect all of gains from replacing its management, the bidder's shareholders will experience no gain from the merger. The second category of hypotheses about mergers, thus, assumes that targets' shareholders receive positive wealth increases as a result of the mergers, but that bidders' gains average zero and are unrelated to the gains to the targets.

The third category of hypotheses assumes that there are *no net gains* from the mergers. Included among these would be mergers arising for speculative motives, out of managerial empire building or purely because of managerial hubris. When a merger produces no net gains, each dollar paid to the shareholders of the target represents a dollar loss to the acquirers' shareholders. The gains to the target's and bidder's shareholders should be inversely related.

As noted above, it is not possible to distinguish a merger motivated by pure hubris from one stemming from managerial empirebuilding. In both cases, the targets' gains are the bidders' losses. It is also possible, however, that managerial hubris may arise with mergers that do generate positive net wealth gains. Out of overoptimism the bidder pays too much for the target. In such a mixed case we would expect a net positive gain from the merger, but a loss to the bidder. Moreover, the bigger the gain to the target, the more likely it is that the bidder overbid, and the bigger its expected loss is.

Mueller and Sirower (2002) tested these various hypotheses by regressing the gains to the bidding firms onto the gains to the targets using a sample of 168 large acquisitions over the period 1978 through 1990. Specifically they estimated the following equation

$$\frac{G}{V_T} = e + f\frac{P}{V_T} + \mu, \tag{8.6}$$

where G is the gain to the bidder in dollars over a 24-month period beginning with the month of the merger,[19] P is the premium paid to the target's shareholders in dollars, and V_T is the market value of the target firm. Matrix 8.1 presents the predicted coefficients for this equation under the four sets of hypotheses described above namely, the synergy hypothesis (SH), the market-for-corporate-control hypothesis (MCCH), the managerial discretion hypothesis (MDH), and the hubris hypothesis (HH).

Matrix 8.1 $G/V_T = e + f\,P/V_T$

Hypothesis	Prediction without HH	Prediction with HH
SH	$e = 0, f = 1$	$e \gtrless 0, f < 1$
MCCH	$e = 0, f = 0$	$e \gtrless 0, f < 0$
MDH	$e = 0, f = -1$	$e = 0, f = -1$

Table 8.1 Relationship between gains to acquirers and premia paid to targets

$$\frac{G}{V_T} = e + f\frac{P}{V_T} + \mu$$

e	f	$\overline{R}^2$	e	f	$\overline{R}^2$
Contested		$n = 44$	Uncontested		$n = 124$
0.03	−0.21	−0.023	0.26	−2.23	0.053
0.06	0.19		0.97	2.81	
Multiple bidders		$n = 45$	Single bidder		$n = 123$
0.48	−1.94	0.051	0.09	−1.34	0.015
1.13	1.84		0.32	1.68	
Related (3 digit)		$n = 95$	Unrelated (3 digit)		$n = 73$
0.20	−0.68	−0.000	0.13	−2.54	0.052
0.79	1.00		0.31	2.23	
Cash only		$n = 90$	Noncash (mixed)		$n = 78$
0.49	−1.46	0.023	0.05	−2.48	0.057
1.42	1.75		0.16	2.38	

Source: Mueller and Sirower (2002).

Note
t-values are under coefficients.

Table 8.1 reports some of their findings. Since each hypothesis is more applicable to some types of mergers than others, Mueller and Sirower (2002) estimated separate regressions for different categories of mergers. Most of the category headings are self explanatory. "Related" mergers are those for which the two firms had at least one three-digit Standard Industrial Classification (SIC) industry in common. "Cash only" mergers were 100 percent financed with cash, "noncash" were at least partly financed through debt or stock transfers.

With respect to the pure synergy hypothesis, however, it did not matter which type of merger they examined. *None* of the eight coefficients on P/V_T is positive. No category of mergers leads to gains that are proportionally shared by the two merging companies.

The MCCH envisages a bidding process for the target and the replacement of its management after the merger. The MCCH seems particularly likely to be applicable to mergers with multiple bidders and for those contested by the targets' managers. Both e and f are insignificantly different from zero in the contested merger sample as the hypothesis predicts. The coefficient on the premium is negative and significant (10 percent level) in the multiple bidder sample, however. Both e and f are also insignificantly different from zero in the related merger sample, but the MCCH is rejected in all of the other regressions. All in all the pure form of the MCCH finds support in only two of the eight regressions.

The MDH predicts a zero intercept, and a coefficient of -1 on P/V_T for mergers. This hypothesis seems most likely to apply to mergers that are not contested, unrelated, and fully financed by cash. All three intercepts for these groups of mergers are insignificantly different from zero, and the three coefficients on P/V_T are all negative, significantly less than zero, and insignificantly different from -1. Thus, these results are consistent with those predicted by the MDH in its pure form, that is, there are no gains whatsoever from mergers, and all are motivated purely for growth, so that each dollar paid in premium to the targets' shareholders is a dollar loss to the bidders. Indeed, each of the point estimates of the coefficient on P/V_T is actually less than -1 suggesting that the mergers may actually be destroying wealth. In total, six of the eight regressions in Table 8.1 support the MDH.

The HH in its pure form assumes that no value is created by a merger and thus makes the same predictions as the MDH. It can also be interpreted as being additive to the other hypotheses. The overbidding predicted by the HH seems most likely with multiple bidders. The intercept for this sample is insignificantly different from zero, and the coefficient on P/V_T is negative and insignificantly different from -1. Thus, the results for multiple bidders' support the pure form of the HH.

The intercept in the multiple bidders' sample, although statistically insignificant, is large in absolute value and implies a mean gain to acquirers, if the premium were zero, of 48 percent. Interpreting this intercept as positive despite its statistical insignificance makes the results for multiple bidders consistent with a combination of MCCH and HH. The mergers generate wealth increases, but the acquirers tend to overbid.

With no positive and significant intercepts and no positive and significant coefficients on P/V_T it is difficult to find much support in Table 8.1 for any of the SH hypotheses in combination with the HH, *unless* one is willing to posit a *tremendous* amount of hubris. A positive intercept and a negative coefficient on P/V_T could arise through a combination of synergy and hubris, if the bidding firm not only did not receive 50 percent of the synergy gains, as assumed under the pure SH, but suffered a loss by bidding a premium *more* than the total synergies generated by the merger.

The HH and MDH make similar predictions and are difficult to separate empirically. In a world in which the MCCH, SH, and MDH are *all* valid for *some* mergers, any sample might contain a mixture of each. Although mergers between firms in related industries seem more likely to produce synergies than mergers between firms in diverse industries, some managers who undertake mergers for empire-building reasons may acquire firms in related industries to reduce the inefficiencies that mergers often bring. Similarly, managerial hubris might lead to overly high prices in any merger. The general pattern of results in Table 8.1 – intercepts that are insignificantly different from zero, coefficients on P/V_T that are both significantly less than zero and insignificantly different from -1 – supports both the MDH and HH.

One of the salient characteristics of mergers is that the variances in gains to the bidding firms tend to be very large relative to the mean. In the data of Mueller and Sirower (2002) the mean "gain" to the bidders was $-\$50$ million, while the variance around this mean was \$3,579,664 million. These large variances help to explain the low $\bar{R}^2$s reported by Mueller and Sirower as well as others (You *et al.*, 1986; Travlos, 1987). Anyone wishing to explain the dispersion of gains to acquiring firm shareholders has a lot of explaining to do.

This high variability in the gains from mergers, and the difficulty in predicting these gains is further support for the MDH and HH. How many people would play in a game in which their expected winnings were $-\$50$, the variance around this expectation was \$3,579,664, and they might lose as much as \$10,000,000 although they could also win as much as \$13,000,000? One assumes not many. Yet, these are the statistics for the acquiring firms in the Mueller/Sirower sample, except that they are measured in millions. Why do the managers of these firms undertake such gambles? One answer is hubris. They believe that they can see value in other firms that no one else can see. Thus, the averages do not apply to them. A second answer is managerial discretion. They are gambling with other people's money. These two hypotheses receive the most support in those studies that have tried to test different hypotheses about the determinants of mergers.[20]

9 The effects of mergers

Three sets of consequences of mergers interest economists. (1) They can affect the performance of the merging firms – their profits, growth rates, and so on. These effects are of obvious interest to the owners, managers, and employees of the firm, and can help us evaluate the weight to be given to the various hypotheses about the determinants of mergers discussed in the previous chapter. (2) They can affect industry and aggregate concentration levels. (3) They can affect social welfare. This latter effect is, to a considerable extent, a product of the first two consequences of mergers.

In this chapter we shall focus on the first set of effects of mergers, since these are most directly related to the theory of the firm. We begin with the effects of mergers on the profitability of the merging firms.

On profitability

Mergers are a form of investment, but they differ in important ways from normal investments in capital equipment.[1] First, they bring to the firm not only plant and equipment, but employees, management teams, customer and supplier relationships, and often new product lines. They do not simply replace that which exists with something similar but newer, as with much of capital equipment purchases, they inevitably add to the firm expanding either its market share, or its vertical structure, or its product line. While a firm might, with great difficulty, expand by 10 percent in a year through the purchase of plant and equipment and the hiring of new employees, it can double its size over night with a large merger or two.

Given the magnitude of the change often brought about by mergers, one expects managers to consider these decisions very carefully prior to making them. If managers maximize profits, then they should expect the profits of their company to rise following a merger. Although all expectations will not be fulfilled, if managers have *rational expectations*, the average merger should generate positive profits.

Perhaps the most surprising finding of the merger literature is that this prediction has not been generally confirmed. This surprising finding holds *even* for the first two great merger waves in the United States in which the mergers were largely horizontal and resulted in many cases in substantial increases in firm size and market shares (Hogarty, 1970).

One of the first investigations of the effects of mergers on profits after the Second World War was by Weston and Mansinghka (1971) (hereafter WM). They examined 63 manufacturing firms, which between 1958 and 1968 undertook a substantial number of diversification mergers, mergers that transformed them into "conglomerates" – the hallmark of the late 1960s merger wave. WM found that these conglomerates went from having significantly lower profit rates than other industrial firms to having about the same profit levels at the end of the decade. They concluded that the mergers represented a successful "defensive diversification" strategy by a group of large mature companies.

Reid (1971) pointed out, however, that the superior performance of WM's conglomerates came to a quick end, once the US economy went into recession. WM's data ended with 1968. Between the end of 1968 and the middle of 1970, the conglomerates' share prices fell by 56 percent, while share prices for the industrials in the WM sample fell only 37 percent. Melicher and Rush (1973, 1974) also reported a relative deterioration in performance for the WM conglomerates based on both accounting profits and various measures of share performance. The articles by Reid (1971) and Melicher and Rush (1973, 1974) suggested that an accurate picture of the effects of the 1960s conglomerate mergers could not be obtained merely by observing their performance during the stock market boom of the late 1960s.

One of the most comprehensive studies of the effects of mergers on profitability is an analysis of nearly 6,000 acquired lines of business between 1950 and 1977 by Ravenscraft and Scherer (1987).[2] They regressed the profits of individual lines of business in the years 1975, 1976, and 1977 on industry dummies and a variable that measured the fraction of the line of business that had been acquired since 1950. In this way they compared the profit rate of an acquired line of business in say the soft drink industry, with the average profit rate in soft drinks of all soft drinks producers. In addition to measuring the fraction of the line of business that was acquired, Ravenscraft and Scherer (1987) attempted to control for other aspects of the merger, as whether it was a hostile takeover or not, and characteristics of the line of business, like its market share, that might affect its profitability. They also distinguished between mergers on the basis of the accounting convention employed by the acquiring firm to evaluate the acquired firm's assets.

To see why the choice of accounting convention can make a difference, consider the following example. Firm A buys firm B, which has 100 in assets and 10 in profits. The market value of B before its acquisition is 100, but A must pay a premium to acquire B and winds up paying 150 for it. If, following the merger, the profit rate of the acquired firm (now one of A's lines of business) is measured relative to the *book value* of its pre-merger assets, the firm continues to earn a return of 0.10. Under this convention the assets of the newly created company are determined by simply *pooling* the book values of the assets of the two merging firms. If, however, the acquired unit's assets are evaluated at the price A paid for them, 150, the *purchase accounting* convention, the post-merger profit rate of the acquired unit is 0.067. Thus, if market values of acquired companies roughly equal the book values of their assets, a more favorable impression of the post-merger profits of acquired units will be obtained, if the pooling accounting convention is employed.[3]

This prediction is confirmed by Ravenscraft and Scherer. A typical regression result follows (Ravenscraft and Scherer, 1987, p. 101)

$$\pi K_{75-77} = [257 \text{ industry dummies}] + 0.68 \text{ POOL} - 2.82 \text{ PURCH} + 0.84 \text{ NEW}$$
$$(0.60) \qquad (2.24) \qquad (0.83)$$

$$+ 1.46 \text{ EQUALS} + 30.15 \text{ SHR} - 3.65 \text{ HOSTILE} - 3.77 \text{ WHITE}$$
$$(1.51) \qquad (5.67) \qquad (1.65) \qquad (1.69)$$

$$- 2.23 \text{ OTHER}$$
$$(1.18)$$

$$R^2 = 0.182, \qquad n = 2{,}732$$

The dependent variable is the profit to asset ratio of a line of business in one of the years, 1975, 1976, or 1977. The variables POOL and PURCH measure the fraction of a line of business that was acquired and whether the assets of the acquired unit were measured as their book value prior to the merger, as under the *pooling* convention, or their *purchase price*. The coefficient on POOL is insignificant implying that the profit rate of an acquired line of business was not significantly different from that of non-acquired lines of business, when the acquired unit's assets were measured at their pre-merger book values. When the profit rates of the acquired lines of business were measured relative to the values paid for these assets, however, they were 2.82 percentage points below those of non-acquired units. The mean profit rate of manufacturing firms over the 1975–77 period was roughly 9.9, so that the lower return earned by acquired units was both economically and statistically significant (*t*-statistic in parentheses).

There is weak evidence that mergers between similar sized firms are somewhat more profitable (coefficient on EQUALS), and that units involved in hostile mergers are less profitable (HOSTILE and WHITE). The latter finding may stem from poorer than average pre-merger performance of hostile targets. The most significant variable in the equation is the firm's market share (SHR). Ravenscraft and Scherer (1987) include this variable to control for the fact that acquired units tend to be smaller and have smaller market shares on average. Unfortunately, to the extent that mergers reduce the efficiency of the acquired units, as implied by the coefficient on PURCH, they also reduce the acquired units' market shares.[4] Thus, the inclusion of market share in the regression actually controls for some of the adverse effects of the mergers, thereby biasing the coefficients on POOL and PURCH upwards.

The null hypothesis of the above equation is that the profit rate of an acquired line of business equals the mean profit rate of similar lines of business as measured by one of the 257 industry dummies. As noted in Chapter 8, however, Ravenscraft and Scherer (1987) found that acquired lines of businesses tended to have *above average* profitability at the time they were acquired. Thus, even a profit

Table 9.1 The effects of mergers on profitability

Country	Authors	Time period	Merger sample	Control group	Profitability measure	Profit change relative to control group
United States	Piper and Weiss, 1974	1947–67	102 acquisitions by 30 bank holding	None	After-tax earnings per share	≈0
	Conn, 1976	1964–70	28 firms acquired by 4 conglomerates	Base industry acquired firm	After-tax profit/total assets	≤0
	Mueller, 1980b	1962–72	247 manufacturing mergers	Base industries; merging firms, size and industry matched firms	Before-tax profit/assets	≤0
			280 manufacturing firms		After-tax profit/assets	≥0
	Mueller, 1986a	1950–72	Merger activity 551 manufacturing firms	Companies in 551 making no acquisitions	After-tax profit/total assets	≤0
	Rhoades, 1987	1968–78	413 acquired banks	3,600 non-acquired banks	After-tax profit/assets	≈0
	Ravenscraft and Scherer, 1987	1950–77	5,966 acquired manufacturing companies	Base industry (line of business)	Before-tax profit/total assets	<0
	Healy et al., 1992	1979–84	50 largest mergers	Base industries	Before-tax-cash-flow assets	>0
	Andrade et al., 2001	1973–98	≈2,000 mergers	Base industries	cash flow/sales	>0
United Kingdom	Singh, 1971	1955–60	77 horizontal mergers	None	Before-tax profit/assets	≈0
					After-tax profit/assets	≈0
	Meeks, 1977	1950–71	1000 + mergers	Base industries	After-tax profit/assets	<0
	Cosh et al., 1980	1967–70	225 manufacturing mergers	Size and industry matched firms	After-tax profit/assets	≥0
					Before-tax profit/assets	≥0

Country	Study	Period	Sample	Control group	Profitability measure	Result
Australia	Kumar, 1985	1967–74	241 mergers	Base industries	After-tax profit/assets	≤ 0
	Cosh et al., 1985	1972–76	66 mergers	Base industries	After-tax profit/assets	$\gtrsim 0$
	McDougall and Round, 1986	1970–81	88 takeovers	Size and industry matched firms	Before-tax profit/assets	≈ 0
Belgium	Kumps and Wtterwulghe, 1980	1962–74	21 mergers	Size and industry matched non-merging firms	After-tax profit/assets	≈ 0
Canada	Baldwin, 1995	1970–79	1,575 acquired plants	Nonacquired plants in same industry	Value-added per worker/shipments	≥ 0
France	Jenny and Weber, 1980	1962–75	40 mergers	Size and industry matched non-merging firms	After-tax profit/asset	≈ 0
Germany	Cable et al., 1980	1964–74	50 mergers	Size and industry matched non-merging firms	After-tax profit/assets	≈ 0
Japan	Ikeda and Doi, 1983	1964–75	49 mergers	None	Before-tax profit/assets	> 0
The Netherlands	Peer, 1980	1962–73	31 mergers	Size and industry matched non-merging firms	After-tax profit/assets	< 0
Sweden	Ryden and Edberg, 1980	1962–76	26 mergers	Size and industry matched non-merging firms	After-tax profit/assets	≈ 0
				Base industry		≤ 1

rate equal to the average would signify a decline. Of course some decline would be anticipated even in the absence of an acquisition as a result of a "regression to the mean" effect. But Ravenscraft and Scherer (1987, pp. 113–17) found that the profitability of acquired units fell toward the mean much faster than for non-acquired units.

Similarly, negative findings were obtained by Meeks (1977) in a study of over 1,000 mergers since the Second World War in the United Kingdom. The post-merger profitability of the merging firms was on average significantly lower than their pre-merger profitability.

Although the studies by Ravenscraft and Scherer (1987) for the United States and Meeks for the United Kingdom are the most ambitious in terms of the numbers of mergers examined, they are by no means the only studies. Table 9.1 summarizes the findings from some 21 studies drawn from different countries and different time periods that have tried to measure the change in profits from before to after mergers. Some find declines, some increases, others find no significant change at all. If one weighs the evidence presented in each study by the number of observations in it, one must conclude that mergers have at best left profitability unchanged, and more likely have actually reduced the profits of the merging firms.

On market shares and growth

To increase profits a merger must either shift the demand schedules of the merging firms, or lower their costs. Demand schedule shifts might come about either because of changes in the market power of the merging firms or because of a change in the quality characteristics perceived by buyers due perhaps to more advertising or R&D having taken place. Each of these effects can in turn affect the market share(s) of the merging firms. An alternative way to measure the effects of mergers is to examine the changes in market shares that accompany them. Since accounting definitions of *sales* do not differ as greatly across companies and countries as definitions of profits and assets, this measure is to be preferred.

Mergers' effects on market shares can be predicted with the help of the following model. Let p_i be the price of firm i's product; x_i be firm i's output; c_i be the unit costs of producing firm i's output; π_i be firm i's profit; m_i be firm i's market share; O_i be firm i's objective function; θ_i be firm i's *degree of cooperation*, the weight it places in its objective function on the profits of other firms in its industry. For simplicity we assume that all firms have the same θ_i and drop the subscript. σ is a measure of the degree of product differentiation in the industry

$$0 \leq \sigma \leq 1.$$

Assume that firm i faces the linear demand schedule

$$p_i = a_i - bx_i - \sigma b \sum_{j \neq i} x_j, \tag{9.1}$$

from which we obtain the objective function

$$O_i = \pi_i + \theta \sum_{j \neq i} \pi_j = \left(a_i - b x_i - \sigma b \sum_{j \neq i} x_j - c_i \right) x_i$$

$$+ \theta \sum_{j \neq i} \left(a_j - b x_j - \sigma b \sum_{k \neq j} x_k - c_j \right) x_j. \tag{9.2}$$

Maximizing (9.2) with respect to x_i yields

$$x_i = \frac{a_i - c_i}{2b} - \frac{\sigma(1 + \theta)}{2} \sum_{j \neq i} x_j. \tag{9.3}$$

The first term in (9.3), $(a_i - c_i)/2b$, we can think of as a quality–efficiency index. It measures the difference between the amount a buyer is willing to pay for a firm's product and the costs of producing it. Calling this term q_i and defining

$$X = \sum_i x_i, \quad Q = \sum_i q_i, \quad r = \frac{\sigma(1 + \theta)}{2},$$

yields upon dividing (9.3) by X and rearranging

$$m_i = \frac{q_i(nr - r + 1)}{(1 - r)Q} - \frac{r}{1 - r}. \tag{9.4}$$

Since r must fall between zero and one, the first term in (9.4) is positive, and $\partial m_i / \partial q_i > 0$.[5] An increase in the quality–efficiency index, that is, an increase in the perceived quality of a firm's product as captured by a shift in its demand schedule, or a reduction in its unit costs should, *ceteris paribus*, lead to an increase in its market share.

Taking the partial derivative of m_i with respect to θ yields

$$\frac{\partial m_i}{\partial \theta} = \frac{(q_i n - Q)\sigma}{2(1 - r)^2 Q}, \tag{9.5}$$

from which we obtain

$$\left(\frac{\partial m_i}{\partial \theta} \geq 0 \right) \longleftrightarrow \left(q_i \geq \frac{Q}{n} \right). \tag{9.6}$$

An increase in the degree of cooperation following a merger increases the relative size of firms, which have quality–efficiency indexes greater than the mean (and thus are above the mean in size), but reduces the size of below average sized firms. The reverse pattern holds for a merger that reduces the degree of cooperation. The reason for this difference in impacts is easy to see from (9.2). The firm chooses output so as to maximize a weighted sum of industry profits. If the weight a firm puts on other firms' profits, θ, increases, the optimal constellation of industry outputs shifts output from the smaller, less profitable firms to the larger, more profitable ones.

Mueller (1985, 1986a, ch. 9) used the above model to examine the effects of mergers for a sample of 209 acquired firms from the 1,000 largest companies of 1950. The methodology compared the market shares of firms acquired between 1950 and 1972 with those of non-acquired firms of similar size in the same industries. A typical regression result looks as follows

$$m_{i72} = 0.011 + 0.885m_{i50} - 0.705Dm_{i50}, \quad n = 313, \quad R^2 = 0.940.$$
$$\quad (2.34) \quad\quad (45.02) \quad\quad\quad (20.09)$$

D represents a dummy variable that takes on a value of 1.0 if the firm was acquired, 0 if it was not. The equation shows that the average non-acquired firm retained 88.5 percent of its 1950s market share in 1972. Firms among the 1,000 largest of 1950s lost market share on average to smaller firms and new entrants over the 1950s and 1960s. An acquired company lost significantly more market share, however. On average it retained only 18 percent of its 1950 market share $(0.885 - 0.705)$. Additional tests showed that the loss of market shares tended to occur *after* the mergers took place. The earlier a firm was acquired, the greater its loss of market share.

These results were for conglomerate and vertical mergers. Companies involved in horizontal mergers, also exhibited market share losses relative to non-merging companies. The losses were smaller for bigger companies suggesting that the horizontal mergers may also have led to increases in the degree of cooperation, but the overwhelming effect of the acquisitions on companies in the largest 1,000 of 1950s was to reduce their market shares, and thus it would seem to have reduced either the quality of their products or the efficiency of their operations.[6]

Baldwin and Gorecki (1990, pp. 53–73; Baldwin, 1995, pp. 242–6) also found significant declines in market shares for Canadian *plants* acquired in horizontal mergers, but observed no significant changes in market shares for other acquired plants. Goldberg (1973) found no significant changes in market shares in the three-and-a-half years following their acquisition for a sample of 44 advertising intensive companies, as did Rhoades (1987) for 413 acquired banks for a period of up to six years following their acquisition.

A similar approach to comparing the market shares of merging firms is to examine their growth rates following mergers relative to matched samples or industry means. Six studies of this type, for Australia, Belgium, France, Germany, Sweden, and the United Kingdom, have found no significant changes in growth rates following mergers.[7] Significant *declines* in growth rates were observed in studies of Holland and the United States.[8]

Thus, we reach a conclusion from studies of the effects of mergers on market shares and relative growth rates similar to what we concluded from the profitability studies. There is no evidence that mergers increase market shares and growth as we would expect, if they increased product quality or efficiency. There is some evidence that mergers have a significantly negative effect on market shares.

Market power or efficiency?

The results regarding the profitability of mergers, although mixed, are clearly more positive than those regarding their impacts on market shares and growth. Although no studies come up with significantly positive effects of mergers on market shares or growth, quite a few find that they increase profitability. Whether these increases in profitability should be interpreted as increases in social welfare or not depends, of course, on whether they are the result of increases in market power or increases in efficiency. In a recent study of mergers occurring in virtually every country of the world, Gugler, Mueller, Yurtoglu, and Zulehner (2002) (hereafter GMYZ) have attempted to distinguish between mergers that increase market power and those that increase efficiency by examining their effects upon *both* profitability and sales.

As the simple model in the previous section indicated, a merger that improves efficiency, broadly defined to include both cost reductions and product improvements, results in an unambiguous increase in the merged firms' market share(s) and profits. Although it is possible to construct examples in which a merger that increases market power also increases the merging firms' market share(s), in most cases – as with a horizontal merger – one expects that the merging companies will take advantage of their increased market power by raising price and thus reducing their output and market share.[9] This reasoning led GMYZ to make the predictions given in the second column of Table 9.2.

In the previous chapter several hypotheses about the causes of mergers were presented that did not rely on the assumption that the managers were maximizing profits. Although these mergers could result in no changes in profits or sales, it is reasonable to assume that some inefficiencies accompany joining different organizational structures and "corporate cultures" and thus that costs rise and profits and sales fall for these mergers – the prediction in the lower right-hand corner of Table 9.2.

The remaining entry in the table has been called "market-power-reducing mergers" in analogy with the entry under 2. No manager is likely to undertake a merger with the purpose of reducing market power and so this combination of effects is a bit of a puzzle, hence the question mark for entry 3.

GMYZ use the changes in sales and profits of the median sized firms in the acquiring and acquired firms' industries to project what the sales and profits of the merging firms would have been had they undertaken no mergers. One of the

Table 9.2 Possible consequences of mergers

	$\Delta \Pi > 0$	$\Delta \Pi < 0$
	1	3
$\Delta S > 0$	Efficiency increase	Market power reduction (?)
	2	4
$\Delta S < 0$	Market power increase	Efficiency decline

Source: GMYZ (2002).

interesting findings of the study is that the effects of mergers on profits and sales are very similar across all countries and across types of mergers. In particular, cross-border mergers are neither more nor less successful than domestic mergers.

Table 9.3 summarizes some of the main findings of GMYZ. Looking first at the effects of mergers on profits we see that 56.7 percent of the mergers resulted in higher profits for the merging firms five years after the mergers than were predicted based on the changes in profits of the median firms in their industries. Across the full sample of 1,250 mergers the profits of the merging companies five years after the mergers averaged $17.8 million more than predicted based on the profits of the median firms in their industry. This difference was statistically significant, but small in comparison to the mean sales of the two merging firms at the time of the merger – $2,553.3 million (GMYZ, tables 2 and 4).

The bottom row of Table 9.3 indicates that a majority of mergers (55.8 percent) resulted in lower than predicted sales for the merging companies five years after the mergers. Thus, the findings of GMYZ with respect to mergers effects on profits and sales are consistent with those of other studies in that they find mergers to be somewhat more successful in terms of their effects on profits than in terms of their effects on sales.

The fraction of all mergers that leads to increases in efficiency ($\Delta \Pi > 0$ and $\Delta S > 0$) is roughly the same as the fraction producing an increase in market power ($\Delta \Pi > 0$ and $\Delta S < 0$), which in turn is nearly equal to the fraction resulting in a decrease in efficiency ($\Delta \Pi < 0$ and $\Delta S < 0$). The somewhat puzzling category

Table 9.3 Classification of mergers by firm size in year $t+5$ (percent of mergers)

		$\Delta \Pi > 0$	$\Delta \Pi < 0$
		1	3
	Small	34.7	17.5
$\Delta S > 0$	Large	23.4*	12.7*
	All	29.1	15.1
		2	4
	Small	20.4	27.4
$\Delta S < 0$	Large	34.8*	29.1
	All	27.6	28.2

Source: GMYZ (2002).

Notes

$\Delta \Pi > 0$ ($\Delta \Pi < 0$) denotes that the mergers resulted in a profit increase (decrease) relative to year t and relative to industry and country peers.

$\Delta S > 0$ ($\Delta S < 0$) denotes that the mergers resulted in a sales increase (decrease) relative to year t and relative to industry and country peers. The first number in each cell is for small firms (total sales less than the median in year $t - 1$), the second number in each cell is for large firms (total sales more than the median in year $t - 1$), and the third number in each cell is the overall proportion. Year t is the year of the merger.

A * means that the proportion of small firms is significantly different from the proportion of large firms at the 1 percent level, two-sided test.

($\Delta \Pi < 0$ and $\Delta S > 0$) accounts for the smallest fraction of mergers. It would seem more likely that mergers between large companies would increase market power, and that mergers between small ones would yield scale economies and other efficiency gains. This conjecture is confirmed in the GMYZ results. A significantly larger fraction of mergers between small firms (34.7 percent) resulted in efficiency increases than for large firms (23.4 percent). The reverse was true for mergers increasing market power. On the other hand, there was no systematic relationship between the size of the merging firms and the likelihood that they would result in a decrease in efficiency. If we assume that increases in market power reduce social welfare, and that decreases in efficiency reduce social welfare, then a majority of the mergers in the GMYZ study reduced social welfare.

Mergers effects on productivity

The strongest evidence that mergers have increased efficiency is contained in studies of changes in *plant ownership* that use plant level data collected by the US Census Bureau. Lichtenberg and Siegel (1987, pp. 643–73), for example, found that between 1972 and 1981 productivity fell in plants before an ownership change and rose afterward. Since many of these ownership changes would have been spin-offs of plants obtained in previous mergers, Lichtenberg and Siegel's findings in part corroborate other work suggesting that mergers in the 1960s lowered company profits and efficiency. Baldwin (1995, pp. 246–53) also found significant increases in productivity for Canadian plants acquired through spin-offs, and through horizontal mergers. McGuckin and Nguyen (1995) also observed plant productivity increases following mergers in the United States. Thus, it would appear that some immediate gains in efficiency at the plant level may result from mergers.

However, these results for *changes* in plant ownership and productivity are at odds with estimates of *levels* of plant productivity for diversified firms. Both Caves and Barton (1990) and Lichtenberg (1992) found that plants held by diversified firms had lower productivity levels than plants held by undiversified firms. Since mergers are the most popular way to diversify, we are left with the puzzle of how mergers can increase productivity at the time that they occur, and yet lead to lower productivity in the long run.

The studies examining mergers' effects on productivity seem to contradict those examining their effects on profitability and sales. One explanation for this inconsistency may be that the studies of productivity effects have used samples of mergers concentrated in the 1970s and early 1980s. As we shall see when we examine mergers' effects on share prices, their effects can differ substantially depending upon when in the business/stock market cycle they occur.

Mergers' effects on share prices – methodological issues

By far the most numerous works on mergers over the last quarter century have been *event studies* of their effects on share prices. Where other studies measure changes in performance for perhaps three or five years following a merger, event studies claim to measure the effects of mergers into the indefinite future, and superiority over other studies in that they do not rely on accounting data. These advantages stem from the use of the CAPM and its attendant assumption of capital market efficiency. With an efficient capital market, the price of a share of firm i at time t, p_{it}, is an unbiased estimate of the discounted present value of the dividends per share of firm i, d_{it}, from t to infinity, given common knowledge about firm i's future profits and dividends, and a cost of capital k.

$$p_{it} = \sum_{t=0}^{\infty} \frac{d_{it}}{(1+k)^t}. \tag{9.7}$$

An announcement that i will acquire another company or be acquired provides new information that can change market expectations regarding future profits and dividends, and thus bring about a change in i's share price. Such changes in share price reflect the market's *expectations of the effects of mergers*, and under the efficient capital market assumption are assumed to be unbiased and thus accurate estimates of what the *actual* effects of mergers will eventually be.

Even if we assume that the effects of mergers can be accurately measured by changes in merging companies' share prices, there are two additional problems in making these measurements: How does one know when the share price change caused by the merger occurs? How does one separate this price change from those caused by other events?

If the stock market fully adjusted to the new information about a merger on the day that it is announced, it might be reasonable to ignore all other events on that day and simply measure the effect of the merger by that day's share price change. A few studies, relying upon a very strong form of the efficient capital market assumption, have more or less done just that. But there is considerable evidence of increases in the volume of trading in target firms and in their share prices *prior* to official announcements of their acquisition, and important information about the merger – will the acquired firm's managers resign, will the antitrust authorities file suit, etc. – often reaches the market after the first announcement. To capture the full effects of a merger, as measured by changes in share price, one must begin measuring these price changes before the merger is announced and continue to do so for some period afterward. This necessity raises the importance of the question of how to separate out the effects of other events.

Two procedures have been followed. (1) A control group is selected and the assumption is made that the acquiring(ed) firm's share prices would have performed over the chosen period exactly as those of the control group did. (2) The performance of the acquiring(ed) firm is measured relative to that of the control group over some period, as say before the merger. Its performance at the time of the merger is then predicted to remain at the same level relative to the control group as it was before the merger.

Measuring the effect of the merger on the acquired firm's share price turns out to be relatively easy. The price of the acquired company's shares tends to start to rise a month or two before the merger is announced, and the merger is consummated on average in about six months following the announcement. If firm A wishes to acquire firm B it almost inevitably must pay a premium for B's shares over their pre-announcement price, because the owners of B's shares hold out for a higher price once they know that A is interested in acquiring them. These premia have generally averaged between 20 and 30 percent of B's pre-bid price, although during the wave of the late 1980s in the United States they averaged between 50 and 100 percent. The announcement of a merger thus produces a large percentage increase in the wealth of acquired firm's shareholders over a fairly short period of time. This increase merely reflects the fact that another firm seeks to acquire it. Whether this is because the managers of the acquiring firm anticipate that the merger will result in an increase in market power or efficiency, or are motivated by one of the other goals discussed in Chapter 8 cannot be deduced from the rise in B's share price caused by A's bid.

The pattern of returns for the acquiring companies is more complicated. One way to predict these returns employs the CAPM

$$R_{it} = \gamma_t + \delta_t \beta_{it} + \mu_{it} \tag{9.8}$$

where R_{it} is the return on firm i's shares in period t, β_{it} is the CAPM's measure of systematic risk for i in t, and μ_{it} is the error term for the equation. Time series observations on R_{it} are first used to estimate a β_{it} for each firm. These are then used along with the returns for each firm in a given period t, say a month, to estimate γ_t and δ_t for that month. These estimated parameters plus the β_{it} for firm i are then used to predict the return on firm i's shares in t

$$\widehat{R}_{it} = \widehat{\gamma}_t + \widehat{\delta}_t \beta_{it} \tag{9.9}$$

The difference between this predicted return, $\widehat{R}_{it}$ and the actual return is the error of the prediction

$$e_{it} = R_{it} - \widehat{R}_{it} \tag{9.10}$$

The efficient capital market assumption implies that the expected value of e_{it} in any period t is zero. The same should be true of the summation of e_{it}s over any span of years. In the absence of new information about i's prospects, cumulated prediction errors should be a slow moving average centered on zero. Should new information on the firm reach the market in a particular period t^*, its returns should adjust immediately to this new information and then continue on again as a random walk. The cumulative residuals for the firm should either jump or fall, and then continue on again as a slow moving average.

A second procedure for predicting an acquiring firm's returns in period t utilizes the *market model*

$$R_{it} - R_{ft} = \alpha_i + \beta_i (R_{mt} - R_{ft}) + \mu_{it} \tag{9.11}$$

where R_{mt} is the return on the market portfolio and R_{ft} is the risk-free rate of return. Under this procedure equation (9.11) is estimated over some benchmark period and the estimated αs and βs are then used to predict R_i in each t and the procedure proceeds as above. Yet, another procedure simply compares actual and predicted share prices using various portfolios of firms as a control group. For each procedure the effects of a merger are measured by examining the differences between actual and predicted values over a particular interval around the announcement date called "the window." Windows in event studies have been as short as a few days around the announcements to several years after them.

We turn now to a review of the findings using these various approaches. The literature is divided into two parts. The following section examines studies appearing up through 1983. This date is chosen as a breaking point, because it marks the publication of a special issue of *The Journal of Financial Economics* devoted to mergers and acquisitions (hereafter M&As), an issue which contained an influential survey of the literature by Jensen and Ruback (1983). Their survey reflects the consensus at that time among finance specialists as to the causes and consequences of M&As. The post-1983 literature reveals much less consensus over mergers' effects, and over the best methodology for studying them.

The first wave – 1972–83

Findings

The application of the event study methodology to M&As was pioneered by Lev and Mandelker (1972), Halpern (1973), and Mandelker (1974). Mandelker's (1974) findings illustrate a pattern that was to be repeated in numerous subsequent studies. The shareholders of the target companies earned a significant 12 percent return as a result of the M&As, while the shareholders of the acquiring firms experienced virtually no change in wealth whatsoever. Mandelker (1974, p. 321) surmised "that for the stockholders of acquiring firms, 'news' of an acquisition may not be worthwhile news."

Two other patterns in Mandelker's results would reappear in future studies. Acquiring firms' shareholders earned an impressive 4.8 percent return above the market portfolio over the 34 months leading up to the mergers, and lost a cumulative 1.5 percent over 40 months beginning in month 7 following the mergers.[10] Both of these figures are much larger than the change in wealth for the acquirers' shareholders in the announcement month.

Several subsequent studies did not report cumulative returns before and after the mergers, but among those that did, the same four patterns Mandelker observed can often be found: (1) the acquired companies' shareholders enjoy large percentage increases in wealth from the time of mergers' announcements until they disappear, (2) acquiring companies' shareholders experience small and often statistically insignificant changes in wealth around the announcements, (3) they experience large and statistically significant increases in wealth over prolonged periods prior to the mergers, and (4) they experience losses in wealth over lengthy periods following the announcements, losses which are sometimes large and statistically significant.

The pattern for the acquiring companies is illustrated in Figure 9.1, constructed from data reported by Asquith (1983) and Dodd and Ruback (1977). Asquith's residuals are estimated using the CAPM and thus the null hypothesis is that the acquiring companies' shares would have performed as the market portfolio did for firms with comparable betas. Acquiring firms begin to earn positive abnormal returns roughly two years prior to the merger announcements. These cumulate to 14.3 percent of the acquirers' market values by the announcement day. On that day, day 0, the bidders earn an average return of 0.002. Points to the right of

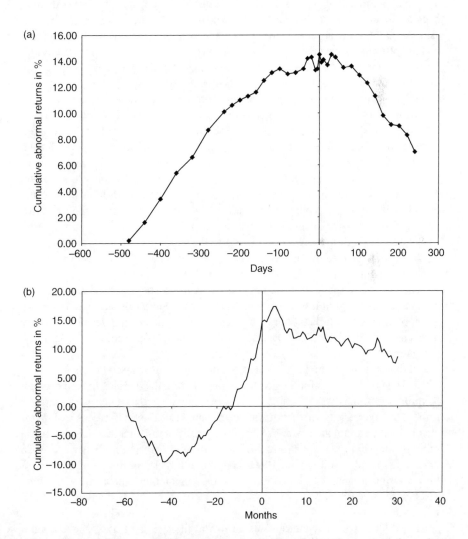

Figure 9.1 Cumulative residuals for successful bidding firms. Constructed from data reported by (a) Asquith, 1983; (b) Dodd and Ruback, 1977.

day 0, represent observations following the consummation of the mergers. Thus, a gap of variable length averaging roughly six months occurs following day 0. Starting at the time that the mergers are completed, the abnormal returns of the acquirers become negative and fall a cumulative 7.0 percent. Thus, over about one year following the mergers, the acquirers' shareholders lost roughly half of the substantial gains that they experienced over the two years leading up to them.

The estimates of Dodd and Ruback are based on the market model. The importance of this choice *vis-à-vis* the CAPM is discussed below. Their cumulative abnormal returns look very similar to Asquith's, except that the upward trend begins almost four years before the announcements. The downward trend begins, as in Asquith's data, around the time when the average merger is completed. Note that in both studies the post-merger declines in returns continue until the data stop. Thus, the cumulative declines to the acquirers would quite likely have been greater than reported had longer post-event periods been chosen.

Table 9.4 reports the findings of eight representative studies. The criteria for inclusion in the table were: (1) that returns were measured in either days or months so that a short window around the announcements could be identified, and (2) abnormal returns were reported for at least 12 months prior and after the announcements. All eight studies report significant gains for the targets' shareholders (mean = 16.3 percent). Six report positive abnormal returns to acquirers when the M&As are announced. But the gains are small with a mean over the eight studies of only 0.3 percent. In stark contrast *all* eight studies report positive abnormal returns over the pre-event period, with the mean gain to acquirers being 11.3 percent. Six of the eight report losses to the acquirers over post-merger intervals ranging from roughly one to six years. The mean cumulative loss to acquirers is −6.2 percent.

What are we to make of these patterns of returns? The returns to the acquired companies are the simplest to explain. To induce a majority of the shareholders of a company to give up their shares, a premium over the pre-merger price usually needs to be paid. The gains to the acquired companies' shareholders reflect these premiums.

Interpreting the patterns of returns to the acquiring firms is less straightforward. The biggest gains for the acquirers come *before* the mergers are announced. Acquirers appear to begin to earn positive abnormal returns as much as 100 months prior to the mergers. Positive movements in share prices so far in advance of mergers obviously cannot have been *caused* by them. The post-merger declines, on the other hand, seem to be consistent with what Reid (1971) and Melicher and Rush (1973, 1974) observed for the 1960s conglomerates. From the point of view of the acquiring companies' shareholders, the merger announcements are worse than just being not worthwhile news, as Mandelker (1974) put it, in fact they should be treated as signals to sell.

This is, however, not the conclusion of the first wave of M&As event studies ending in 1983. As already noted, several either ignored the post-merger performance of acquirers entirely or tracked it for only short intervals.[11] This

Table 9.4 Returns to acquiring and acquired companies' shareholders, first wave

Study	Time period (country)	Returns prior to merger announcement acquiring firms	Returns in announcement day (d), month (m), acquiring firm	Post-merger returns in days (d), months (m) after merger acquiring firms	Acquired firms' returns	Sample	Benchmarks
Mandelker, 1974	1941–63 (USA)	0.048^b ($m = -34, -1$)	0.003^b ($m = 0, 6$)	-0.015^b ($m = 7, 46$)	0.120^*	241 large mergers	CAPM[a]
Ellert, 1976	1950–72 (USA)	0.233^* ($m = -100, -1$)[c]	-0.018^d	-0.016 ($m = 1, 48$)		205 mergers challenged by Justice Dept. or FTC between 1950 and 1972	CAPM
Dodd and Ruback, 1977	1958–78 (USA)	0.117^* ($m = -60, -1$)	0.028 ($m = 0$)	-0.059^b ($m = 1, 60$)	0.206^*	136 tender offers	Market model[a] ($m = -72, -13$) ($m = +13, +72$) ($m = +13, +72$)
Kummer and Hoffmeister, 1978	1956–74 (USA)	0.170^b ($m = -40, -1$)	0.052^b ($m = 0$)	0.006^b ($m = 1, 20$)	0.187^*	88 cash tender offers	CAPM
Langetieg, 1978	1929–69 (USA)	0.136^* ($m = -64, -1$)	-0.028 ($m = 0, 5$)	-0.262 ($m = 7, 78$)	0.128^*	149 mergers of all kinds	Market portfolio and industry index
Firth, 1980	1969–75 (USA)	0.014^b ($m = 48, -1$)	-0.063^* ($m = 0$)	0.001^b ($m = 1, 36$)	0.363	434 mergers of all kinds	Market model ($m = -48, -13$) ($m = +13, +36$)
Asquith, 1983	1962–72 (USA)	0.143^b ($d = -480, -1$)	0.002 ($m = 0$)	-0.072^* ($d = 1, 240$)	0.133^*	196 mergers of all kinds	CAPM
Malatesta, 1983	1969–74 (USA)	0.043^* ($m = -60, -1$)	0.009 ($m = 0$)	-0.079^* ($m = 1, 12$)	0.168^*	256 mergers of all kinds	Market model ($m = -62, -13$) ($m = 13, 60$)

Notes

Returns are measured as differences between merging companies' returns and control group returns in all cases. In those studies in which the data were centered around the date of final consummation, the series were displaced backwards by six months to allow for the fact that announcements generally precede mergers by six months.

$*$ Statistically significant at the 0.05 level or better.

[a] A CAPM implies the predicted performance given a firm's β if it performed as the market portfolio performs. Market model predicts firm i's returns using the α and β from $R_{it} = \alpha_i + \beta_i + \mu_{it}$, or some variant thereof. If only one time interval was used to estimate all residuals, only one is given. When three are given, the residuals prior to announcement are estimated from market model estimated over the first interval, the announcement residual from the second interval, and the post-announcement from the third.

[b] Reported data do not allow calculation of statistical significance.

[c] Month 0 in the Ellert study is the month in which a complaint is filed.

[d] Announcement of a merger in Ellert study is measured as period from judicial complaint through settlement.

choice reflected a strong belief in the efficiency of the capital market. The capital market was assumed to make an unbiased evaluation of a merger's effect on future profits at the time it was announced. Mergers' full long-run effects could be measured by changes in share prices over short intervals around their announcements. As was true for several of the studies in Table 9.4, those that ignored the post-merger performance of acquiring companies tended to find small and often insignificant changes in acquirers' share prices around the announcements. The acquirers' shareholders were judged not to have lost as a result of the mergers, the acquired shareholders were clear winners, and thus the studies that ignored the post-merger performance of acquiring companies concluded that M&As increased total shareholder wealth.

Somewhat surprisingly, this was also the conclusion reached by several studies *that did report post-merger returns.* Of the eight cited in Table 9.4, only Firth and Malatesta concluded that the acquiring companies' shareholders had suffered significant losses. In Firth's case all losses occurred in the announcement month, in Malatesta's they occurred over the year following the mergers. Interestingly, Firth and Malatesta were among the very few first wave studies to add up the absolute wealth changes for both groups of shareholders. Both found that the aggregate losses to the acquiring companies' shareholders *exceeded* the gains in wealth of the targets. The remaining studies that reported post-merger losses for acquiring companies dismissed them as "surprising" or "puzzling," or simply ignored them.

Even if one ignores the post-merger losses for acquiring companies' shareholders, their small and often insignificant gains at the merger announcements seem inconsistent with the premise that their managers are maximizing shareholder wealth. Although the managers of a target of a tender offer or of some other unwelcomed overture may be reluctant participants in the marriage of two companies, the acquirers' managers clearly are not. If the "synergistic" gains that justify a merger are some form of scale or scope economy, or an increase in market power, then a straightforward application of Nash's (1950) bargaining theory would imply that the gains from the merger would be shared equally by the two companies. When one takes into account the size disparity between acquirers and targets, if anything one expects that a larger fraction of the gains from mergers go to the acquirers. How is it that the much smaller targets walk off with most or all, or perhaps *even more than all* of the gains from M&As?

The answer given by most first-wave finance studies was that M&As' gains come from replacing the targets' managers, as hypothesized in Manne's (1965) much-cited article about "the market for corporate control."[12] Once a company with poor management has been identified, bidding for it begins and continues until the premium paid reflects all potential gains from replacing its managers. Thus, all of the wealth gains go to the target's shareholders. Additional support for this interpretation was provided by those studies that found significant *below normal* returns for the targets in the months prior to their acquisition.[13]

After an exhaustive survey of the first generation finance literature on M&As, Jensen and Ruback (1983, p. 47) concluded that

> ... the evidence seems to indicate that corporate takeovers generate positive gains, that target firm shareholders benefit, and that bidding firm shareholders do not lose. Moreover, the gains by corporate takeovers do not appear to come from the creation of market power. Finally, it is difficult to find managerial actions related to corporate control that harm shareholders ...

This statement succinctly summarizes the consensus among nearly all contributors to the early literature as to the impact of M&As on shareholder wealth.[14]

Commentary

The efficient capital market theory claims that at each point in time the market is capable of making an unbiased prediction of future share prices of firms. Yet, at stock market peaks, these predictions greatly overestimate future share prices. To understand *why* the stock market's implicit forecasts of corporate performance can be wide off the mark, one must relax or abandon the strong forms of rational behavior assumptions that underlie the efficient capital market hypothesis. In periods like the late 1920s, 1960s, and 1990s investors seem to be seized by "irrational exuberance," to use Alan Greenspan's apt term, and stock prices reflect an overly optimistic view of future growth in corporate earnings.[15] Each share price increase reinforces the optimism that led to it, and in turn stimulates even more optimism and share purchases (Shiller, 2000, ch. 3).

The optimism feeding stock market booms is often underpinned by various "theories" advanced by market analysts as to why a given company's or sector's stocks are good values. The shares of these companies come into vogue and their prices are driven up even faster than the average share as, for example, occurred at the end of the 1990s with the dramatic run-ups in share prices of the high tech, new economy, and dot-com companies.

The evidence that investors are overly optimistic about future earnings at stock market peaks is highly relevant for the use of event studies to determine the effects of mergers, since history shows that M&As come in waves, and that the crests of these waves coincide with stock market peaks.[16] Thus, a disproportionate fraction of any sample that includes a stock market peak consists of mergers that occurred when the market was seized by overoptimism. The possibility must be entertained that M&A announcements during stock market booms are also greeted by overoptimism, and thus that estimates of the *effects* of these mergers based upon share price movements at the announcements are biased upward.

This possibility is enhanced by the fact that "theories" about why certain sorts of mergers produce large gains also abound during stock market booms. During the late 1960s, theories as to why conglomerate mergers would increase shareholder wealth appeared in great number, and the word "synergy" first came into popular use to describe efficiency gains that did not fall under any of the conventional headings. The market's optimism about the conglomerates was reflected in their high price/earnings ratios (P/Es). Indeed, the conglomerates' high P/E s became the basis for yet another hypothesis about how they created wealth – they did it by "P/E magic" (Mead, 1969). The market would re-evaluate the earnings of a company with a P/E of 10 at 30 immediately upon its acquisition by a conglomerate with a P/E of 30. The investors' psychology that would support P/E magic is very similar to that which supports all forms of Ponzi schemes and drives stock market booms (Shiller, 2000, ch. 3).

The arithmetic of P/E magic could justify premiums of 200 and 300 percent, and thus made all companies with low P/Es look like bargains so long as the magic held. Even the premiums actually paid represented a great deal of optimism as to the effect of the mergers, however.[17] The sample periods of five of the studies in Table 9.4 include the 1960s stock market boom. All report positive abnormal returns of more than 10 percent for acquiring firms prior to the acquisitions.[18] Whether the share prices of these companies were driven up by announcements of unexpected increases in earnings and other sorts of good news, or by irrational exuberance cannot be determined. If the acquiring companies' pre-merger share performance reflected real improvements in performance relative to other firms, then the post-merger performance of their shares implies that the acquirers suddenly shifted from outperforming other companies to underperforming them at the time of their acquisitions. If the acquiring companies' pre-merger share performance reflected merely overoptimism by the stock market, then the post-merger performance of their shares can easily be explained as the elimination of the market's overoptimism that drove up the prices of the acquirers prior to the acquisitions. In either case one obtains a false impression of the *effects* of the mergers by only examining the market's reaction at their announcements.

The second wave – post-1983

Up until the mid-1980s, the finance literature on M&As exhibited a remarkable consensus about both the methodology to be used to determine their causes and consequences, and what these causes and consequences were. In the mid-1980s, however, disagreements emerged about the motives of the managers who undertake M&As, about their effects, and about the proper methodology for measuring these effects. This latter debate has revolved around the questions of the proper benchmark for and length of "window" for measuring returns.

The proper benchmark

The market model can give quite different results depending upon the benchmark period used to estimate its parameters. When, for example, estimates using the CAPM imply significant positive abnormal returns for acquirers before merger announcements, then estimates of α from (9.1) over a pre-announcement period will be positive and large. Differences between actual and predicted returns will, accordingly, be lower than if a period of normal returns is used as a benchmark. The reverse will be true, if a period of low normal returns – like that following merger announcements – is used as a benchmark.

The natural choice for a benchmark period is some interval *before* the merger announcements, since one wishes to measure the *changes* in performance as a result of the mergers. However, several studies, including that of Dodd and Ruback (1977) from which Figure 9.1b was constructed, estimated post-merger abnormal returns using a post-merger period to estimate equation (9.11). This choice resulted in much lower estimates of post-merger losses to acquirers than using a pre-merger benchmark. For example, using a benchmark period from 36 to 3 months before the announcement month, Magenheim and Mueller (1988) calculated cumulative losses to acquirers of a significant 11.3 percent over the first 12 months after the announcements. Using a post-announcement benchmark the losses were an insignificant 3.2 percent.[19] Thus, studies that estimate the effects of mergers using the market model with post-merger returns estimated against a post-merger benchmark, *have underestimated the change in performance* that occured at the time of the announcements.

Franks and Harris, however, suggest that the use of the market model estimated over a pre-event period is inappropriate. With αs and βs estimated from before the announcements, they estimate a cumulative return to acquirers over the two years following the announcements of -12.6 percent (see Table 9.5). They dismiss these negative returns, however, stating several possible alternative explanations for them including that "bidders time mergers to take advantage of recent abnormal returns in their own stock prices... positive [pre-merger] αs, if unsustainable, would introduce a negative drift in abnormal returns, which could be interpreted as 'too' high a control return rather than poor performance by bidders" (Franks and Harris, 1989, p. 246, footnote omitted). They do not discuss, however, why the acquirers in their sample outperformed the market portfolio by almost 1 percent per month for a period of five years before the mergers, and why this extraordinarily good performance happened to come to an end at the time when the companies announced their acquisitions.

More fundamentally, however, their argument raises doubts about whether one can conclude anything about the effects of mergers on the operating performance of the merging firms from data on shareholder returns. If we should not interpret declines in acquirers' abnormal returns following mergers as being *caused* by the mergers, should we not also question whether the gains to the targets' shareholders reflect real synergies caused by the mergers? As noted above, several studies reported that targets earned significant negative abnormal returns prior to being taken over. The usual explanation for this is that they were badly managed and that the takeovers occurred to replace their managers. But perhaps their shares were merely *undervalued* prior to the takeovers, just as the acquirers' shares might have been *overvalued*. The premiums paid may then not have reflected the creation of wealth through the replacement of bad managers or other synergies, but merely reflected the return of the targets' market values to their unbiased levels just as, following Franks and Harris, the decline in returns to the acquirers was merely

Table 9.5 Returns to acquiring and acquired companies' shareholders with long post-merger windows

Study	Time period (country)	Returns prior to merger announcement acquiring firms	Returns in announcement day (d), month (m), acquiring firm	Post-merger returns in days (d), months (m), after merger, acquiring firms	Acquired firm's returns	Sample	Benchmarks
Magenheim and Mueller, 1988	1976–81 (USA)	0.127* 0.280* (m = −24, −4)				51 mergers 26 tender offers	Market model (m = −60, −25)
			−0.004 0.014 −0.007 0.007 (m = 0)	−0.277* 0.089 −0.491* −0.273* (m = −3, 36)		51 mergers 26 tender offers 51 mergers 26 tender offers	(m = −60, −4) (m = −36, −4)
Franks and Harris, 1989	1960–85 (UK)		0.010* (m = 0)	−0.126* 0.045* (m = 1, 24)	0.233* (m = 0)	1,048 M&As	Market model (m = −71, −12) CAPM
Franks et al., 1991	1975–84 (USA)		−0.010 (m = 0)	−0.040[a] (m = 1, 36)	0.280* (m = 0)	399 M&As	Portfolio which control for size, dividends and past returns
Agrawal et al., 1992	1955–87 1955–59 1960–69 1970–79 1980–87 1975–84 (USA)			−0.103* −0.232* −0.151* 0.041 −0.194* −0.028 (m = 1, 60)		765 M&As 51 M&As 299 M&As 247 M&As 168 M&As 290 M&As	CAPM with adjustments for firm size
Loderer and Martin, 1992	1966–86 1966–69 1970–79 1980–86 (USA)			0.075[b] −0.612*[b] 0.300[b] 0.175[b] (d = 1, 1250)		1,298 M&As 261 M&As 598 M&As 439 M&As	Market model with adjustments for firm size (t = 1, 1,250)
Leeth and Borg, 1994	1905–30 (USA)	0.330* (m = −60, −4)	−0.001 (m = 0)	−0.238* (m = 1, 36)		191 M&As in mining and manufacturing	CAPM

Study	Period (Country)				Sample	Benchmark
Gregory, 1997	1984–92 (UK)	−0.005 (m = 0)		−0.125* (m = 0, 24)	408 M&As	CAPM with adjustments for firm size
Loughran and Vijh, 1997	1970–89 (USA)			−0.065 / −0.242* / 0.185 / −0.096 (m = 1, 60)	947 M&As / 405 stock financed / 314 cash financed / 228 stock/cash financed	Firms matched by size and BV/MV[c]
Higson and Elliott, 1998	1975–90 (UK)	0.002 (m = 0)	0.315* (m = 0)	0.008 (m = 1, 36)	830 M&As / 722 M&As	Firms matched by size
	1975–80			−0.100*	305 M&As	
	1981–84			0.263*	156 M&As	
	1985–90			−0.062* (m = 1, 24)	315 M&As	
Rau and Vermaelen, 1998	1980–91 (USA)			−0.040*	2,823 mergers	Returns of firms of similar size and BV/MV
				0.089*	316 tender offers	
				−0.173*	932 mergers, firms with low BV/MV	
				−0.042	105 tender offers with low BV/MV	
				0.076*	931 mergers, firms with high BV/MV	
				0.155* (m = 1, 36)	104 tender offers, firms with high BV/MV	
Andrade et al., 2001	1973–98	−0.038 (t = −20, c)[d]	0.238 (t = −20, c)[d]		3,688 mergers	(CAPM?)
	1961–93 (USA)			−0.050* (m = 0, 36)	2,068 mergers	
Conn et al., 2001	1984–2000 (UK)	0.012* (m = 0)		−0.057* (m = 0, 36)	3,260 takeovers	Returns of firms in same industry matched by size + BV/MV

Notes

* Indicates significant at 0.05 level or better.

a Franks et al. report only the α of the market model estimated over months +1 to +36. To make their results comparable to the others in the table, I have multiplied their estimate of α by 36.

b Loderer and Martin report only the α of the market model estimated over days +1 to +1,250. To make their results comparable to the others in the table, I have multiplied their estimate of α by 1,250. Only the negative estimate was statistically significant.

c BV/MV = (Book value)/(Market value).

d c = completion of merger.

a return to normalcy. Should we not treat the two possibilities symmetrically? This methodological issue is taken up again below.

The returns to acquirers over long post-merger windows

Most of the post-1983 studies, which have estimated abnormal returns to acquirers over long post-merger windows, have used either the CAPM or portfolios of companies of similar size, dividend payout ratios, book to market ratios, etc. Twelve such studies are briefly summarized in Table 9.5. All but one cover M&As since the Second World War. Leeth and Borg (1994) examine mergers from 1905 to 1930 and show that large positive pre-merger abnormal returns and large negative post-merger returns are not a new phenomenon.

Of particular interest is the article by Agrawal, Jaffe, and Mandelker (1992) (AJM). They estimate returns over five year post-announcement periods. Over the 1955–87 period, the cumulative abnormal returns to acquirers are a significant −10 percent. Significant negative post-merger returns were also estimated for the 1950s, 1960s, and 1980s. Insignificantly positive abnormal returns were estimated, however, for the 1970s. This pattern is consistent with the hypothesis that merger waves are fueled in part by stock market speculation and that acquiring companies undertake wealth-destroying M&As out of empire-building motives when their share prices and/or cash flows are high, or simply out of hubris fed by their companies' high share prices. The depressed share prices of the 1970s may have brought about a more sober approach to M&As.

Of interest, also, are AJM's results for the period 1975–84. This time period is identical to that used by Franks, Harris, and Titman (1991) (FHT). FHT claimed that the significant negative returns reported in earlier studies were the result of inappropriate benchmark portfolios. Their preferred benchmark yielded an insignificant monthly abnormal return of −0.11 percent. Half of FHT's sample period falls in the 1970s, however, where AJM observed slightly positive post-merger residuals. AJM also obtained small and insignificant negative post-merger abnormal returns for the time period used by FHT, but this finding was not representative of M&As over the entire 1955–87 period, nor of three of the four sub-periods in the AJM data.

It is also worth noting that FHT's monthly abnormal return of −0.11 implies a cumulative loss to the acquirers after 36 months amounting to 4 percent of their market values. Such a loss would offset the 28 percent gains to the targets, if the acquirers were seven times larger than the targets, which is about the case in most studies.[20] Thus, even using FHT's preferred benchmark leads one to conclude that the net wealth gains from the M&As in their sample were insignificantly different from zero.

Estimates of returns by Loderer and Martin (1992) and Higson and Elliott (1998) are also sensitive to the time period in which the M&As occurred. Loderer and Martin obtained only one significant estimate of a post-announcement abnormal return – a negative return for M&As between 1966 and 1969.[21] This finding is, of course, consistent with the hypothesis that booming stock markets are associated with disproportionate numbers of ill-conceived M&As. Unlike AJM, Loderer and Martin did not estimate negative post-announcement returns for M&As during the 1980s, however.

The patterns of post-merger returns reported by Gregory (1997) and Higson and Elliott (1988) are quite interesting. Higson and Elliott find that mergers in the United Kingdom between 1975 and 1980, and again between 1985 and 1990 were followed by significant wealth losses to acquirers. Mergers between 1981 and 1984, on the other hand, were followed by significant positive abnormal returns. Gregory's data extend those of Higson and Elliott's end. He estimates a significant −12.5 percent abnormal return for acquirers for M&As between 1984 and 1992. Putting these two UK studies together, we see that M&As have been followed by negative abnormal returns to acquirers for every time period between 1975 and 1992, except for 1981–84, when stock prices in the UK were flat.[22]

Finally, mention must be made of the study of Rau and Vermaelen (1998)(RV). They estimate significant post-announcement returns of −4 percent for a sample of 2,823 acquirers, and significant positive returns for 316 tender offers (time period 1980–91). They also provide considerable support for the hypothesis that high share prices fueled by overoptimism are associated with wealth destroying mergers. Acquirers with high market values relative to their capital stocks earned a −17.3 percent abnormal return over the three years following merger announcements. In contrast companies with relatively low market values had positive post-announcement returns. RV conclude "that these findings are consistent with the hypothesis that the market overextrapolates the past performance of the bidder management when it assesses the benefits of an acquisition decision. As a result, the market, as well as the management, the board of directors and large shareholders overestimate the ability of the glamour bidder to manage other companies" (Rau and Vermaelen, 1998, p. 251).[23]

Commentary

Anyone understanding the logic of event studies, but unfamiliar with their application to M&As, would undoubtedly, upon seeing Figure 9.1, conclude that the most important *events* affecting the acquiring companies in these two studies were those that led to the continual upward movements in the acquirers' abnormal returns over the 2–4 years prior to the acquisition announcements, and the steady and sizeable declines that began afterward. This person would certainly be surprised to learn that the preponderance of M&A event studies have ignored both the pre-announcement run-ups in returns to acquirers and the post-merger declines, concentrating instead upon the tiny changes occurring around the announcements.

A few studies have tried to explain the post-merger losses to acquirers as the result of poor benchmark choices. Fama and French (1993), for example, criticized the use of the CAPM and market model to estimate gains to acquirers, because these models fail to account for the systematic effects of firm size and book-to-market ratios on company returns. They speculated that the acquirers' negative post-merger returns would disappear, once these characteristics were accounted for.[24] But the studies by AJM and others reviewed above indicate that the poor post-acquisition performance of the acquirers' shares does not disappear, even when these and other suggested changes in benchmarks are made. Substantial fractions of the M&As of the last half century have been followed by steady declines in the returns to the acquiring companies' shareholders over long time intervals.

There are two possible interpretations of these patterns. One is to assume that the positive abnormal returns preceding the merger announcements indicate that unexpected positive information about the current and future performance of prospective acquirers continually reached the market over periods of two, three, or more years prior to the announcements. Conversely, the steady stream of negative abnormal returns commencing afterward indicates that unexpected negative information about the current and future performance of the acquiring companies continually reached the market over several years after the announcements. To assume that this dramatic change in the nature of the unexpected information about the acquirers' performance occurred around the time of the mergers and yet was totally independent of them seems hardly plausible.

The second possible interpretation of the pre- and post-announcement returns of acquirers allows the market's evaluation of shares to be subject to fads and overoptimism. The market begins mistakenly to bid up the share prices of some group of firms. These firms undertake mergers while their shares are overpriced. The post-merger declines in returns to acquirers are not *caused* by the mergers, but merely reflect the market's return to a more objective evaluation of these companies' prospects.

There is much in the evidence to support this latter interpretation. RV's findings that the acquisitions of low book-to-market "glamour" firms had significantly lower post-merger returns than did high book-to-market firms is consistent with it. They also report that glamour acquirers more frequently issued stock to finance their mergers, suggesting perhaps that the managers thought that their stock was "overvalued." In further support of this interpretation are the findings of several studies that post-merger cumulative returns are much lower for M&As financed through exchanges of shares than for those financed out of cash.[25]

Further support for this interpretation is provided by analyses of the market's evaluation of diversification and conglomerate mergers during the 1960s. Servaes (1996) found that the market values of diversified companies were already significantly discounted in the late 1960s and early 1970s. Matsusaka (1993) reports, however, that announcements of conglomerate acquisitions at that time were coupled with *positive* and significant abnormal returns. Why would the market bid down the shares of companies, which had already diversified, and simultaneously bid up the shares of companies announcing moves in that direction? An obvious answer is that conglomerate mergers were in vogue at the time. The conglomerates' managers were thought to be capable of adding value to any company they acquired. The price–earnings ratios of the conglomerates were bid up accordingly and each newly announced acquisition was greeted with still more enthusiasm. That this enthusiasm was unfounded is revealed in the significant negative post-merger returns for the mergers of the 1960s reported in most of the studies in Tables 9.4 and 9.5.

The possibility that the acquirers' shares are overvalued calls into question the interpretations of studies like those of Lang *et al.* (1989) and Doukas (1995). Both found, using very short event windows, that firms with high Tobin's qs earned higher returns upon announcing M&As than low q acquirers. Both interpreted high qs as indicators of managerial talent and argued that acquisitions by companies with talented managers were more successful. Their index of managerial talent, a high q, is, however, very similar to RV's (1998) index of glamour – a low book-to-market ratio. RV's findings of poor *post-merger* performance of glamour firms' shares suggests that declaring the acquisitions of high q firms a success based on short event windows at their announcements is premature.

More fundamentally, the possibility that the pre-announcement positive abnormal returns reflect overoptimism and an overvaluation of acquirers' shares calls into question the common practice in event studies of measuring the effects of M&As using short windows. If the market can overvalue a group of companies' shares for a period of three to four years, it is possible that it continues to overvalue them for a few days or even a month or two around the announcements of acquisitions. Indeed, if the reason for the overvaluation of acquirers prior to the M&As' announcements is due to a mistaken acceptance of a "theory" about the synergistic effects of mergers – as seems to have been true of the conglomerates – then the market's reaction to M&A announcements is certain to have an upward bias. Thus, explaining post-merger declines in acquirers' share prices by assuming their overvaluation prior to the announcements casts a shadow of doubt over both the efficient capital market hypothesis and the event study literature that rests upon it.[26]

Before closing this discussion of long-run event windows I would like the reader to engage in the following *Gedankenexperiment*. Imagine that the pattern of returns observed in studies like that of Dodd and Ruback (1977), Langetieg (1978), Asquith (1983), and many others did not resemble those presented in Figure 9.1, but rather the reverse. Instead of an inverse-U peaking around the time of the mergers, a normal-U with a trough near the time of the mergers was observed. Would the most plausible interpretation of such a pattern not be that the acquirers were continually releasing unexpected information of bad operating performance to the market over several years prior to the mergers? Would it not also be natural to interpret the post-merger increases in returns to continually released unexpected information of improving operating performance after the mergers? Would it not be reasonable to conclude that the mergers had *caused* the turnaround in operating performance implied by the pattern of pre- and post-merger returns? Would the literature that evaluates the effects of mergers by looking at changes in returns on common shares not have taken into account the changes to the acquirers over a much longer time span than have most of the contributions so far, if the long-run pattern of returns to acquirers had taken the form of a U instead of an inverted U?

Table 9.6 Returns to acquiring and acquired companies' shareholders with short-event windows

Study	Time period (country)	Returns in announcement day (d), month (m), acquiring firm	Acquired firm's returns	Sample	Benchmarks
Dennis and McConnell, 1986	1962–80 (USA)	0.032*c (d = −6, +6)	0.137*c (d = −6, +6)	90 acquirers 76 targets	CAPM
Bradley et al., 1988	1963–84 (USA)	0.001 (d = −5, +5)a	0.312*	236 tender offers	Market model (d = −300, −60)
Lang et al., 1989	1968–86 (USA)			87 tender offers	Market model (d = −300, −60)
		−0.049	0.320*	Low q bidder/high q target	
		0.002b	0.418*b	Low q bidder/low q target	
		0.102*b	0.390*b	High q bidder/low q target	
		−0.023b (d = −5, +5)a	0.466*b	High q bidder/high q target	
Bhagat et al., 1990	1984–86 (USA)	−0.009 (d = −3, +3)		32 hostile takeovers	Market model (d = −260, −0)
Kang, 1993	1975–88 (Japan, USA)	0.007	0.124*	119 Japanese bidders + 102 US targets	Market model (d = −220, −20)
		0.000 (d = −20, +20)	0.137* (d = −20, +20)	119 US bidders + 102 US targets	
Houston and Ryngaert, 1994	1985–91 (USA)	−0.023* (d = −4, 0)d	0.144* (d = −4, 0)d	131 large bank mergers	Market model (d = −230, −31)
Smith and Kim, 1994	1980–86 (USA)	−0.016	0.328*	56 high cash flow bidders	Market model (d = −100, −61)
			0.286* (d = −5, +5)	57 low cash flow bidders	
Hubbard and Palia, 1995	1985–91 (USA)	0.017* (d = −5, +5) −0.004* (d = −4, +4)		354 mergers	CAPM

Study	Period			Sample	Benchmark model
Doukas, 1995	1975–89 (US acquirers)	0.004* −0.002 ($d = -1, 0$)		Foreign acquisitions by US firms 270 with $q > 1$ 193 with $q < 1$	Market model ($d = -220, -21$)
Maquieira et al., 1998	1963–96 (USA)	−0.048 0.061* ($m = -2, +2$)[e]	0.416* 0.381* ($m = -2, +2$)[e]	47 conglomerate mergers 55 nonconglomerate mergers All mergers stock-for-stock transactions	Market index for common stock
Eckbo and Thorburn, 2000	1964–82 (USA, Canada)	0.013* −0.002 ($m = 0$)	0.036* ($m = 0$)	1261 Canadian bidders 390 US bidders 332 Canadian targets	Market model ($m = -60, -13$)
Becher, 2000	1980–97	−0.011* ($d = -5, +5$)	0.171* ($d = -5, +5$)	558 bank mergers	Market index
Bhagat et al., 1999	1962–97 (USA)	0.006* ($d = -5, +5$)	0.293* ($d = -5, +5$)	510 takeovers	Market model ($d = -5, +5$)

Notes

* Indicates significant at 0.05 level or better.

a Window is from five days before first bid until five days after successful bid, so that window is longer than 11 days whenever more than one bid occurs.

b Estimates from a regression with low q bidder/low q target's returns as intercept and other returns estimated with dummy variables. Bidder's return for high q bidders/low q targets is the only one significantly different from the intercept, one cannot tell from the data, whether it is significantly different from zero. High qs are qs > 1 over three years before the takeover.

c Returns are to common shareholders.

d Day-4 is four days before authors identify information about bidder (target) reaching market. Window is closed on day agreement announced. Window is five days when leakage and agreement dates are the same, larger otherwise.

e Window ends two months after effective data of merger.

The effects of M&As with short windows

Although the post-1983 literature does contain several studies that estimate returns to acquirers over long-post event windows, much of the recent literature continues to estimate the effects of M&As over very short windows around the announcements. Table 9.6 summarizes the findings of 14 such studies. Five estimated zero or negative returns to at least some groups of acquirers, and concluded that agency problems and/or managerial hubris accounted for these mergers (Morck *et al.*, 1990; Houston and Ryngaert, 1994; Smith and Kim, 1994; Hubbard and Palia, 1995; Doukas, 1995). The other nine studies claimed support for some form of synergy hypothesis – even when the acquirers' shareholders obtained zero gains or losses – so long as the combined wealth changes around the announcements were positive. These nine studies can be seen as reconfirming the consensus view of M&As reached in the first wave of the literature.

Additional findings

Several additional findings in the finance literature on mergers are relevant to the issues discussed in this chapter. Three of these are briefly discussed in the following section.

Managerial discretion and the gains to acquirers

In support of an agency theory of mergers, Hubbard and Palia reported that the acquirers' shareholders' gains were positively related to the managers' stakes in their companies. Managers with small stakes "tend to 'overpay' when they acquire a target firm," causing their shareholders to lose money (Hubbard and Palia, 1995, p. 783). Denis *et al.* (1997) find that managerial share holdings are negatively related to corporate diversification which, as we will see in the next section, is negatively related to company performance.[27]

As discussed in the previous chapter *every* study, which has regressed the gains to the acquiring companies' shareholders onto the gains to the targets, has found a negative relationship. The more acquirers pay, the more they lose. This finding is inconsistent with both synergy hypotheses about mergers and the market-for-corporate-control hypothesis, but is exactly what both the MDH and HH predict.

The discount for diversification

The early finance literature that tried to account for the wave of conglomerate mergers hypothesized the existence of synergistic gains from diversification, $2 + 2 = 5$.[28] Following the end of the stock market boom of the 1960s, the market's evaluation of the synergies from diversification seemed to reverse – two plus two became equal to three. Several studies have reported losses to acquirers' shareholders at the time diversification mergers are announced (Sicherman and Pettway, 1987; Morck *et al.*, 1990; Kaplan and Weisbach, 1992). Indexes of diversification have also been found to be negatively related to returns on shares (Comment and Jarrell, 1995), Tobin's q (Wernerfelt and Montgomery, 1988; Lang and Stulz, 1994; Servaes, 1996) and the market value of a given company (Berger and Ofek, 1995). Moreover, the discount for diversification is quite large. Berger and Ofek (1995), for example, estimate market values of diversified companies over the 1986–91 period some 13–15 percent below the values that of their assembled assets could realize as stand alone companies. These studies imply that the creation of diversified companies – almost always through M&As – destroys wealth.[29]

The gains from undiversifying

The process of diversification destroys wealth, reversing this process seems to create it. Spin-offs of previously acquired assets are greeted positively by the market, and the stock market gain is larger, the more negative the market's reaction was to the assets' acquisition (Allen *et al.*, 1995). Assets remaining in a company after a spin-off or sale of unrelated assets perform better (John and Ofek, 1995). Diversified companies with low market to book value ratios are more likely to be taken over through a leveraged buyout, and experience the biggest sell-off of their assets after the takeover (Berger and Ofek, 1995). Diversifying acquisitions are four times more likely to be spun-off later (Ravenscraft and Scherer, 1987, ch. 6; Kaplan and Weisbach, 1992). Desai and Jain (1999) found that spin-offs between 1975 and 1991 that increased focus were greeted with larger increases in share prices than non-focus-increasing spin-offs, and were followed by improvements in the operating performance of the more focused company. John and Ofek (1995) confirmed the latter result for 321 divestures in the late 1980s, and finally spin-offs during the 1990s were also followed by share price increases (Mulherin and Boone, 2000).

The motives of managers once again

In an early effort to explain how conglomerate mergers create synergy, Lintner (1971) proposed as the test for synergy, whether the market value of the combined company after the merger, V_C, was greater than the sum of the market values of the two merging companies V_A and V_B. Although most of the finance literature has measured the effects of mergers by examining the percentage changes in returns to the two merging firms separately, a recent paper by Bhagat, Hirshleifer, and Noah (1999) (BHN) has to some extent brought the literature on M&As full circle, for they judge the success of takeovers by seeing whether $V_C > V_A + V_B$. They find that it is on average for a sample of 510 takeovers spanning the years 1962 through 1997 and conclude that M&As increase corporate wealth.

BHN do not report estimates for long post-merger windows, however. Thus, using their methodology, mergers between July, 1962 and June, 1968 increased the acquirers' market values by a significant 3.44 percent (Table 2.2, Panel B). BHN, like numerous other studies, find that the market judges the mergers of the 1960s a success – at the time they were announced.[30] Yet, *every* study that has isolated the post-merger returns to acquirers from the mergers of the 1960s has found them to be negative and significant (see Tables 9.4 and 9.5).[31] Which findings are we to believe?

Even if we ignore the post-merger losses to acquirers, there is something awkward about the persistent findings of negligible returns to acquirers from the point of view of the theory of the firm. If the managers of the acquirers are trying to maximize their shareholders' wealth, why do they continually undertake highly risky investments like M&As, which have near zero expected returns? If they are not trying to maximize shareholder wealth, is it legitimate to assume that they do so anyway?

The behavior of the acquirers' managers becomes even more puzzling, when it is contrasted with how they behave when they negotiate their compensation contracts. A standard result from the principal/agent literature is that the optimal compensation contract for managers trades off the advantages of aligning the interests of managers and shareholders by tying managerial compensation to changes in shareholder wealth against the utility losses suffered by risk-averse managers from such ties. The more risk averse the manager is, the more his compensation contract resembles a fixed wage. The empirical literature on managerial compensation would seem to imply that managers are highly risk averse, since their compensation is very weakly tied to the wealth of their shareholders.[32] Why are managers so highly risk averse when it comes to negotiating their compensation contracts, and then behave like river boat gamblers when they become bidders in the market for corporate control? An obvious answer is that in one case it is *their own* income that is at issue, in the other it is someone else's.[33] Hubbard and Palia (1995) buttressed this interpretation by finding a significant relationship between the fraction of shares owned by an acquirers' managers and the returns to its shareholders from an acquisition. This finding in turn is consistent with both the MDH and HH.

Conclusions

Even if every manager's primary goal were to expand her company, or if every manager suffered from hubris, *some* mergers would increase efficiency or market power. A growth-maximizing manager should never pass up an opportunity to increase profits, since any increase in profits provides more resources to pursue further growth. Thus, all mergers that would occur if managers maximized shareholder wealth should also take place even if they maximize growth or are vulnerable to hubris. The agency/hubris hypotheses lead one to expect additional mergers, however, mergers that may not increase shareholder wealth or even destroy it. The paramount questions for the theory of the firm are to determine how many mergers are wealth enhancing, how many merely redistribute corporate wealth between bidder and target shareholders, and how many destroy it? For those interested in the effects of mergers on social welfare, it is also necessary to determine whether any increases in wealth stemming from mergers are a result of efficiency or market power increases.

The studies of post-merger share performance clearly suggest that mergers at some points of time are *not* followed by long declines in returns to acquirers. Moreover, these seemingly successful mergers tend to occur when the stock market is *not* at a peak. This finding from the event study literature may help to explain why studies of the effects of ownership changes on plant productivity in the 1970s found such positive effects relative to studies of mergers effects on profitability and sales. The latter studies have often included many mergers from stock market boom periods, since this is when most mergers occur.

In addition to the timing of the mergers, their nature and means of payment have also been found to be important. Several studies found the returns to acquirers in tender offers and hostile takeovers to be larger than for friendly mergers. M&As financed by cash have higher returns than those financed by issuing shares, and so on. Of course, if the strong form of the efficient capital market does not hold, any differences in returns to acquirers observed at the acquisitions' announcements might just reflect differences in overoptimism among traders. Conglomerates were the fad of the 1960s, hostile takeovers the fad of the 1980s (Matsusaka, 1993, p. 377). When, however, positive abnormal returns at the announcements are sustained over long post-merger windows, as has been the case for tender offers in some studies,[34] one's confidence in a finding is enhanced.

Results like these both demonstrate that *some* acquisitions create wealth and suggest why they do so. The necessity of having to resort to a tender offer suggests that the targets' managers were not ready partners to the deal. This in turn calls to mind the market-for-corporate-control hypothesis and indicates why tender offers may create wealth. The fact that the targets of the tender offers were often diversified firms that had diversified through mergers, also lends support to the agency theory of mergers, however, and calls into question the event studies that concluded that these mergers were successes based on the market's short-run reaction to their announcements. More generally, it emphasizes the importance of determining the fractions of mergers, which enhance wealth and the fraction that destroy it. The Bhagat *et al.* (1990) sample of *all* hostile takeovers from 1984 through 1986, where the price paid for the target was at least $50 million, contained only 62 acquisitions. Rau and Vermaelen (1998) put together an exhaustive sample of mergers and tender offers between 1980 and 1991 and came up with 2,823 mergers and 316 tender offers, and during the 1990s hostile tender offers have essentially disappeared (Andrade *et al.*, 2001, pp. 105–6). Even if one feels confident that tender offers generate wealth by replacing bad managers, one is left with a lot of other mergers to account for both with respect to their effects on wealth and their underlying motivation. Our review of the finance literature in the latter part of this chapter suggests that its methodology is inadequate for answering the basic questions about mergers posed at the beginning of this chapter. This conclusion in turn leads us back to an examination of their effects on profitability, sales, and productivity. Here too, the literature contains some ambiguities, but I think that it can be safely concluded that this literature does not suggest that the average merger increases social welfare.

10   Conclusion

The future of the corporation and the future of capitalism

In 1983, in the conclusion of his survey of the literature on takeovers, Michael Jensen requested more "knowledge of this enormously productive social invention: the corporation" (Jensen and Ruback, 1983, p. 47). Six years later, after presumably acquiring the required knowledge, Jensen stated that the inefficiencies inherent in the corporate form with its separation of ownership and control and attendant agency problems were so severe, that this "enormously productive social invention" was soon to disappear (Jensen, 1989). Which perception of the corporation comes closest to the truth? What do these different perspectives imply about the future of the corporate form, or even of corporate capitalism itself? These questions will concern us in this brief concluding chapter.[1]

The future of the corporation

Chandler (1977, 1990) has described the corporate organizational form that developed in the United States and Germany at the end of the nineteenth and beginning of the twentieth centuries as one of the most important, if not *the* most important innovations of the modern capitalist era. Chandler depicts the managers who led this "organizational revolution" as empire-builders ever interested in more investment, ever seeking to expand their companies. Chandler's historical accounts of the rise and triumph of the modern corporation largely come to an end with the Second World War. Up through the middle of the twentieth century, indeed up until the mid-1960s, the opportunities in the United States to invest and grow internally were such, that most managers could satisfy their desires for growth – and their shareholders' desires for high returns – through internal expansion. By the mid-1960s the post-Second World War economic boom was slowing down in the United States and many firms in the textiles, food, tobacco, and other slow-growth industries took advantage of a booming stock market to grow via mergers. Many of these mergers made little economic sense in terms of either efficiency or market power as was subsequently revealed during the long and dismal decade of the 1970s, in which corporate productivity ceased growing, markets were lost to foreign competition, and companies undid some of the damage of the 1960s merger wave by spinning off assets that they had acquired.

Although the economic revival of the 1980s buoyed profits and stock prices, many corporations continued to make poor investment decisions, and many markets continued to be lost to foreign competition. Over the period from the end of 1969 to the end of 1988 four out of five large US corporations earned an average return on their investments that was less than their costs of capital. General Motors alone effectively squandered $150 billion by investing its shareholders' money in projects with low rates of return (Mueller and Reardon, 1993). It was roughly about this time that Jensen formed his pessimistic assessment of the corporation's future.

Ironically, it was also precisely at this time that the institutions of corporate capitalism began to fulfill their potential as a constraint on managerial discretion. During the merger wave of the 1980s several hostile takeovers took place with the objective of replacing the managers of the target firms and undoing their past mistakes, which usually had been a series of bad mergers. Some twenty years after Marris (1964) and Manne (1965) had described how "the market for corporate control" could discipline managers, it began to perform as advertised.

Managers responded in two ways. First, they begin to "downsize" their corporate empires. Assets were spun and sold off, so that companies could concentrate on their "core competencies." Increasing "shareholder value" replaced increasing the size of the firm as a primary managerial goal. Companies in great numbers began to do what here-to-fore had been an almost unheard of practice – using their cash to buy up their own shares rather than investing it in low return projects.[2]

Managers' second reaction to the takeovers wave of the 1980s was to approach the legislatures in the states in which their companies were incorporated and urge them to pass legislation to make hostile takeovers more difficult. The legislatures, of course, obliged, and hostile takeovers of the kind that occurred in the late 1980s disappeared from the corporate landscape (Roe, 1993b).

The $24.7 billion RJR Nabisco takeover at the end of the 1980s merger wave was the first merger of the twentieth century to surpass the value of United States Steel merger of 1901, when both mergers are valued at 1991 prices (*The Economist*, April 27, 1991, p.11). During the peak of the merger wave of the late 1990s, mergers exceeding this value were announced almost every week. One century after its first great merger wave, the United States experienced the largest merger wave in its entire history in terms of the number of acquisitions and their size, even controlling for the increased size of the economy, and by the end of this merger wave it had spread to include virtually all major countries around the world. When one views the breadth and scale of this merger wave, and the sizes of some of the companies that it created (see again Chapter 1), the first words that enter one's mouth are not "downsizing" and "core competencies." As the twenty-first century began, giant corporations could be found operating in most of the highly developed countries of the world, and a great number of truly multinational companies were operating in all of them. Will this also be true at the end of the twenty-first century?

Some observers think not. Drucker (2001) points out that General Motors – the company that introduced the M-form organizational structure under Alfred Sloan – has abandoned it. Informational technologies have so reduced the costs of transacting that companies like General Motors – long favorite examples of firms that vertically integrated to save on transaction costs – have now sold off many of their parts divisions, and prefer to purchase parts from other firms with which they often have long and close contractual relationships. Technological change and in particular the accessability of information about different products and their prices on the market have so reduced the transaction costs in using the market that one might legitimately speculate that the Coasian firm might someday disappear.

We shall not speculate further on whether the Coasian firm is an endangered species or not. What seems very clear is that the Schumpeterian firm is alive and well, and is likely to continue to thrive into the indefinite future. Successful innovators like Microsoft, Intel, and Nokia have quickly become giant multinational companies with large shares of their respective markets and large profits to prove it. This sequence of innovation, monopoly, and high profitability looks no different today than it did a century ago when Schumpeter first described it. If anything has changed, it is perhaps only that the pace of imitation and creative destruction has quickened, and thus the successful innovator/monopolist of today must work even harder to maintain any first-mover advantages that it has, if it is going to survive until tomorrow.

Thus, I do not see a dramatic difference in the future of the corporation – or perhaps it would be better to describe it as the future of the firm – from what it has been like over the past century. Firms will continue to come into existence, because some entrepreneurs believe that they have an idea for making a profit. Most will fail to do so, and in a few years will be gone. A tiny few will have a great idea and will grow to be the dominant firms in the industry that they enter or create. Some will soon lose this position of dominance as other firms imitate and surpass their innovation. Some, however, will have sufficient first-mover advantages to remain atop their industries for long periods of time. As their markets mature and their internal growth rates decline, their managers will be tempted to resort to mergers to sustain and expand their companies. Neither innovative firms, merging firms, nor giant firms are likely to disappear in the foreseeable future.

The spread of information and the globalization of markets will, however, have some important effects on this cycle of growth. As already noted, innovators may lose their leadership positions more quickly than before, or will have to work harder to retain them. More intense competition in product markets reduces managerial discretion by denying managers resources to pursue their own goals. The globalization of capital markets should bring about a convergence in institutional structures and constraints on managers – a race to the top, in which countries will only be able to attract capital if their institutions offer capital suppliers adequate protection against managers who place their own interests above those of outside or minority shareholders. Thus, intensified product market competition and improved corporate governance structures around the world should reduce, but most likely not eliminate, problems of managerial discretion. The corporation will survive as a leaner and more efficient entity – if governments allow it to do so.

The future of corporate capitalism

When the communist regime in the Soviet Union fell in 1991 following the collapse of similar regimes in East Europe two years earlier, it seemed to many that capitalism and democracy had both triumphed in the great struggle of competing ideologies and institutions over the twentieth century. Surely it would only be a *short* time before these institutional systems would displace their competitors around the world. Eleven years later, this prediction looks naively optimistic. Many countries remain resiliently immune to the introduction of democratic institutions, and anti-capitalism sentiment seems once again on the rise. In particular, the following set of challenges to corporate capitalism can be identified.

External terrorists. The terrorist acts of September 11th, 2001 were, of course, directed at the United States, but the choice of the twin Trade Towers as one of the targets symbolizes a growing animosity in some parts of the world to capitalist institutions. The world is visibly separated into a set of rich countries, which have successfully adopted capitalist institutions and prospered from them, and those that have not adopted these institutions and remain in poverty. Among the latter, one must include those countries, which have half-heartedly adopted capitalism, and thus have not enjoyed most of the benefits that come with it. Rather than blame their own governments for keeping them in poverty by not introducing market institutions and capitalist development, some of those living in "second world" countries prefer to blame the capitalist countries. Future attacks like September 11th provide a continuing threat to individual companies in capitalist countries, if not to the whole institutional structure.

Internal terrorists. Any meeting of an international body to discuss future trade liberalization or similar questions today is accompanied by violent protests by persons from within and without the country holding the meeting. Every capitalist country today can expect challenges, often violent, against companies that symbolize success. In most cases these result "only" in a loss of life and property, and do not threaten the set of capitalist institutions themselves. When, however, as in France, a farmer who blows up a McDonald's outlet in protest against American Capitalism becomes a national hero of sorts, rather than an inmate of the local jail, such a threat seems present.

Foreign governments. Taxing foreigners has always been a popular way to raise revenue among non-democratic and democratic countries alike. Foreigners do not vote. For similar reasons, attacking foreign companies to benefit local companies and citizens is a tempting way to win votes or popularity for most politicians. In addition to taxation, this can take the form of repealing patent protection, ignoring infringements on trademarks and copyrights, introducing tariff barriers, and the like. When undertaken by a poor country, such actions often seem to have desirable distributional consequences. But in the long run many of these actions harm both poor and rich countries by injuring the competitive process and making property rights less secure, thereby reducing the incentives to produce the very products that the poorer countries need and want.

Domestic governments. Just as every country contains some people who are ready to engage in violence to overturn capitalist institutions, every country contains some interest groups and politicians, who seek to use the political process to overturn capitalist institutions already in place, or prevent their spread. A half century ago, Joseph Schumpeter (1950) famously predicted that democratic institutions would force capitalism to give way to socialism. In most European countries he was only half right. The state in these countries accounts for between 50 and 70 percent of economic activity. In most European countries, "neo-liberal" is a pejorative label applied to people who favor market processes over state intervention in the allocation of private goods and services. The spectacular success of countries that adopted liberal market institutions during the last couple of decades of the twentieth century from Singapore to Ireland led many countries to adopt liberal market institutions. But the opponents of market institutions have not gone away, they merely have been placed at bay and are waiting for an opportunity – a world financial crisis, a world recession – which will allow them to proclaim that capitalism has failed, and to push forward with a political agenda that focuses upon transferring and destroying wealth rather than creating it.

In a competitive environment, there is no substitute for success. Each country of the world today is in competition with every other country in the sense that the performance of its institutions in terms of making its citizens better off can be compared with that of every other country. The superiority of capitalist systems over the long run in this regard is so great that one need not fear that it will disappear entirely. But it will continue to have periods in which it increases in popularity and periods in which its popularity wanes. As long as some countries continue to employ capitalist institutions and to prosper with them, others will continue to imitate them. The dynamics of competition across countries is not that much different than across firms, it simply works much more discontinuously and slowly.

Notes

1 Introduction

1 *Statistical Abstract of the United States*, 2001, table 710, and *Historical Statistics, Colonial Times to 1970*, Part II, p. 911.
2 Automobiles are among the durable goods that Mitsubishi manufactures.

2 The nature of profits

1 Small Spill is in fact in two businesses, the oil tanker business and the insurance business, where its only client is itself. One could say that Small Spill had a profit of $100 this year in its insurance business.
2 The entrepreneur cannot in reality guarantee the other factor owners their incomes unless she has the capital to back up the guarantee. If the entrepreneur is without capital, the contracts may allow the other factor owners to have the satisfaction of seeing the entrepreneur in jail, but not of collecting their incomes.

3 The nature of the firm

1 If the future was known with perfect certainty, no landlord would rent to a person, who would not pay her rent in the future. Certainty about the future would force everyone who did not wish to sleep on the street to pay their rents. Rental contracts serve to induce this same behavior in the presence of uncertainty.
2 As we shall see in Chapter 6, it is also necessary to assume that owner–entrepreneurs are risk neutral, or to assume something equally extreme, to make the decisions, which maximize the owner–entrepreneur's utility to be consistent with profits maximization.
3 Although the displacement of the putting out system by factories due to the latter's lower transaction costs seems to provide a plausible explanation for this development in England (Williamson, 1985, ch. 8), Herrigal (1996, ch. 2) recounts that this system of production survived in some parts of Germany into the twentieth century without appearing to suffer from a serious cost disadvantage relative to the large corporations emerging in other parts of Germany.

4 The Schumpeterian firm

1 Schumpeter's most famous account of the innovation process is contained in a short monograph, first published in German in 1911, and then in an English translation in 1934.
2 See, Mueller and Tilton (1969), and Acs and Audretsch (1990).
3 Jewkes *et al.* (1959) discuss these cases and many more.
4 See also, Scherer *et al.* (1975).

5 Klepper and Simons (2000b) name this hypothesis "the emerging-competitive-advantage hypothesis."

6 The hazard rate for any firm at time t is the probability that it will exit at t given that it has not already exited.

7 See also, Klepper and Simons (1999, 2000a) and Klepper (1999).

8 This figure neglects entry by very small firms. Including the small firms, the entry rate between 1977 and 1982 was 51.7 percent (DRS, table 2).

9 Since the first census interval was only four years, column 6 is column 5 divided by 4.75.

10 DRS report entry via plant acquisitions as new firm entry.

11 Over a ten-year period in Canada, Baldwin (1995, ch. 2) found that the growth rate in size of survivors more than offset their loss in numbers, however.

12 See surveys by Schmalensee (1989), Scherer and Ross (1990, ch. 11), and Martin (1994, ch. 7). Logically, the concentration variable should have a positive effect on profitability only in industries with relatively homogeneous products, since when product heterogeneity is significant, firms will price independently of one another, and their profitability will depend largely upon the characteristics of their own products and their demand schedules. Recent works by Bloch (1994) and Mueller and Raunig (1999) indicate that the concentration variable can be highly significant, when the set of industries included in the study is limited to those that appear to be relatively homogeneous.

13 See also the studies in Geroski and Schwalbach (1991) and the review by Cable and Schwalbach (1991).

14 For a discussion of these, see Katz and Shapiro (1985, 1986, 1994).

15 The model discussed in this section was first presented by Schmalensee (1982).

16 See Grabowski and Vernon (1992).

17 Robinson and Fornell (1985) test various hypotheses about first-movers using PIMS data for consumer goods industries. The PIMS data have several disadvantages in that the researcher does not know which products the data are for, the data are only for the largest US manufacturers, etc. Nevertheless, several of Robinson and Fornell's findings are consistent with the hypotheses discussed here. For example, first-movers are perceived to have higher quality products, and quality is positively associated with market share. First-movers do particularly well in convenience good products. Their most important finding that was inconsistent with these hypotheses was that first-movers did not have higher prices than their rivals. Their market leadership seemed to arise from the perception that their products were of higher quality, and yet their prices were the same.

While this picture certainly fits some first-movers, like perhaps McDonalds in the United States, it does not fit companies like Kelloggs, Gerbers, and Campbell's Soups that are both perceived to have higher quality products and charge higher prices than their rivals, which include supermarket brands. It is possible that some firms that market supermarket brands are not in the PIMS sample.

18 A similar objection can be raised against Diamond's (1971) *search costs* model as an explanation for first-mover advantages. In the Diamond model, the presence of search costs induces firms to engage in a kind of reverse Bertrand competition, raising prices in the knowledge that buyers will not desert them because of the presence of search costs. For the products listed above, however, information is gathered more or less costly over time as one shifts between the first-mover's and followers' products, and thus does not seem to be a likely explanation for the quasi-monopoly positions we observe. In a broader sense, however, Diamond's search costs might be interpreted as switching costs as discussed below.

19 See, Staddon (1983) and Mueller (1986b).

20 Nelson (1974) and Porter (1974).

21 For discussions of habit formation in the context of demand analysis, see Boyer (1983), Pollak (1970, 1976), Spinnewyn (1981), and von Weizsäcker (1971).

22 On the importance of sunk costs, see Baumol and Willig (1981) and Sutton (1991).

23 Arthur (1989), David (1985, 1992), and Silverberg *et al.* (1988).
24 See Preston and Keachie (1964), Rapping (1965), Baloff (1966), Dudley (1972), Smiley and Ravid (1983), and Lieberman (1984).
25 These began with Mueller (1977), and include Geroski and Jacquemin (1988), Connolly and Schwartz (1985), Mueller (1986a), Odagiri and Yamawaki (1986), Levy (1987), and the studies in Mueller (1990).
26 See Boyle (1970), Stevens (1973), Mueller (1980b, pp. 279–83), and Ravenscraft and Scherer (1987, ch. 3).
27 The inequalities defined by the second-order condition for maximizing or minimizing behavior also prove helpful on many occasions.
28 Dynamic neoclassical models, as for example neoclassical growth models, tend to be static equilibrium models in which the equilibrium is preserved and moves through time, or is approached as a steady state.

5 The managerial corporation

1 See discussion in next chapter.
2 The discussion follows Jensen and Meckling (1976).
3 The discussion in this section follows the classic article by Tibor Scitovsky (1943).
4 This interpretation does not require that we assume a separable utility function as in equation (5.2).
5 In the Marris' model sales, assets and employment all grow at the same rate, so the managers can be viewed as maximizing any of these measures of firm size.
6 There is no reason to expect today's captains of industry to be any less inclined toward empire building than their predecessors.
7 As mentioned above, Marris' analysis is in terms of V rather than M, but with K fixed, V is proportional to M.
8 See Williamson (1966).
9 See, Solow (1968) and Jensen and Meckling (1976).
10 The life-cycle variant on the growth-maximization hypothesis was first presented by Mueller (1972).
11 See again, Mueller (1977, 1986a, 1990) and Mueller and Supina (2002).
12 Neither the top managers of a middle manager's own firm nor outside companies are likely to be able to obtain sufficiently accurate information of his abilities to make this market function perfectly. Eugene Fama (1980), who emphasizes the role of the market for managers in limiting managerial discretion, points out that other managers can observe a given manager's behavior well, even if the board of directors or shareholders cannot. The potential of their informing on a manager who does not maximize profits should curb this behavior. Perhaps, but if top managers pursue their own goals at shareholders' expense, they are unlikely to reward this type of corporate "whistle blowing." "Ratting" on one's boss is not likely to get one promoted nor quickly hired by other, similar bosses.
13 See Levinthal (1988) and Tirole (1988, ch. 0).
14 Shareholders need not be literally risk neutral. If a given company is only a small fraction of the shareholders' portfolios, then changes in the earnings of the company have a small impact on their incomes and it will appear *as if* they are risk neutral.
15 For completeness, note that $\beta < 0$ implies $E(U'u) > 0$, and thus that both sides of (5.35) are negative. But this is impossible if $\beta < 0$, so that the Pareto-optimal contract must have $\beta > 0$.
16 The pioneering contribution to this literature is by Aghion and Bolton (1992). Oliver Hart (2001) provides an accessible review of the literature to which he and John Moore have made several important contributions, for example, Hart and Moore (1990).
17 For surveys of this literature, see Ciscel and Carroll (1980), and Hay and Morris (1991, pp. 299–301).

18 For surveys of this literature see Baker *et al.* (1988) and Rosen (1992).
19 For a direct test of this assertion and supporting evidence for "poorly governed firms," see Bertrand and Mullainathan (2000).
20 See Williamson (1967).

6 Corporate governance

1 For a survey of this literature, see Shleifer and Vishny (1997).
2 Recent contributions to this literature include, Cheffins (2000): and La Porta, Lopez-De-Silanes, Shleifer and Vishny (1997, 1998, 2000).
3 See, again Shleifer and Vishny (1997), as well as Edwards and Fischer (1994), and Masuyama (1994).
4 Exceptions always exist. Fans of the American football team from Green Bay, a town of some 70,000 inhabitants, have from time to time purchased shares in the team to ensure that it survives and remains in Green Bay. Shareholdings are widely dispersed, although concentrated in the Wisconsin area, and the prospects of the team ever paying a dividend are virtually nil. The only reward for buying them seems to be the knowledge that the shareholder owns a part of the Green Bay Packers.
5 For surveys of this literature, see Ciscel (1974), Benston (1985), and Short (1994).
6 For profits maximization always to be equivalent to utility maximization regardless of the rate of transformation of effort into profits, the owner–entrepreneur must have a constant marginal utility of income. See discussion in Chapter 5.
7 See the interesting case studies assembled in McCraw (1997).
8 See, Blumberg (1968) and Poole (1986).
9 A second explanation for the great amount of seemingly nonoptimal trading that we observe could be that a large majority of portfolio managers think that they are much better than the average portfolio manager in spotting "bargains" on the market. This seemingly irrational belief would be consistent with Roll's (1986) hubris hypothesis to explain mergers.
10 Stigler (1971). Although Stigler's capture hypothesis was developed in the context of state-regulated firms rather than state-owned firms, the logic of the argument applies equally well in the latter situation.
11 See surveys by Benston (1985) and Short (1994).
12 See also, Nyman and Silberston (1978), Lawriwsky (1984), and Mueller (1986a, ch. 7).
13 Gedajlovic and Shapiro (1998) also test for a relationship between performance and ownership concentration, but their results are difficult to compare with the other studies, since they do not distinguish among the identities of owners, and also interact ownership with diversification.
14 Demsetz and Lehn (1985). They only test for a linear relationship between performance and ownership concentration, however, and do not distinguish among types of owners. Thus, it is certainly possible that a nonlinear relationship between managerial holdings and performance was present in their data.
15 This literature is surveyed in Vining and Boardman (1992) and Mueller (2003, ch. 16).
16 As quoted by Chandler (1962, p. 313).
17 For a survey of the literature that is skeptical about the beneficial effects of outside directors on firm performance, see Bhagat and Black (2000).
18 See, Kosnik (1987), Weisbach (1988), Rosenstein and Wyatt (1990), Byrd and Hickman (1992), Brickley *et al.* (1994), Lai and Sudarsanam (1997), Goergen and Renneboog (2000), and Renneboog (2000).
19 See LLSV (1997, p. 1138). A few countries that LLSV did not classify are also included in Table 6.2, because they are part of the GMY study. Blank entries in columns 2–5 imply that the country was not part of the LLSV study, blank entries in columns 6–7 imply that the country was not part of the GMY study.
20 See also Faccio *et al.* (2001).

21 The methodology used to estimate q_ms relates changes in market values of firms to their investments. It is described in detail in Chapter 8.
22 The standard errors of the estimated q_ms for some countries, like Australia and Luxembourg, do not allow one to reject the hypothesis that q_m equals 1.0.
23 For additional early references and discussion, see Mueller (1992).
24 See special issue of *The Journal of Law and Economics*, 1983, devoted to the proceedings of the conference.
25 See Zingales (1994), Modigliani and Perotti (1997), Yurtoglu (2000) and discussion and references in Gugler (2001c, p. 207).

7 Investment

1 This equation can be derived in an alternative manner taking into account the fact that today's capital stock is the result of past investment decisions, each of which was related to the firm's output at that point in time. Because capital depreciates, one expects that more recent output levels will have more influence on the size of today's capital stock, then outputs far in the past. This assumption can be captured by writing today's capital stock, K_t, as

$$K_t = b' \sum_{i=0}^{\infty} \lambda_{t-i} Q_{t-i}, \tag{N7.1}$$

where $\lambda_{t-i-1} < \lambda_{t-i}$. A particularly simple way to incorporate this assumption is to make $\lambda_{t-i} = \lambda^{t-i}$, with $0 < \lambda < 1$. This assumption is usually referred to as the Koyck transformation in recognition of the person who first employed it in this context (Koyck, 1954).

Using this transformation we can rewrite equation (N7.1) as

$$K_t = b'Q_t + b'\lambda Q_{t-1} + b'\lambda^2 Q_{t-2} + b'\lambda^3 Q_{t-3} + \cdots \tag{N7.2}$$

and analogously for K_{t-1}

$$K_{t-1} = b'Q_{t-1} + b'\lambda Q_{t-2} + b'\lambda^2 Q_{t-3} + \cdots \tag{N7.3}$$

Multiplying (N7.3) by λ and subtracting from (N7.2), we obtain

$$K_t - \lambda K_{t-1} = b'Q_t. \tag{N7.4}$$

After subtracting $(1 - \lambda)K_{t-1}$ from both sides of (N7.4), we obtain

$$I_t = K_t - K_{t-1} = b'Q_{t-1} - (1 - \lambda)K_{t-1}, \tag{N7.5}$$

which is the same as (7.6) with the adjustment factor, a replaced by $(1 - \lambda)$, and $b' = b(1 - \lambda)$.
2 A production function with constant returns to scale is also called a linear homogeneous production function, and satisfies the following condition

If $Q = f(K, L)$, then $\alpha Q = f(\alpha K, \alpha L)$.

Equation (7.19) is often called the Euler condition after the person, who first derived it.
3 Fama (1978) lists eight conditions in his proof of the theorem, but only the following four require special emphasis.
4 A risk averse individual's utility function has the characteristics that $U'(Y) > 0$, and $U''(Y) < 0$.
5 G&M did not use the ratio of profits to market value as the cost of capital as Jorgenson and Siebert did. This ratio equals the M&M cost of capital under the assumption that

the firm's profits remain the same in perpetuity. When profits can grow or decline, this measure combines the firm's cost of capital with market expectations of its future growth. For an unlevered firm its market value is the product of its share price, P_S, and the number of shares outstanding, N_S. The ratio of its profits to market value, $\pi/P_S N_S$, equals the ratio of the earnings per share of the firm ($E_S = \pi/N_S$) to its share price, P_S, and thus is simply the reciprocal of the price/earning ratio, a common index of market expectations in finance.

As measures of the neoclassical cost of capital, G&M used the CAPM β, and a measure linked to the variance of a firm's share returns. Both measures' coefficients were of the right sign and significant in the R&D equation, both were of the wrong sign in the investment equation.

6 Somewhat more mixed support for the MDH using data from the petroleum industry was presented by Griffin (1988).

7 For related evidence, see Oliner and Rudebusch (1992), Carpenter *et al.* (1994, 1998), Carpenter (1995), Chirinko and Schaller (1995), Carpenter and Rondi (2000), and Audretsch and Elston (2002).

8 See also, Vogt (1994) and Carpenter (1995).

9 These include Whittington (1972, 1978), Brealey *et al.* (1976), Hiller (1978), and McFetridge (1978).

10 Real returns on common shares over the 1975–84 period were around 6 percent.

11 Poterba (1991) reports estimates of costs of capital for the 1980s from several studies that lie in the range 9.7–18.7 percent. These are somewhat higher than the implied costs of capital from the SDFA and M&R studies. If the estimates Poterba reports are taken as the true values, than either the SDFA estimates of r are too low, or the M&R estimates of q_m are too high on average.

12 The differences in country legal systems were discussed in the previous chapter.

8 The determinants of mergers

1 See, Nelson (1959, 1966), Melicher *et al.* (1983), and Geroski (1984).

2 See, Hannah (1976), Hannah and Kay (1977), and Geroski (1984).

3 When we examine the effects of mergers in the next chapter, we shall see that mergers between small firms are more likely to produce the changes in profits and sales that one expects are caused by cost reductions, however.

4 A line of business is essentially an industry in which a firm is operating. For example, if an acquired firm sells tires, glass, and televisions, its profits in each of these three lines of business were compared to the average profits of other companies' activities in tires, glass, and television.

5 See, Kumps and Wtterwulghe (1980), Cable *et al.* (1980), Jenny and Weber (1980), Cosh *et al.* (1980), Peer (1980), Rydén and Edberg (1980), and McDougall and Round (1986).

6 Sorenson (2000) also found acquirers in the United States to be significantly more profitable than their targets for mergers in 1996.

7 This is not the assumption made about individual expectations in the proofs of the fundamental CAPM theorems (Chapter 7), but it is probably a more realistic assumption about real world capital markets than assuming that all investors have the same (homogeneous) expectations.

8 Gort (1969, p. 628), who first proposed the economic disturbance hypothesis, argued that differences in expectations during market downturns did not lead to large numbers of mergers, because shareholders suffered from the "sunk costs" irrationality. During an upswing in the market, shareholders are offered 60 for shares currently selling at 50, and gladly accept, because they originally paid only 40 for the shares. During a downturn shareholders are offered 60 for shares currently selling at 50, and refuse, because they originally paid 70 for the shares. Although it is somewhat awkward to build economic

theories on assumptions of individual irrationality, Gort is neither the first nor the last to question the rationality of shareholders' behavior during market swings.

9 See also, Loughran and Vijh (1997), Rau and Vermaelen (1998), and Agrawal and Jaffe (2000).

10 For a discussion of these and other possible financial motives for mergers, see Lintner (1971).

11 $10(0.09)/0.06 = 15$.

12 Ninty-five percent of the potential gains from diversification can be achieved with portfolios of 9 or 10 shares, however (Evans and Archer, 1968).

13 Of course, firms might undertake horizontal and vertical mergers for growth reasons also, but the number of these available to any firm will be more limited than is true of diversification mergers. Thus, the latter should dominate for any firm's management seeking substantial growth through merger.

14 The (over)optimism that accompanies stock market expansions may also increase the likelihood that the market's reaction to the announcement of the merger will be positive during these periods.

15 Additional corroborating evidence is provided by Hubbard and Palia (1995), conflicting evidence by Andrade and Stafford (1997).

16 Given the similarities in their predictions and the nature of the hypotheses there is really no way to differentiate the hubris from the managerial-discretion-hypothesis. The former predicts that managers make mistakes out of hubris, the latter that they are conscious that they are likely to lower their firm's share price, but go ahead anyway. Without psychoanalyzing the managers at the time of the merger, there is no way to separate these two hypotheses empirically.

17 The literature questioning the consistency of share price movements and rational actor models is by now large. See for example, Shiller (1981, 1984, 2000).

18 See, Mandelker (1974), Asquith (1983), Jensen and Ruback (1983, pp. 42–5), and Bradley *et al.* (1988).

19 The issue of the proper length of "window" for measuring gains to acquirers is quite controversial and is taken up in the next chapter. Mueller and Sirower (2002) obtained similar results to those reported in Table 8.2 for a much shorter window.

20 Those studies that have related the gains to the acquirers to those of the targets invariably find a negative relationship – the more the bidders pay, the lower their gain. See, Gort and Hogarty (1970), Nielsen and Melicher (1973), Piper and Weiss (1974), Firth (1980), Varaiya and Ferris (1987), Berkovitch and Narayanan (1993), and Denis *et al.* (1997).

9 The effects of mergers

1 For an effort to treat mergers as *just* investments in capital equipment, see Bittlingmayer (1996).

2 A "line of business" comes close in most cases to an economic definition of an industry tires, soap, etc.

3 Ravenscraft and Scherer (1987, pp. 229–38) found that the choice of accounting convention was related to the pre-merger ratio of market to book value of assets of the acquired firm. The lower this ratio, the more likely it was that the purchase accounting convention was used. Thus, managers (accountants?) tended to employ the accounting procedure that cast the most favorable light on the acquired unit's post-merger profitability, and thus on the profitability of the combined entity.

4 See discussion in the following section.

5 $$\frac{\partial m_i}{\partial q_i} = \frac{(nr - r + 1)}{(1-r)Q} - \frac{q_i(nr - r + 1)(1 - r)}{(1-r)^2 Q^2} = \frac{(Q - q_i)(nr - r + 1)}{(1-r)Q^2} > 0.$$

6 Antimerger policy was very strict in the 1950s and 1960s, and thus horizontal mergers among major competitors were rare. But, under the more relaxed antimerger policy

of the 1980s, more significant horizontal mergers did take place. Stewart and Kim (1993) have found that mergers during 1985–86 led to significant increases in market concentration and welfare losses.

7 McDougall and Round (1986, pp. 157–9); Kumps and Wtterwulghe (1980); Jenny and Weber (1980); Cable *et al.* (1980); Rydén and Edberg (1980); and Cosh *et al.* (1980).

8 Peer (1980) and Mueller (1980b).

9 In a Cournot oligopoly Farrell and Shapiro (1990, pp. 112–13) have proved that a merger that generates no synergies must lead to a higher price.

10 The statistical significance of these figures cannot be determined with the data reported.

11 For example, Halpern (1973), Franks *et al.* (1977), Bradley (1980), Dodd (1980), Asquith *et al.* (1983), and Bradley *et al.* (1983).

12 Mandelker (1974), Dodd and Ruback (1977), Kummer and Hoffmeister (1978), Asquith (1983), and Bradley *et al.* (1983) all conclude that their results support or at least are consistent with the market-for-corporate-control hypothesis.

13 See, Mandelker (1974), Smiley (1976), Asquith (1983), and Malatesta (1983). Not all studies found targets underperforming the market prior to being acquired, however, (Dodd and Ruback, 1977; Kummer and Hoffmeister, 1978; and Langetieg, 1978). As we saw in the previous chapter, the hypothesis that targets are poorly performing companies has received mixed empirical support.

14 Of the studies cited so far, Firth (1980) would be the only exception, although Langetieg (1978) admitted the possibility of other motives.

15 See Shiller (1981, 1984, 1989, 2000), and DeBondt and Thaler (1985). See also Scherer (1988).

16 See, Nelson (1959, 1966), Melicher *et al.* (1983), and Geroski (1984). Although there has been some controversy over whether mergers actually come in waves, this issue seems now to be resolved (Golbe and White, 1993; Linn and Zhu, 1997).

17 Alberts and Varaiya (1989) calculated, for example, that to justify the premiums paid in M&As in the 1970s and 1980s, the earnings' growth rates of acquired companies would have to rise from being on average at the median of the distribution of growth rates to being in the top decile.

18 These are Ellert (1976), Dodd and Ruback (1977), Kummer and Hoffmeister (1978), Langetieg (1978), and Asquith (1983). For evidence consistent with P/E magic accounting for some conglomerate mergers, see Conn (1973).

19 Dodd and Ruback (1977) also used the post-merger period as the benchmark for calculating the returns to acquirers in the announcement month. They measured a statistically significant 2.8 percent return to acquirers in this month and concluded that the acquisitions generated wealth for both acquirers and targets. This is a rather curious way to measure success, however. Although the acquirers' shares underperform the market for several years after the mergers, they are deemed successful, because the acquirers' shares did better in the announcement month than afterward.

20 Franks and Harris (1989) report bidders being eight times larger than their targets, Higson and Elliott (1998) and GMYZ six times larger.

21 Loderer and Martin, like FHT, report only estimates of α. Since they are made using daily observations, they are infinitesimally small. The figures in Table 9.5 are the daily estimates multiplied by 1,250 to make them comparable to the others in the table. They seem too large in absolute value, however.

22 The results of Franks and Harris (1989) also are consistent with these findings for the United Kingdom, if one uses the pre-merger estimates of the market model as a benchmark.

23 This is also the interpretation favored by Agrawal and Jaffe (2000) in their survey of the "post-merger puzzle." Philippatos and Baird (1996) compare *differences* between market and book values before mergers and post-merger performance and also find that relatively high pre-merger market values are associated with poorer post-merger share performance.

24 Fama and French (1993, pp. 45–55). See also, Franks and Harris (1989) and FHT (1991).
25 In addition to RV, see Travlos (1987), FHT, Gregory (1997), and Loughran and Vijh (1997).
26 Fama (1998) has recently taken up the challenge to the efficient capital market assumption posed by estimates of post-merger losses to acquirers and by other event studies using long windows. Fama concludes that these studies *do not* undermine the efficient capital market assumption. The downward drifts in post-merger returns to acquirers are the result of chance overreactions to the merger announcements. Space precludes our taking up Fama's arguments in detail. Suffice it to say that if he is correct, then the losses to the acquirers are real and are a *delayed* result of the M&As.
27 See, also, Lewellen *et al.* (1985) and You *et al.* (1986). Mann and Sicherman (1991) also present evidence in support of the agency hypothesis. Amihud *et al.* (1986), however, interpret their evidence as consistent with the hypothesis that *both* managers and shareholders benefit from mergers.
28 See, Weston (1970) and Weston *et al.* (1972).
29 Studies that try to relate firm diversification to profitability paint a more mixed picture. Positive correlations between diversification and profitability have been reported by Rhoades (1973), Carter (1977), and Lecraw (1984); negative correlations by Rhoades (1974) and Mueller (1986b, ch. 7); and an insignificant relationship by Miller (1969), Imel and Helmberger (1971), Vernon and Nourse (1973), Bloch (1974), and Geroski (1982). Moreover, the studies by Scott (1993) and Evans and Kessides (1994) imply that any observed positive correlation may be due to enhanced market power from multimarket contact rather than enhanced efficiency.
30 These would include, Weston *et al.* (1972), Asquith (1983), Schipper and Thompson (1983), and Matsusaka (1993).
31 See, Scherer (1988, pp. 71–2).
32 See, for example, Jensen and Murphy (1990) and the survey by Rosen (1992). As the stock market advanced by leaps and bounds during the 1990s, managerial compensation contracts shifted toward a greater alignment with shareholder interests. But the contracts that were in place when all but the most recent mergers took place are accurately characterized as in the text.
33 Ravenscraft and Scherer (1987, p. 215) speculate that the conglomerates' managers may have been risk takers spurred on by a highly skewed distribution of returns to mergers. See also, Gort and Hogarty (1970).
34 See Magenheim and Mueller (1988) and Rau and Vermaelen (1998).

10 Conclusion

1 The somewhat schizophrenic conceptions of the corporate organizational form among economists are discussed in Mueller (1992).
2 In the late 1960s, I suggested to a vicepresident of the Xerox Corporation that the higher tax on dividends than on capital gains at that time did not justify Xerox's investing in low return projects so that the shareholders received their returns in the form of capital gains and not dividends. The money could be returned to them as capital gains, if Xerox would merely repurchase its shares with it. The executive looked at me somewhat astonished, and then exclaimed, "but that would be self-cannibalization!"

References

Acs, Zoltan J. and David B. Audretsch (1990) *Innovation and Small Firms*, Cambridge MA: MIT Press.

Aghion, Philippe and Patrick Bolton (1992) "An Incomplete Contracts Approach to Financial Accounting," *Review of Economic Studies*, **59**, 473–94.

Agrawal, Anup and Jeffrey F. Jaffe (2000) "The Post-Merger Performance Puzzle," in *Advances in Mergers and Acquisitions*, 1, Amsterdam: Elsevier, 7–41.

Agrawal, Anup, Jeffrey F. Jaffe, and Gershon N. Mandelker (1992) "The Post-Merger Performance of Acquiring Firms: A Re-examination of an Anomaly," *Journal of Finance*, **47**, 1605–21.

Agrawal, Anup and Charles R. Knoeber (1996) "Firm Performance and Mechanisms to Control Agency Problems between Managers and Shareholders," *Journal of Financial and Quantitative Analysis*, **31**, 377–97.

Alberts, William W. and Nikhil P. Varaiya (1989) "Assessing the Profitability of Growth by Acquisition: A 'Premium Recaptur' Approach," *International Journal of Industrial Organization*, **7**, March, 133–49.

Alchian, Armen (1963) "Reliability of Progress Curves in Airframe Production," *Econometrica*, **31**, 679–93.

Alchian, Armen A. and Harold Demsetz (1972) "Production, Information Costs, and Economic Organization," *American Economic Review*, **62**, 777–95.

Allen, Jeffrey W., Scott L. Lummer, John J. McConnell, and Debra K. Reed (1995) "Can Takeover Losses Explain Spin-Off Gains?," *Journal of Financial and Quantitative Analysis*, **30**, 465–85.

Amihud, Yakov and Baruch Lev (1981) "Risk Reduction as a Managerial Motive for Conglomerate Mergers," *Bell Journal of Economics*, **12**, 605–17.

Amihud, Yakov, Peter Dodd, and Mark Weinstein (1986) "Conglomerate Mergers, Managerial Motives and Stockholder Wealth," *Journal of Banking and Finance*, **10**, 401–10.

Andrade, Gregor and Erik Stafford (1997) "Investigating the Characteristics and Determinants of Mergers and Other Forms of Investment," mimeo, University of Chicago.

Andrade, Gregor, Mark Mitchell, and Erik Stafford (2001)"New Evidence and Perspectives on Mergers," *Journal of Economic Perspectives*, **15**, 103–20.

Arthur, W.B. (1989) "Competing Technologies, Increasing Returns, and Lock-in by Historical Events," *Economic Journal*, **99**, 116–31.

Asquith, Paul (1983) "Merger Bids, Uncertainty, and Stockholder Returns," *Journal of Financial Economics*, **11**, 51–83.

Asquith, Paul, Robert F. Bruner, and David W. Mullins, Jr (1983) "The Gains to Bidding Firms From Merger," *Journal of Financial Economics*, **11**, 121–39.

Audretsch, David B. (1991) "New-Firm Survival and the Technological Regime," *Review of Economics and Statistics*, **73**(3), 441–50.

Audretsch, David B, and Julie A. Elston (2002) "Does Firm Size Matter? Evidence on the Impact of Liquidity Constraints on Firm Investment Behavior in Germany," *International Journal of Industrial Organization*, **20**(1), 1–17.

Axelrod, Robert (1984) *The Evolution of Cooperation*, New York: Basic Books.

Bain, Joe S. (1956) *Barriers to New Competition*, Cambridge: Harvard University Press.

Baker, George, Michael Gibbs, and Bengt Holmström (1994) "The Internal Economics of the Firm: Evidence from Personnel Data," *Quarterly Journal of Economics*, **109**(4), 881–919.

Baker, George P., Michael C. Jensen, and Kevin J. Murphy (1988) "Compensation and Incentives: Practice vs. Theory," *Journal of Finance*, **43**(3), 593–616.

Baldwin, John R. (1995) *The Dynamics of Industrial Competition*, Cambridge: Cambridge University Press.

Baldwin, John and Paul Gorecki (1990) "Mergers Placed in the Context of Firm Turnover," in Bureau of the Census, *1990 Annual Research Conference Proceedings*, Washington, DC: US Department of Commerce, 53–73.

Baloff, N. (1966) "The Learning Curve: Some Controversial Issues," *Journal of Industrial Economics*, **14**, 275–82.

Baumol, William J. (1967) *Business Behavior, Value and Growth*, New York: Macmillan; first published (1959).

Baumol, William J., Peggy Heim, Burton G. Malkiel, and Richard E. Quandt (1970) "Earnings Retention, New Capital and the Growth of the Firm," *Review of Economics and Statistics*, **52**(4), 345–55.

Baumol, William J. and R. Willig (1981) "Fixed Cost, Sunk Cost, Entry Barriers and Sustainability of Monopoly," *Quarterly Journal of Economics*, **96**, 405–31.

Baumol, William J., Peggy Heim, Burton G. Malkiel, and Richard E. Quandt (1973) "Efficiency of Corporate Investment: Reply," *Review of Economics and Statistics*, **55**, 128–31.

Baysinger, Barry and Henry Butler (1985) "Corporate Governance and the Board of Directors: Performance Effects of Changes in Board Composition," *Journal of Law, Economics and Organization*, **1**, 101–24.

Becher, David A. (2000) "The Valuation Effects of Bank Mergers," *Journal of Corporate Finance*, **6**, 189–214.

Benston, George J. (1985) "The Validity of Profits–Structure with Particular Reference to the FTCs Line of Business Data," *American Economic Review*, **75**, 37–67.

Berger, Philip G. and Eli Ofek (1995) "Diversifications Effect on Firm Value," *Journal of Financial Economics*, **37**, 39–65.

Berglöf, Erik and Enrico Perotti (1994) "The Governance Structure of the Japanese Financial Keiretsu," *Journal of Financial Economics*, **36**, 259–84.

Berkovitch, Elazar and M.P. Narayanan (1993) "Motives for Takeovers: An Empirical Investigation," *Journal of Financial and Quantitative Analysis*, **28**, 347–62.

Berle, Adolf A. (1960) *Power without Property*, London: Sidgwick & Jackson.

Berle, Adolf A. and Gardner C. Means (1932) *The Modern Corporation and Private Property*, New York: Commerce Clearing House; rev. edn. New York: Harcourt, Brace, Jovanovich, 1968.

Bertrand, Marianne and Sendhil Mullainathan (2000) "Do CEOs Set Their Own Pay?," MIT Working Paper 00-26.

Bhagat, Sanjai and Bernard Black (2000) "Board Independence and Long Term Firm Performance," mimeo, University of Colorado.

Bhagat, Sanjai, David Hirshleifer, and Robert Noah (1999) "The Effects of Takeovers on Shareholder Value," mimeo, University of Colorado.

Bhagat, Sanjai, Andrei Shleifer, and Robert W. Vishny (1990) "Hostile Takeovers in the 1980s: The Return to Corporate Specialization," *Brookings Papers on Economic Activity, Microeconomics,* 1–84.

Bittlingmayer, George (1985) "Did Antitrust Policy Cause the Great Merger Wave?," *Journal of Law and Economics,* **XXVII**(1), 77–118.

Bittlingmayer, George (1996) "Mergers as a Form of Investment," *Kyklos,* **49**, 127–53.

Bloch, Harry (1974) "Advertising and Profitability: A Reappraisal," *Journal of Political Economy,* **82**, 267–86.

Bloch, Harry (1994) "Sample-Selection Procedures for Estimating the Relationship between Concentration and Profitability from Cross-Industry Data," *Review of Industrial Organization,* **9**, 71–84.

Blumberg, Paul (1968) *Industrial Democracy: The Sociology of Participation,* London: Constable.

Boardman, Anthony E and Aidan R. Vining (1989) "Ownership and Performance in Competitive Environments: A Comparison of the Performance of Private, Mixed, and State-Owned Enterprises," *Journal of Law and Economics,* **32**, 1–33.

Boehmer, Ekkehart (2001) "Germany," in K. Gugler, 2001a, 96–120.

Bøhren, Øyvind and Bernt Arne Ødegaard (2001) "Corporate Governance and Economic Performance," mimeo, Norwegian School of Management, Oslo.

Boyer, M. (1983) "Rational Demand and Expenditures Patterns Under Habit Formation," *Journal of Economic Theory,* **31**, 27–53.

Boyle, Stanley E. (1970) "Pre-merger Growth and Profit Characteristics of Large Conglomerate Mergers in the United States, 1948–68," *St. Johns Law Review,* special edition **44**, 152–70.

Bradley, Michael (1980) "Interfirm Tender Offers and the Market for Corporate Control," *Journal of Business,* **53**, 345–76.

Bradley, Michael, Anand Desai, and E. Han Kim (1983) "The Rationale Behind Interfirm Tender Offers: Information or Synergy?," *Journal of Financial Economics,* **11**, 183–206.

Bradley, Michael, Anand Desai, and E. Han Kim (1988) "Synergistic Gains from Corporate Acquisitions and their Division between the Stockholders of Target and Acquiring Firms," *Journal of Financial Economics,* **21**, 3–40.

Brealey, R.A., S.D. Hodges, and D. Capron (1976) "The Return on Alternative Sources of Finance," *Review of Economics and Statistics,* **58**, 469–77.

Brickley, James A., Jeffrey L. Coles, and Rory L. Terry (1994) "Outside Directors and the Adoption of Poison Pills," *Journal of Financial Economics,* **35**, 371–90.

Bronfenbrenner, Martin (1960) "Reformulation of Naive Profit Theory," *Southern Economic Journal,* **27**, 300–9.

Byrd, John W. and Kent A. Hickman (1992) "Do Outside Directors Monitor Managers?: Evidence from Tender Offer Bids," *Journal of Financial Economics,* **32**, 195–222.

Cable, J.R., J.P.R. Palfrey, and J.W. Runge (1980) "Federal Republic of Germany, 1964–1974," in D.C. Mueller (ed.), *The Determinants and Effects of Mergers: An International Comparison,* Cambridge, MA: Oelgeschlager, Gunn, and Hain, 99–132.

Cable, John and Joachim Schwalbach (1991) "International Comparisons of Entry and Exit," in Geroski and Schwalbach (eds), *Entry and Market Contestability: An International Comparison*, Oxford: Basil Blackwell, 257–81.

Carpenter, Robert E. (1995) "Finance Constraints or Free Cash Flow? A New Look at the Life Cycle Model of the Firm," *Empirica*, **22**(3), 185–209.

Carpenter, Robert E. and Laura Rondi (2000) "Italian Corporate Governance, Investment and Finance," *Empirica*, **27**(4), 365–88.

Carpenter, Robert E., Steven M. Fazzari, and Bruce C. Petersen (1994)"Inventory Investment, Internal Finance Fluctuations, and the Business Cycle," *Brookings Papers on Economic Activity*, 75–122.

Carpenter, Robert E., Steven M. Fazzari, and Bruce C. Petersen (1998) "Financing Constraints and Inventory Investment: A Comparative Study with High-Frequency Panel Data," *Review of Economics and Statistics*, **80**, 513–19.

Carter, John R. (1977) "In Search of Synergy: A Structure–Performance Test," *Review of Economics and Statistics*, **59**, 279–89.

Caves, Richard E. (1998) "Industrial Organization and New Findings on the Turnover and Mobility of Firms," *Journal of Economic Literature*, **36**, 1947–82.

Caves, Richard E. and David R. Barton (1990) *Efficiency in U.S. Manufacturing Industries*, Cambridge: Cambridge University Press.

Caves, Richard E. and Masu Uekusu (1976) *Industrial Organization in Japan*, Washington, DC: Brookings Institution.

Chandler, Alfred D. (1962) *Strategy and Structure*, Cambridge, MA: MIT Press.

Chandler, Alfred D., Jr (1977) *The Visible Hand*, Cambridge, MA: Harvard University Press.

Chandler, Alfred D., Jr (1990) *Scale and Scope*, Cambridge, MA: Harvard University Press.

Chandler, Alfred D. (1992) "Organizational Capabilities and the Economic History of the Industrial Enterprise," *Journal of Economic Perspectives*, **6**, 79–100.

Charkham, Jonathan P. (1994) *Keeping Good Company: A Study of Corporate Governance in Five Countries*, Oxford: Clarendon Press.

Cheffins, Brian (2000) "Does Law Matter? The Separation of Ownership and Control in the United Kingdom," University of Cambridge, ESRC Centre for Business Research, Working Paper No. 172.

Chirinko, Robert S. (1993) "Business Fixed Investment Spending: Modeling Strategies, Empirical Results, and Policy Implications," *Journal of Economic Literature*, **31**, 1875–911.

Chirinko, Robert S. (1994) "Finance Constraints, Liquidity, and Investment Spending: Cross-Country Evidence,"*Federal Reserve Bank of Kansas City*, WP-94-05, August.

Chirinko, Robert S. and Huntley Schaller (1995) "Why Does Liquidity Matter in Investment Equations?," *Journal of Money, Credit and Banking*, **27**, 527–48.

Cho, Myeong-Hyeon (1998) "Ownership Structure, Investment, and the Corporate Value: An Empirical Analysis," *Journal of Financial Economics*, **47**, 103–21.

Ciscel, David H. (1974) "The Determinants of Executive Compensation," *Southern Economic Journal*, **40**, 613–17.

Ciscel, David H. and Thomas M. Carroll (1980) "The Determinants of Executive Salaries: An Econometric Survey," *Review of Economics and Statistics*, **62**, 7–13.

Coase, Ronald H. (1937) "The Nature of the Firm," *Economica*, **4**, 386–405; reprinted in *Readings in Price Theory*, Homewood, IL: Irwin, 1952, 331–51.

Coase, Ronald H. (1960) "The Problem of Social Cost," *Journal of Law and Economics*, **3**, 1–44.

Comanor, William S. (1967) "Vertical Mergers, Market Power, and the Antitrust Laws," *American Economic Review*, **57**, 254–65.

Comment, Robert and Gregg A. Jarrell (1995) "Corporate Focus and Stock Returns," *Journal of Financial Economics*, **37**, 67–87.

Commons, John R. (1924) *Legal Foundations of Capitalism*, New York: Macmillan.

Conn, Robert L. (1973) "Performance of Conglomerate Firms: Comment," *Journal of Finance*, **28**, 154–8.

Conn, Robert L. (1976) "The Failing Firm/Industry Doctrines in Conglomerate Mergers," *Journal of Industrial Economics*, **24**(3), 181–7.

Conn, Charlie, Andrew D. Cosh, Paul Guest, and Alan Hughes (2001) "Long-run Share Performance of U.K. Firms Engaging in Cross-Border Acquisitions," ESRC Centre for Business Research, University of Cambridge, Working Paper No. 214.

Connolly, Robert A. and Steven Schwartz (1985) "The Intertemporal Behavior of Economic Profits," *International Journal of Industrial Organization*, **3**, 379–400.

Conyon, Martin J. (1997) "Corporate Governance and Executive Compensation," *International Journal of Industrial Organization*, **15**, 493–509.

Cosh, Andrew D., Paul M. Guest, and Alan Hughes (2000) "Managerial Discretion and Takeover Performance," mimeo, Centre for Business Research, Cambridge University.

Cosh, Andrew D., Alan Hughes, M.S. Kumar, and Ajit Singh (1985) *Institutional Investment Company Performance and Mergers: Empirical Evidence for the UK*, London: Office of Fair Trading.

Cosh, Andrew D., Alan Hughes, Kevin Lee, and Ajit Singh (1998) "Takeovers, Institutional Investment and the Persistence of Profits," in Ian Begg and S.G.B. Henry (eds), *Applied Economics and Public Policy*, Cambridge: Cambridge University Press, 107–44.

Cosh, Andrew, Alan Hughes, and Ajit Singh (1980) "The Causes and Effects of Takeovers in the United Kingdom: An Empirical Investigation for the Late 1960s at the Microeconomic Level," in D.C. Mueller (ed.), *The Determinants and Effects of Mergers: An International Comparison*, MA: Oelgeschlager, Gunn, and Hain, 227–70.

David, Paul A. (1985) "Clio and the Economics of QWERTY," *American Economic Review*, **75**(2), 332–7.

David, Paul A. (1992) "Heroes Herds and Hysteresis in Technological History," *Industrial and Corporate Change*, **1**, 129–79.

DeBondt, Werner and Richard H. Thaler (1985) "Does the Stock Market Overreact?," *Journal of Finance*, **40**, 793–805.

De-Jong, Henk (1997) "The Governance Structure and Performance of Large European Corporations," *Journal of Management and Governance*, **1**(1), 5–27.

Demirgüç-Kunt, Asli and Vojislaw Maksimovic (1998) "Law, Finance, and Firm Growth," *Journal of Finance*, **53**, 2107–37.

Demsetz, Harold (1983) "The Structure of Ownership and the Theory of the Firm," *Journal of Law and Economics*, **26**, 375–90.

Demsetz, Harold and Kenneth Lehn (1985) "The Structure of Corporate Ownership: Causes and Consequences," *Journal of Political Economy*, **93**, 1155–77.

Deneckere, Raymond and Carl Davidson (1985) "Incentives to Form Coalitions with Bertrand Competition," *Rand Journal of Economics*, **16**, 473–86.

Denis, David J., Diane K. Denis, and Atulya Sarin (1997) "Agency Problems, Equity Ownership, and Corporate Diversification," *Journal of Finance*, **52**, 135–60.

Dennis, Debra K. and John J. McConnell (1986) "Corporate Mergers and Security Returns," *Journal of Financial Economics*, **16**, 143–87.

Desai, Hemang and Prem C. Jain (1999) "Firm Performance and Focus: Long-run Market Performance Following Spinoffs," *Journal of Financial Economics*, **54**, 75–101.

Devereux, Michael and Fabio Schiantarelli (1990) "Investment, Financial Factors, and Cash Flow: Evidence from U.K. Panel Data," in R. Glenn Hubbard (ed.), *Asymmetric Information, Corporate Finance, and Investment*, Chicago: University of Chicago Press, 279–306.

Dewey, Donald (1961) "Mergers and Cartels: Some Reservations about Policy," *American Economic Review*, **51**, 255–62.

Diamond, Peter A. (1971) "A Model of Price Adjustment," *Journal of Economic Theory*, **3**, 158–68.

Dodd, Peter (1980) "Merger Proposals, Management Discretion and Stockholder Wealth," *Journal of Financial Economics*, **8**, 105–37.

Dodd, Peter and Richard Ruback (1977) "Tender Offers and Stockholder Returns: An Empirical Analysis," *Journal of Financial Economics*, **5**, 351–74.

Doeringer, Peter B. and Michael J. Piore (1971) *Internal Labor Markets and Manpower Analysis*, Lexington: Lexington Heath.

Doukas, John (1995) "Overinvestment, Tobins q and Gains from Foreign Acquisitions," *Journal of Banking and Finance*, **19**, 1185–303.

Drucker, Peter (2001) "The Next Society," *The Economist*, November 3rd, 3–22.

Dudley, L. (1972) "Learning and Productivity Change in Metal Products," *American Economic Review*, **62**, 662–9.

Duesenberry, James S. (1958) *Business Cycles and Economic Growth*, New York: McGraw Hill.

Dunne, Timothy, Mark J. Roberts, and Larry Samuelson (1988) "Patterns of Firm Entry and Exit in U.S. Manufacturing Industries," *Rand Journal of Economics*, **19**, 495–515.

Eckbo, B. Espen and Karin S. Thorburn (2000), "Gains to Bidder Firms Revisited: Domestic and Foreign Acquisitions in Canada," *Journal of Financial and Quantitative Analysis*, **35**, 1–25.

Edwards, Jeremy and Klaus Fischer (1994) *Banks, Finance and Investment in Germany*, Cambridge: Cambridge University Press.

Ellert, J.C. (1976) "Mergers, Antitrust Law Enforcement and Stockholder Returns," *Journal of Finance*, **31**, 715–32.

Elliott, J. Walter (1973) "Theories of Corporate Investment Behavior Revisited," *American Economic Review*, **63**(1), 195–207.

Evans, J.L. and S.H. Archer (1968) "Diversification and the Reduction of Dispersion: An Empirical Analysis," *Journal of Finance*, **23**, 29–40.

Evans, William N. and Ioannis N. Kessides (1994) "Living by the Golden Rule: Multimarket Contact in the U.S. Airline Industry," *Quarterly Journal of Economics*, **109**, 341–66.

Faccio, Mara, Larry H.P. Lang, and Leslie Young (2001) "Dividends and Expropriation," *American Economic Review*, **91**, 54–78.

Fama, Eugene F. (1978) "The Effects of a Firms Investment and Financing Decisions on the Welfare of its Security Holders," *American Economic Review*, **68**(3), 272–84.

Fama, Eugene F. (1980) "Agency Problems and the Theory of the Firm," *Journal of Political Economy*, **88**, 288–307.

Fama, Eugene F. (1998) "Market Efficiency, Long-Term Returns, and Behavioral Finance," *Journal of Financial Economics*, **49**, 283–306.

Fama, Eugene F. and Kenneth R. French (1993) "Common Risk Factors in the Returns on Stocks and Bonds," *Journal of Financial Economics*, **33**, 3–56.

Farrell, Joseph and Carl Shapiro (1990) "Horizontal Mergers: An Equilibrium Analysis," *American Economic Review*, **80**, 107–26.

Fazzari, Steven M., R. Glenn Hubbard, and Bruce C. Peterson. (1988) "Financing Constraints and Corporate Investment," *Brookings Papers on Economic Activity*, **1**, 141–95.

Firth, Michael (1980) "Takeovers, Shareholder Returns, and the Theory of the Firm," *Quarterly Journal of Economics*, **94**, 315–47.

Fisher, L. and J.H. Lorie (1964) "Rates of Return on Investments in Common Stocks," *Journal of Business*, **37**, 1–21.

FitzRoy, Felix and Dennis C. Mueller (1984) "Cooperation and Conflict in Contractual Organizations," *Quarterly Review of Economics and Business*, **24**, 24–49.

Florence, P. Sargent (1961) *Ownership, Control and Success of Large Companies*, London: Sweet and Maxwell.

Franks, J.R., J.E. Broyles, and M.J. Hecht (1977) "An Industry Study of the Profitability of Mergers in the United Kingdom," *Journal of Finance*, **32**, 1513–25.

Franks, Julian R. and Robert S. Harris (1989) "Shareholder Wealth Effects of Corporate Takeovers," *Journal of Financial Economics*, **23**, 225–49.

Franks, Julian, Robert Harris, and Sheridan Titman (1991) "The Postmerger Share-Price Performance of Acquiring Firms," *Journal of Financial Economics*, **29**, 81–96.

Franks, Julian and Colin Mayer (1997) "Ownership and Control of German Corporations," *Review of Financial Studies*, **14**(4), 943–77.

Friend, Irvin and Frank Husic (1973) "Efficiency of Corporate Investment," *Review of Economics and Statistics*, **55**, 122–7.

Geroski, Paul A. (1982) "Simultaneous Equations Models of the Structure–Performance Paradigm," *European Economic Review*, **19**, 145–58.

Geroski, Paul A. (1984) "On the Relationship Between Aggregate Merger Activity and the Stock Market," *European Economic Review*, **25**, 223–33.

Geroski, Paul A. (1991) *Market Dynamics and Entry*, Oxford: Basil Blackwell.

Geroski, Paul and Alexis Jacquemin (1988) "The Persistence of Profits: A European Perspective," *Economic Journal*, **98**, 375–89.

Gedajlovic, Eric R. and Daniel M. Shapiro (1998) "Management and Ownership Effects: Evidence from Five Countries," *Strategic Management Journal*, **19**, 533–53.

Geroski, Paul A. and Joachim Schwalbach (eds) (1991) *Entry and Market Contestability: An International Comparison*, Oxford: Basil Blackwell.

Gilson, Ronald J. and Mark J. Roe (1993) "Understanding the Japanese Keiretsu: Overlaps between Corporate Governance and Industrial Organization," *Yale Law Journal*, **102**, 871–906.

Goergen, Marc and Luc Renneboog (2000) "Insider Control by Large Investor Groups and Managerial Disciplining in Belgian Listed Companies," *Managerial Finance*, **26**(10), 22–41.

Golbe, Devra L. and Lawrence J. White (1993) "Catch a Wave: The Time Series Behavior of Mergers," *Review of Economics and Statistics*, **75**, 493–9.

Goldberg, Lawrence G. (1973) "The Effect of Conglomerate Mergers on Competition," *Journal of Law and Economics*, **16**, 137–58.

Górriz, Carmen Galve and Vicente Salas Fumás (1996) "Ownership Structure and Firm Performance: Some Empirical Evidence from Spain," *Managerial Decision Economics*, **17**, 575–86.

Gort, M. (1969) "An Economic Disturbance Theory of Mergers," *Quarterly Journal of Economics*, **83**, 624–42.

Gort, M. and T.F. Hogarty (1970) "New Evidence on Mergers," *Journal of Law and Economics*, **13**, 167–84.

Grabowski, Henry and Dennis C. Mueller (1972) "Managerial and Stockholder Welfare Models of Firm Expenditures," *Review of Economics and Statistics*, **54**, 9–24.

Grabowski, Henry and Dennis C. Mueller (1975) "Life-Cycle Effects on Corporate Returns on Retentions," *Review of Economics and Statistics*, **57**, 400–9.

Grabowski, Henry G. and John M. Vernon (1992) "Brand Loyalty, Entry, and Price Competition in Pharmaceuticals After the 1984 Drug Act," *Journal of Law and Economics*, **35**(2), 331–50.

Gregory, Alan (1997) "An Examination of the Long Run Performance of UK Acquiring Firms," *Journal of Business Finance and Accounting*, **25**, 971–1002.

Griffin, James M. (1988) "A Test of the Free Cash Flow Hypothesis: Results from the Petroleum Industry," *Review of Economics and Statistics*, **70**, 76–82.

Grossman, Sanford J. and Oliver Hart (1986) "The Costs and Benefits of Ownership: A Theory of Vertical and Lateral Integration," *Journal of Political Economy*, **94**(4), 691–719.

Grunfeld, Yehuda (1960) "The Determinants of Corporate Investment," in A.C. Harberger (ed.), *The Demand for Durable Goods*, Chicago: Chicago University Press, 211–66.

Gugler, Klaus (1998) "Corporate Ownership Structure in Austria," *Empirica*, **25**, 285–307.

Gugler, Klavs (ed.) (2001a) *Corporate Governance and Economic Performance*, Oxford: Oxford University Press.

Gugler, Klaus (2001b) "Austria," in K. Gugler (2001a), 71–84.

Gugler, Klaus (2001c) "Conclusion and Policy Implication," in K. Gugler (2001a), 201–15.

Gugler, Klaus (2002) "Corporate Governance and Investment," mimeo, University of Vienna.

Gugler, Klaus, Dennis C. Mueller, and B. Burcin Yurtoglu (2002a) "Marginal q, Tobins q, Cash Flow and Investment," mimeo, University of Vienna.

Gugler, Klaus, Dennis C. Mueller, and B. Burcin Yurtoglu (2002b)"Corporate Governance, Capital Market Discipline and Returns on Investment," mimeo, University of Vienna.

Gugler, Klaus, Dennis C. Mueller, B. Burcin Yurtoglu, and Christine Zulehner (2002) "The Effects of Mergers: An International Comparison," *International Journal of Industrial Organization*, in press.

Halpern, Paul J. (1973) "Empirical Estimates of the Amount and Distribution of Gains to Companies in Mergers," *Journal of Business*, **46**, 554–75.

Hannah, Leslie (1976) *The Rise of the Corporate Economy*, Baltimore: Johns Hopkins University Press.

Hannah, Leslie and John A. Kay (1977) *Concentration in Modern Industry*, London: Macmillan.

Harford, Jarrod (1999) "Corporate Cash Reserves and Acquisitions," *Journal of Finance*, **54**, 1969–97.

Harris, Robert S., John F. Stewart, and Willard T. Carleton. (1982) "Financial Characteristics of Acquired Firms," in M. Keenan and L.J. White (eds), *Mergers and Acquisitions: Current Problems in Perspective*, Lexington, MA: Lexington Books, 223–41.

Hart, Oliver (2001) "Financial Contracting," *Journal of Economic Literature*, **39**, 1079–101.

Hart, Oliver and John Moore (1990) "Property Rights and the Nature of the Firm," *Journal of Political Economy*, **98**(6), 1119–58.

Hay, Donald A. and Derek J. Morris (1991) *Industrial Economics and Organization*, 2nd edn, Oxford: Oxford University Press.

Healy, Paul M., Krishna G. Palepu, and Richard S. Ruback (1992) "Does Corporate Performance Improve After Mergers?," *Journal of Financial Economics*, **31**, 135–75.

Hermalin, Benjamin E. and Michael S. Weisbach (1991) "The Effect of Board Composition and Direct Incentives on Firm Performance," *Financial Management*, **21**(4), 101–12.

Herrigal, Gary (1996) *Industrial Constructions*, Cambridge: Cambridge University Press.

Higson, Chris and Jamie Elliott (1998) "Post-takeover Returns: The UK Evidence," *Journal of Empirical Finance*, **5**, 27–46.

Hiller, John R. (1978) "Long-Run Profit Maximization: An Empirical Test," *Kyklos*, **31**, 475–90.

Hirschman, Albert O. (1970) *Exit, Voice and Loyalty*, Cambridge, MA: Harvard University Press.

Hogarty, Thomas F. (1970) "Profits from Mergers: The Evidence of Fifty Years," *St. John's Law Review*, **44**, special edition, 378–91.

Hoshi, Takeo, Anil Kashyap, and David Scharfstein (1991) "Corporate Structure, Liquidity, and Investment: Evidence from Japanese Industrial Groups," *Quarterly Journal of Economics*, **106**(1), 33–60.

Houston, Joel F. and Michael D. Ryngaert (1994) "The Overall Gains from Large Bank Mergers," *Journal of Banking and Finance*, **18**, 1155–76.

Hubbard, R. Glenn and Darius Palia (1995) "Benefits of Control, Managerial Ownership, and the Stock Returns of Acquiring Firms," *Rand Journal of Economics*, **26**, 782–92.

Hubbard, R. Glenn, Anil K. Kashyap, and Toni M. Whited (1995) "International Finance and Firm Investment," *Journal of Money, Credit and Banking*, **27**, 683–701.

Hundley, Greg and Carol K. Jacobson (1998) "The Effects of the Keiretsu on the Export Performance of Japanese Companies: Help or Hindrance?," *Strategic Management Journal*, **19**(10), 927–37.

Ikeda, Katsuhiko and Noriyuki Doi (1983) "The Performances of Merging Firms in Japanese Manufacturing Industry: 1964–75," *Journal of Industrial Economics*, **31**(3), 257–66.

Imel, Blake and Peter Helmberger (1971) "Estimation of Structure–Profit Relationships with Application to the Food Processing Sector," *American Economic Review*, **61**, 614–27.

Jacquemin, Alexis and Elizabeth de Ghellinck (1980) "Family Control, Size and Performance in the Largest French Firms," *European Economic Review*, **13**, 81–91.

Jenny, Frédéric and André-Paul Weber (1980) "France, 1962–72," in D.C. Mueller (ed.), *The Determinants and Effects of Mergers: An International Comparison*, Cambridge, MA: Oelgeschlager, Gunn, and Hain, 133–62.

Jensen, Michael C. (1986) "Agency Costs of Free Cash Flow, Corporate Finance and Takeovers," *American Economic Review*, **76**, 323–29.

Jensen, Michael C. (1989) "The Eclipse of the Corporation," *Harvard Business Review*, September/October, 61–74.

Jensen, Michael C. and William H. Meckling (1976) "The Theory of the Firm: Managerial Behavior, Agency Costs and Ownership Structure," *Journal of Financial Economics*, **3**, 305–60.

Jensen, Michael C. and Kevin J. Murphy (1990) "Performance Pay and Top-Management Incentives," *Journal of Political Economy*, **98**(2), 225–64.

Jensen, Michael C. and Richard S. Ruback (1983) "The Market for Corporate Control," *Journal of Financial Economics*, **11**, 5–50.

Jewkes, John, John Sawers, and Richard Stillerman (1959) *The Sources of Invention*, New York: W.W. Norton; 2nd edn (1969).

John, Kose and Eli Ofek (1995) "Asset Sales and Increase in Focus," *Journal of Financial Economics*, **37**, 105–26.

Jorgenson, Dale W. and Calvin D. Siebert (1968) "A Comparison of Alternative Theories of Corporate Investment Behavior," *American Economic Review*, **58**(4), 681–712.

Jovanovic, Boyan and Glenn M. MacDonald (1994) "The Life Cycle of a Competitive Industry," *Journal of Political Economy*, **102**, 322–47.

Kang, Jun-Koo (1993) "The International Market for Corporate Control," *Journal of Financial Economics*, **34**, 345–71.

Kaplan, Steven N. and Michael S. Weisbach (1992) "The Success of Acquisitions: Evidence from Divestitures," *Journal of Finance*, **47**, 107–38.

Kathuria, Rajat and Dennis C. Mueller (1995) "Investment and Cash Flow: Asymmetric Information or Managerial Discretion," *Empirica*, **22**(3), 211–34.

Kato, Takao (1997) "Chief Executive Compensation and Corporate Groups in Japan: New Evidence from Micro Data," *International Journal of Industrial Organization*, **15**, 455–67.

Katz Michael L. and Carl Shapiro (1985) "Network Externalities, Competition, and Compatibility," *American Economic Review*, **75**(3), 424–40.

Katz Michael L. and Carl Shapiro (1986) "Technology Adoption in the Presence of Network Externalities," *Journal of Political Economy*, **94**, 822–41.

Katz Michael L. and Carl Shapiro (1994) "Systems Competition and Network Effects," *Journal of Economic Perspectives*, **8**(2), 93–115.

Kester, W. Carl (1986) "Capital and Ownership Structure: A Comparison of United States and Japanese Manufacturing Corporations," *Financial Management*, Spring, 5–16.

Keynes, John Maynard (1936) *The General Theory of Employment, Interest and Money*, New York: Harcourt.

Klein, April (1998) "Firm Performance and Board Committee Structure," *Journal of Law and Economics*, **41**(1), 275–303.

Klemperer, P. (1987) Markets with Consumer Switching Costs. *Quarterly Journal of Economics*, **102**, 375–94.

Klepper, Steven (1996) "Entry, Exit, Growth, and Innovation over the Product Life Cycle," *American Economic Review*, **86**, 562–83.

Klepper, Steven (1999) "Firm Survival and the Evolution of Oligopoly," mimeo, Carnegie Mellon University.

Klepper, Steven and Elisabeth Graddy (1990) "Industry Evolution and the Determinants of Market Structure: The Evolution of New Industries and the Determinants of Market Structure," *Rand Journal of Economics*, **21**, 27–44.

Klepper, Steven and Kenneth Simons (1999) "Entry of Prior Radio Producers and Competitive Ramifications in the U.S. Television Receiver Industry," mimeo, Carnegie Mellon University.

Klepper, Steven and Kenneth Simons (2000a) "The Making of an Oligopoly: Firm Survival and Technological Change in the Evolution of the U.S. Tire Industry," *Journal of Political Economy*, **108**, 728–60.

Klepper, Steven and Kenneth Simons (2000b) "Industry Shakeouts and Technological Change," mimeo, Carnegie Mellon University.

Knight, Frank H. (1965) *Risk, Uncertainty, and Profit*, New York: Harper and Row; first edn. (1921).

Kole, Stacey R. (1995) "Measuring Managerial Equity Ownership: A Comparison of Sources of Ownership Data," *Journal of Corporate Finance*, **1**, 413–35.

Kole, Stacey R. (1996) "Managerial Ownership and Firm Performance: Incentives or Rewards?," *Advances in Financial Economics*, **2**, 413–35.

Kosnik, Rita D. (1987) "Greenmail: A Study of Board Performance in Corporate Governance," *Administrative Science Quarterly*, **32**, 163–85.

Koyck, L.M. (1954) *Distributed Lags and Investment Analysis*, Amsterdam: North-Holland.

Kumar, M.S. (1985) "Growth, Acquisition Activity and Firm Size: Evidence from the United Kingdom," *Journal of Industrial Economics*, **33**(3), 327–38.

Kummer, Donald R. and J. Ronald Hoffmeister (1978) "Valuation Consequences of Cash Tender Offers," *Journal of Finance*, **33**, 505–16.

Kumps, Anne-Marie and Robert Wtterwulghe (1980) "Belgium, 1962–74," in D.C. Mueller (ed.), *The Determinants and Effects of Mergers: An International Comparison*, Cambridge, MA: Oelgeschlager, Gunn, and Hain, 67–97.

Lai, J. and S. Sudarsanam (1997) "Corporate Restructuring in Response to Performance Decline: Impact of Ownership, Governance and Lenders," *European Finance Review*, **1**, 197–233.

Lamont, Owen (1997) "Cash Flow and Investment: Evidence from Internal Capital Markets," *Journal of Finance*, **52**, 83–109.

Lang, Larry H.P. and René M. Stulz (1994) "Tobins q, Corporate Diversification and Firm Performance," *Journal of Political Economy*, **102**, 1248–80.

Lang, Larry H.P., René M. Stulz, and Ralph A. Walking (1989) "Managerial Performance, Tobins Q, and the Gains from Successful Tender Offers," *Journal of Financial Economics*, **24**, 137–54.

Langetieg, Terrence C. (1978) "An Application of a Three-Factor Performance Index to Measure Stockholder Gains from Merger," *Journal of Financial Economics*, **6**, 365–84.

La Porta, Rafael, Florencio Lopez-De-Silanes, Andrei Shleifer, and Robert W. Vishny (1997) "Legal Determinants of Finance," *Journal of Finance*, **52**, 1131–50.

La Porta, Rafael, Florencio Lopez-De-Silanes, Andrei Shleifer, and Robert W. Vishny (1998) "Law and Finance," *Journal of Political Economy*, **106**, 1113–55.

La Porta, Rafael, Florencio Lopez-De-Silanes, Andrei Shleifer, and Robert W. Vishny (2000) "Agency Problems and Dividend Policies Around the World," *Journal of Finance*, **55**, 1–33.

Larner, Robert J. (1966) "Ownership and Control in the 200 Largest Nonfinancial Corporations, 1929 and 1963," *American Economic Review*, **56**, 777–87.

Lawriwsky, Michael L. (1984) *Corporate Structure and Performance*, London: Croom Helm.

Lecraw, Donald J. (1984) "Diversification Strategy and Performance," *Journal of Industrial Economics*, **33**, 179–98.

Leeth, John D. and J. Rody Borg (1994) "The Impact of Mergers on Acquiring Firm Shareholder Wealth: The 1905–1930 Experience," *Empirica*, **21**, 221–44.

Lev, B. and Gershon N. Mandelker (1972) "The Microeconomic Consequences of Corporate Mergers," *Journal of Business*, **45**, 85–104.

Levine, Ross and Sara Zervos (1998) "Stock Markets, Banks and Economic Growth," *American Economic Review*, **88**, 537–58.

Levinthal, D. (1988) "A Survey of Agency Models of Organizations," *Journal of Economic Behavior and Organization*, **9**, 153–85.

Levy, David (1987) "The Speed of the Invisible Hand," *International Journal of Industrial Organization*, **5**, 79–92.

Levy, Haim (1983) "The Capital Asset Pricing Model: Theory and Empiricism," *Economic Journal*, **93**, 145–65.

Lewellen, Wilbur, Claudio Loderer, and Ahron Rosenfeld (1985) "Merger Decisions and Executive Stock Ownership in Acquiring Firms," *Journal of Accounting and Economics*, **7**(1–3), 209–31.

Lichtenberg, Frank R. (1992) "Industrial De-diversification and its Consequences for Productivity," *Journal of Economic Behavior and Organization*, **18**(3), 427–38.

Lichtenberg, Frank R. and George M. Pushner (1994) "Ownership Structure and Corporate Performance in Japan," *Japan and the World Economy*, **6**, 239–61.

Lichtenberg, Frank R. and Donald Siegel (1987) "Productivity and Changes in Ownership of Manufacturing Plants," *Brookings Papers on Economic Activity*, **3**, 643–73.

Lieberman, M.B. (1984) "The Learning Curve and Pricing in the Chemical Processing Industries," *Rand Journal of Economics*, **15**, 213–28.

Linn, Scott and Zhen Zhu (1997) "Aggregate Merger Activity: New Evidence on the Wave Hypothesis," *Southern Economic Journal*, **64**, 130–46.

Lintner, John (1971) "Expectations, Mergers and Equilibrium in Purely Competitive Securities Markets," *American Economic Review*, **61**, 101–11.

Loderer, Claudio and Kenneth Martin (1992) "Postacquisition Performance of Acquiring Firms," *Financial Management*, **21**, 69–91.

Loderer, Claudio and Kenneth Martin (1997) "Executive Stock Ownership and Performance: Tracking Faint Traces," *Journal of Financial Economics*, **45**, 223–55.

Loughran, Tim and Anand M. Vijh (1997) "Do Long-Term Shareholders Benefit from Corporate Acquisitions?," *Journal of Finance*, **52**, 1765–90.

McConnell, John J. and Henri Servaes (1990) "Additional Evidence on Equity Ownership and Corporate Value," *Journal of Financial Economics*, **27**, 595–612.

McConnell, John J. and Henri Servaes (1995) "Equity Ownership and the Two Faces of Debt," *Journal of Financial Economics*, **39**, 131–57.

McCraw, Thomas K. (ed.) (1997) *Creating Modern Capitalism*, Cambridge, MA: Harvard University Press.

McDougall, Fred M. and David K. Round (1986) *The Determinants and Effects of Corporate Takeovers in Australia, 1970–1981*, Victoria: Australian Institute of Management.

McEachern, William A. (1975) *Managerial Control and Performance*, Lexington, MA: Heath.

McFetridge, Donald G. (1978) "The Efficiency Implications of Earnings Retentions," *Review of Economics and Statistics*, **60**, 218–24.

McGowan, John J. (1965) "The Effect of Alternative Antimerger Policies on the Size Distribution of Firms," *Yale Economic Essays*, **5**, 423–74.

McGuckin, Robert H. and Sang V. Nguyen (1995) "On the Productivity and Plant Ownership Change: New Evidence from the Longitudinal Research Database," *Rand Journal of Economics*, **26**(2), 257–76.

Magenheim, Ellen and Dennis C. Mueller (1988) "Are Acquiring-Firm Shareholders Better Off after an Acquisition?," in J. Coffee, L. Lowenstein, and S. Rose-Ackerman (eds), *Knights, Raiders and Targets*, Oxford: Oxford University Press, 171–93.

Mahoney, Paul G. (2001) "The Common Law and Economic Growth: Hayek might be Right," *Journal of Legal Studies*, **30**, 503–25.

Malatesta, Paul H. (1983) "The Wealth Effect of Merger Activity and the Objective Functions of Merging Firms," *Journal of Financial Economics*, **11**, 155–81.

Mandelker, Gershon N. (1974) "Risk and Return: The Case of Merging Firms," *Journal of Financial Economics*, **1**, 303–35.

Mann, Steven V. and Neil W. Sicherman (1991) "The Agency Costs of Free Cash Flow: Acquisition Activity and Equity Issues," *Journal of Business*, **64**, 213–27.

Manne, Henry G. (1965) "Mergers and the Market for Corporate Control," *Journal of Political Economy*, **73**, 110–20.

Maquieira, Carlos P., William P. Megginson, and Lance Nail (1998) "Wealth Creation versus Wealth Redistribution in Pure Stock-for-Stock Mergers," *Journal of Financial Economics*, **48**, 3–33.

Marglin, Stephen A. (1974) "What do Bosses Do? The Origins and Functions of Hierarchy in Capitalist Production," *Review of Radical Political Economics*, **6**, 33–60.

Marris, Robin (1963) "A Model of the Managerial Enterprise," *Quarterly Journal of Economics*, **77**, 185–209.

Marris, Robin (1964) *The Economic Theory of Managerial Capitalism*, Glencoe: Free Press.

Marris, Robin (1998) *Managerial Capitalism in Retrospect*, London: Macmillan.

Martin, Stephen (1994) *Industrial Economics*, 2nd edn, Englewood Cliffs, NJ: Prentice Hall.

Masuyama, Seiichi (1994) "The Role of Japanese Capital Markets: The Effect of Cross-Shareholdings on Corporate Accountability," in N. Dimsdale and M. Prevezer (eds), *Capital Markets and Corporate Governance*, Oxford: Oxford University Press, 325–41.

Matsusaka, John G. (1993) "Takeover Motives During the Conglomerate Merger Wave," *Rand Journal of Economics*, **24**, 357–79.

Mead, W.J. (1969) "Instantaneous Merger Profit as Conglomerate Merger Motive," *Western Economic Journal*, **7**, 295–306.

Meeks, Geoffrey (1977) *Disappointing Marriage: A Study of the Gains from Merger*, Cambridge, England: Cambridge University Press.

Melicher, Ronald W., Johannes Ledolter, and Louis J. D'Antonio (1983)"A Time Series Analysis of Aggregate Merger Activity," *Review of Economics and Statistics*, **65**, 423–30.

Melicher, Ronald W. and David F. Rush (1973) "The Performance of Conglomerate Firms: Recent Risk and Return Experience," *Journal of Finance*, **28**, 381–8.

Melicher, Ronald W. and David F. Rush (1974) "Evidence on the Acquisition-Related Performance of Conglomerate Firms," *Journal of Finance*, **29**, 141–9.

Miller, Richard A. (1969) "Market Structure and Industrial Performance, Relation of Profit Rates to Concentration, Advertising Intensity, and Diversity," *Journal of Industrial Economics*, **17**, 104–18.

Modigliani, Franco and Merton Miller (1958) "The Cost of Capital, Corporation Finance, and the Theory of Investment," *American Economic Review*, **48**, 261–97.

Modigliani, Franco and Merton Miller (1961) "Dividend Policy, Growth, and the Valuation of Shares," *Journal of Business*, **34**(4), 411–33.

Modigliani, Franco and Enrico Perotti (1997) "Protection of Minority Interest and the Development of Security Markets," *Managerial Decision Economics*, **18**, 519–28.

Morck, Randall, Andrei Shleifer, and Robert W. Vishny (1988a)"Management Ownership and Market Valuation: An Empirical Analysis," *Journal of Financial Economics*, **20**, 293–315.

Morck, Randall, Andrei Shleifer, and Robert W. Vishny (1988b)"Characteristics of Targets of Hostile and Friendly Takeovers," in A. Auerbach (ed.), *Corporate Takeovers: Causes and Consequences*, Chicago: University of Chicago Press, 101–29.

Morck, Randall, Andrei Shleifer, and Robert W. Vishny (1990) "Do Managerial Objectives Drive Bad Acquisitions?," *Journal of Finance*, **45**, 31–48.

Morito, Ario, Edwin M. Reingold, and Mitsuko Shimomuna (1988) *Made in China*, New York: Signet.

Mowery, David C. and Nathan Rosenberg (1998) *Paths of Innovation*, Cambridge: Cambridge University Press.

Mueller Dennis C. (1969) "A Theory of Conglomerate Mergers," *Quarterly Journal of Economics*, **LXXXIII**, 643–59; reprinted in G. Marchildon (ed.), *Mergers and Acquisitions*, London: Edward Elgar (1991).

Mueller, Dennis C. (1972) "A Life Cycle Theory of the Firm," *Journal of Industrial Economics*, **20**, 199–219.

Mueller, Dennis C. (1976) "Information, Mobility and Profit," *Kyklos* 29, Fasc. 3, 419–48; reprinted in: D.B. Audretsch and S. Klepper (eds), *"Innovation, Evolution of Industry and Economic Growth,"* Cheltenham: Edward Elgar, vol. 2 (2000).

Mueller, Dennis C. (1977) "The Persistence of Profits Above the Norm," *Economica*, **44**, 369–80.

Mueller, Dennis C. (ed.) (1980a) *The Determinants and Effects of Mergers: An International Comparison*, Cambridge, MA: Oelgeschlager, Gunn, and Hain.

Mueller, Dennis C. (1980b) "The United States, 1962–1972," in D.C. Mueller (ed.), *The Determinants and Effects of Mergers: An International Comparison*, Cambridge, MA: Oelgeschlager, Gunn, and Hain, 271–98.

Mueller, Dennis C. (1985) "Mergers and Market Shares," *Review of Economics and Statistics*, **67**(2), 259–67.

Mueller, Dennis C. (1986a) *Profits in the Long Run*, Cambridge: Cambridge University Press.

Mueller, Dennis C. (1986b) "Rational Egoism Versus Adaptive Egoism as Fundamental Postulate for a Descriptive Theory of Human Behavior," *Public Choice*, **51**, 3–23.

Mueller, Dennis C. (1987) *The Corporation: Growth, Diversification, and Mergers*, London: Harwood Academic Publishers.

Mueller, Dennis C. (1992) "The Corporation and the Economist," *International Journal of Industrial Organization*, **10**, 147–70; reprinted in D. Hausman (ed.), *The Philosophy of Economics: An Anthology*, 2nd edn, Cambridge: Cambridge University Press (1993).

Mueller, Dennis C. (ed) (1990) *The Dynamics of Company Profits*, Cambridge, England: Cambridge University Press.

Mueller, Dennis C. (2003) *Public Choice III*, Cambridge: Cambridge University Press.

Mueller, Dennis C. and Burkhard Raunig (1999) "Heterogeneities within Industries and Structure–Performance Models," *Review of Industrial Organization*, **15**(4), 303–20.

Mueller, Dennis C. and Elizabeth Reardon (1993) "Rates of Return on Investment," *Southern Economic Journal*, **60**, 430–53.

Mueller, Dennis C. and Mark L. Sirower (2002) "The Causes of Mergers: Tests Based on the Gains to the Acquiring Firms' Shareholders and the Size of Premia," *Managerial and Decision Economics*, in press.

Mueller, Dennis C. and Dylan Supina (2002) "Goodwill Capital," *Small Business Economics*, **19**, 233–53.

Mueller, Dennis C. and John E. Tilton (1969) "Research and Development Costs as a Barrier to Entry," *Canadian Journal of Economics*, November, 570–79; reprinted in D.B. Audretsch and S. Klepper (eds), "*Innovation, Evolution of Industry and Economic Growth*," Cheltenham: Edward Elgar, Vol. 1, 2000, 3–12.

Mueller, Dennis C. and Lawrence Yun (1997) "Managerial Discretion and Managerial Compensation," *International Journal of Industrial Organization*, **15**, 441–54.

Mueller, Dennis C. and B. Burcin Yurtoglu (2000) "Country Legal Environments and Corporate Investment Performance," *German Economic Review*, **1**(2), 187–220.

Mueller, Willard F. (1962) "The Origins of the Basic Inventions Underlying DuPont's Major Product and Process Innovations, 1920 to 1950," in NBER, *The Rate and Direction of Innovative Activity*, Princeton: Princeton University Press, 323–46.

Mulherin, J. Harold and Audra L. Boone (2000) "Comparing Acquisitions and Divestitures," *Journal of Corporate Finance*, **6**, 117–39.

Murrell, Peter (1990) *The Nature of Socialist Economies*, Princeton: Princeton University Press.

Myers, Stuart and Nicholas Majluf (1984) "Corporate Financing and Investment Decisions when Firms have Information that Investors do not have," *Journal of Financial Economics*, **13**, 187–221.

Nakatani, Iwao (1984) "The Economic Role of Financial Corporate Grouping," in M. Aoki (ed.), *The Economic Analysis of the Japanese Firm*, Amsterdam: North-Holland, 227–58.

Nash, John F. (1950) "The Bargaining Problem," *Econometrica*, **18**, 155–62.

Nelson, P. (1974) "Advertising as Information," *Journal of Political Economy*, **82**, 729–54.

Nelson, Ralph L. (1959) *Merger Movements in American Industry, 1895–1956*, Princeton: Princeton University Press.

Nelson, Ralph L. (1966) "Business Cycle Factors in the Choice Between Internal and External Growth," in W. Alberts and J. Segall (eds), *The Corporate Merger*, Chicago: University of Chicago Press.

Nelson Richard R. and Sidney G. Winter (1982) *An Evolutionary Theory of Economic Change*, Cambridge, MA: Harvard University Press.

Nickell, Stephen, Daphne Nicolitsas, and Neil Dryden (1997) "What Makes Firms Perform Well?," *European Economic Review*, **41**, 783–96.

Nielsen, J.F. and R.W. Melicher (1973) "A Financial Analysis of Acquisition and Merger Premiums," *Journal of Financial and Quantitative Analysis*, **8**, 139–48.

Nyman, S. and Aubrey Silberston (1978) "The Ownership and Control of Industry," *Oxford Economic Papers*, **30**, 74–101.

Odagiri, Hiroyuki and Hideki Yamawaki (1986) "A Study of Company Profit–Rate Time Series: Japan and the United States," *International Journal of Industrial Organization*, **4**, 1–23.

Oliner, Stephen D. and Glenn D. Rudebusch (1992) "Sources of the Financing Hierarchy for Business Investment," *Review of Economics and Statistics*, **74**, 643–54.

Orr, Dale (1974) "The Determinants of Entry: A Study of the Canadian Manufacturing Industries," *Review of Economics and Statistics*, **56**, 58–66.

Pavitt, Keith, M. Robson, and J. Townsend (1987) "The Size Distribution of Innovating Firms in the UK: 1945–83," *Journal of Industrial Economics*, **55**, 291–316.

Peer, Henk (1980) "The Netherlands, 1962–1973," in D.C. Mueller (ed.), *The Determinants and Effects of Mergers: An International Comparison*, Cambridge, MA: Oelgeschlager, Gunn, and Hain, 163–91.

Perry, Martin K. and Robert H. Porter (1985) "Oligopoly and the Incentive for Horizontal Merger," *American Economic Review*, **75**, 219–27.

Petersen, Mitchell A. and Raghuram G. Rajan (1994) "The Benefits of Lending Relationships: Evidence from Small Business Data," *Journal of Finance*, **49**, 3–37.

Philippatos, George C. and Philip L. Baird III (1996) "Postmerger Performance, Managerial Superiority and the Market for Corporate Control," *Managerial and Decision Economics*, **17**, 45–55.

Piper, T.F. and S.J. Weiss (1974) "The Profitability of Multibank Holding Company Acquisitions," *Journal of Finance*, **29**, 163–74.

Pollak, R.A. (1970) "Habit Formation and Dynamic Demand Functions," *Journal of Political Economy*, **78**, 745–63.

Pollak, R.A. (1976) "Habit Formation and Long-Run Utility Functions," *Journal of Economic Theory*, **13**, 272–97.

Poole, Michael (1986) *Towards a New Industrial Democracy*, London: Routledge & Kegan Paul.

Porter, Michael E. (1974) "Consumer Behavior, Retailer Power and Market Performance in Consumer Goods Industries," *Review of Economics and Statistics*, **56**, 419–36.

Poterba, James B. (1991) "Comparing the Cost of Capital in the United States and Japan: A Survey of Methods," *Federal Reserve Bank of New York Quarterly*, **15**, 20–32.

Prais, S.J. (1976) *The Evolution of Giant Firms in Britain: A Study of the Growth of Concentration in Manufacturing Industry in Britain, 1909–70*, Cambridge: Cambridge University Press.

Preston, L.E. and E.C. Keachie (1964) "Cost Functions and Progress Functions: An Integration," *American Economic Review*, **54**, 100–7.

Rajan, Raghuram G. and Luigi Zingales (1998) "Financial Dependence and Growth," *American Economic Review*, **88**, 559–86.

Rapping, L. (1965) "Learning and World War II Production Functions," *Review of Economics and Statistics*, **47**, 81–6.

Rau, P. Raghavendra and Theo Vermaelen (1998) "Glamour, Value and the Post-acquisition Performance of Acquiring Firms," *Journal of Financial Economics*, **49**, 223–53.

Ravenscraft, David J. and F.M. Scherer (1987) *Mergers, Sell-Offs, and Economic Efficiency*, Washington, DC: The Brookings Institution.

Reid, Samuel R. (1971) "A Reply to the Weston/Mansinghka Criticisms Dealing with Conglomerate Mergers," *Journal of Finance*, **26**, 937–46.

Renneboog, Luc (2000) "Ownership, Managerial Control and the Governance of Poorly Performing Companies Listed on the Brussels Stock Exchange," *Journal of Banking and Finance*, **24**, 1959–95.

Rhoades, Stephen A. (1973) "The Effect of Diversification on Industry Profit Performance in 241 Manufacturing Industries," *Review of Economics and Statistics*, **55**, 146–55.

Rhoades, Stephen A. (1974) "A Further Evaluation of the Effect of Diversification on Industry Profit Performance in 241 Manufacturing Industries," *Review of Economics and Statistics*, **56**, 557–9.

Rhoades, Stephen A. (1987) "The Operating Performances of Acquired Firms in Banking," in R.L. Wills, J.A. Caswell, and J.D. Culbertson (eds), *Issues After a Century of Federal Competition Policy*, Lexington, MA: Lexington Books, 277–92.

Roe, Mark J. (1993a) "Some Differences in the Corporate Structure in Germany, Japan, and the United States," *Yale Law Journal*, **102**, 1927–2001.

Roe, Mark J. (1993b) "Takeover Politics," in M.B. Blair (ed.), *The Deal Decade*, Washington, DC: Brookings Institution, 321–53.

Roe, Mark J. (1999) "Political Preconditions to Separating Ownership from Control: The Incompatibility of the American Public Firm with Social Democracy," mimeo, Columbia University.

Romano, Roberta (1987) "The Political Economy of Takeover Statutes," *Virginia Law Review*, **73**, 111–99.

Robinson, W.T. and C. Fornell (1985) "Sources of Market Pioneer Advantages in Consumer Goods Industries," *Journal of Marketing Research*, **22**, 305–17.

Roll, Richard (1986) "The Hubris Hypothesis of Corporate Takeovers," *Journal of Business*, **59**, 197–216.

Rosen, Sherwin (1992) "Contracts and the Market for Executives," in L. Werin and H. Wijkander (eds), *Contract Economics*, Oxford: Basil Blackwell, 181–211.

Rosenstein, Stuart and Jeffrey G. Wyatt (1990) "Outside Directors, Board Independence, and Shareholder Wealth," *Journal of Financial Economics*, **26**, 175–91.

Rydén, Bengt and Jan-Olof Edberg (1980) "Large Mergers in Sweden, 1962–1976," in D.C. Mueller (ed.), *The Determinants and Effects of Mergers: An International Comparison*, Cambridge, MA: Oelgeschlager, Gunn, and Hain, 193–226.

Sakuma, Kyoko (2001) "Japan," in Gugler (2001a), 139–55.

Salant, Stephen W., Sheldon Switzer, and Robert J. Reynolds (1983) "Losses from Horizontal Merger: The Effects of an Exogenous Change in Industry Structure on Cournot–Nash Equilibrium," *Quarterly Journal of Economics*, **98**, 185–99.

Scherer, F.M. (1988) "Corporate Takeovers: The Efficiency Arguments," *Journal of Economic Perspectives*, **2**, 69–82.

Scherer, F.M. and David Ross (1990) *Industrial Market Structure and Economic Performance*, 3rd edn, Boston: Houghton Mifflin.

Scherer, F.M., Alan Beckenstein, Erich Kaufer, and R.D. Murphy (1975) *The Economics of Multi-Plant Operation: An International Comparisons Study*, Cambridge, MA: Harvard University Press.

Schiantarelli, Fabio and Alessandro Sembenelli (2000) "Form of Ownership and Financial Constraints: Panel Data Evidence from Flow of Funds and Investment Equations," *Empirica*, **27**(2), 175–92.

Schipper, Katherine and Rex Thompson (1983) "Evidence on the Capitalized Value of Merger Activity for Acquiring Firms," *Journal of Financial Economics*, **11**(1–4), 85–119.

Schmalensee, Richard (1982) "Product Differentiation Advantages of Pioneering Brands," *American Economic Review*, **72**, 349–65.

Schmalensee, Richard (1989) "Inter-Industry Studies of Structure and Performance," in R. Schmalensee and R.D. Willig (eds), *Handbook of Industrial Organization*, Cambridge MA: MIT Press, 951–1009.

Schumpeter, Joseph A. (1934) *The Theory of Economic Development*, Cambridge, MA: Harvard University Press; first published in German, pp. 1911.

Schumpeter, Joseph A. (1950) *Capitalism, Socialism and Democracy*, New York: Harper and Row.

Scitovsky, Tibor (1943) "A Note on Profit Maximization and its Implications," *Review of Economic Studies*, **11**, 57–60.

Scott, John T. (1982) "Multimarket Contact and Economic Performance," *Review of Economics and Statistics*, **64**, 368–75.

Scott, John T. (1993) *Purposive Diversification and Economic Performance*, Cambridge: Cambridge University Press.

Servaes, Henri (1996) "The Value of Diversification During the Conglomerate Merger Wave," *Journal of Finance*, **51**, 1201–25.

Sharpe, William F. (1964) "Capital Asset Prices: A Theory of Market Equilibrium Under Conditions of Risk," *Journal of Finance*, **19**, 425–42.

Shiller, Robert J. (1981) "Do Stock Prices Move Too Much to be Justified by Subsequent Changes in Dividends?," *American Economic Review*, **71**, 421–36.

Shiller, Robert J. (1984) "Stock Prices and Social Dynamics," *Brookings Papers on Economic Activity*, December, 457–98.

Shiller, Robert J. (1989) *Market Volatility*, Cambridge MA: MIT Press.

Shiller, Robert J. (2000) *Irrational Exuberance*, Princeton: Princeton University Press.

Shinnar, Reuel, Ofer Dressler, C.A. Feng, and Alan I. Avidan. (1989) "Estimation of the Economic Rate of Return for Industrial Companies," *Journal of Business*, **62**(3), 417–45.

Shleifer, Andrei and Robert W. Vishny (1997) "A Survey of Corporate Goverance," *Journal of Finance*, **52**, 737–83.

Shleifer, Andrei and Robert W. Vishny (2001) "Stock Market Driven Acquisitions," NBER Working Paper No. 8439.

Short, Helen (1994) "Ownership, Control, Financial Structure and the Performance of Firms," *Journal of Economic Surveys*, **8**, 203–50.

Short, Helen and Kevin Keasey (1999) "Managerial Ownership and the Performance of Firms: Evidence from the UK," *Journal of Corporate Finance*, **5**, 79–101.

Sicherman, Neil W. and Richard H. Pettway (1987) "Acquisition of Divested Assets and Shareholders' Wealth," *Journal of Finance*, **42**(5), 1261–73.

Silverberg, Gerald, Giovanni Dosi, and Luigi Orsenigo (1988) "Innovation, Diversity and Diffusion: A Self Organizing Model," *Economic Journal*, **98**, 1032–54.

Singh, Ajit (1971) *Take-overs: Their Relevance to the Stock Market and the Theory of the Firm*, Cambridge: Cambridge University Press.

Smiley, Robert (1976) "Tender Offers, Transactions Costs and the Theory of the Firm," *Review of Economics and Statistics*, **58**, 22–32.

Smiley, Robert H. and Abraham S. Ravid (1983) "The Importance of Being First: Learning Price and Strategy," *Quarterly Journal of Economics*, **98**, 353–62.

Smith, Adam (1776) *The Wealth of Nations*, New York: Random House (1937).

Smith, Richard L. and Joo-Hyun Kim (1994) "The Combined Effects of Free Cash Flow and Financial Slack on Bidder and Target Stock Returns," *Journal of Business*, **67**, 281–310.

Solow, Robert M. (1968) "The Truth Further Refined: A Comment on Marris," *Public Interest*, **11**, 47–52.

Sorenson, Donald E. (2000) "Characteristics of Merging Firms," *Journal of Economics and Business*, **52**, 423–33.

Spinnewyn, Frans (1981) "Rational Habit Formation," *European Economic Review*, **15**, 91–109.

Staddon, J.E.R. (1983) *Adaptive Behavior and Learning*, Cambridge: Cambridge University Press.

Steiner, Peter O. (1975) *Mergers: Motives, Effects, Policies*, Ann Arbor: University of Michigan Press.

Stevens, D.L. (1973) "Financial Characteristics of Merged Firms: A Multivariate Analysis," *Journal of Financial and Quantitative Analysis*, **8**, 149–58.

Stewart, John F. and Sang-Kwon Kim (1993) "Mergers and Social Welfare in U.S. Manufacturing 1985–86," *Southern Economic Journal*, **59**, 701–20.

Stigler, George J. (1950) "Monopoly and Oligopoly by Merger," *American Economic Review*, **40**, 23–34; reprinted in R.B. Heflebower and G.W. Stocking (eds), *Readings in Industrial Organization and Public Policy*, 1958, Homewood, Ill.: Irwin, 69–80.

Stigler, George J. (1971) "The Theory of Economic Regulation," *Bell Journal of Economics and Management Science*, **2**, 137–46.

Sutton, John (1991) *Sunk Costs and Market Structure*, Cambridge, MA: MIT Press.

The Economist (1991) April 27, p. 11.

Thomsen, Steen and Torben Pedersen (2000) "Ownership Structure and Economic Performance in the Largest European Companies," *Strategic Management Journal*, **21**, 689–705.

Tirole, Jean (1988) *The Theory of Industrial Organization*, Cambridge, MA: MIT Press.

Tobin, James (1969) "A General-Equilibrium Approach to Monetary Theory," *Journal of Money, Credit and Banking*, **1**, 15–29.

Travlos, Nickolaos G. (1987) "Corporate Takeover Bids, Methods of Payment, and Bidding Firms Stock Returns," *Journal of Finance*, **42**(4), 943–63.

Utterback, James and Fernando Suarez (1993) "Innovation, Competition and Industry Structure," *Policy Research*, **22**, 1–22 or 21.

Varaiya, Nikhil and K.R. Ferris (1987) "Overpaying in Corporate Takeovers: The Winners Curse," *Financial Analysts's Journal*, May–June, 64–73.

Vernon, John M. and Robert E. Nourse (1973) "Profit Rates and Market Structure of Advertising Intensive Firms," *Journal of Industrial Economics*, **22**, 1–20.

Vining, Aidan R. and Anthony E. Boardman (1992) "Ownership Versus Competition: Efficiency in Public Enterprise," *Public Choice*, **73**, 205–39.

Vogt, Stephen C. (1994) "The Role of Internal Financial Sources in Firm Financing and Investment Decisions," *Review of Financial Economics*, **4**(1), 1–24.

Weinstein, David and Yishay Yafeh (1998) "On the Costs of a Bank-Centered Financial System: Evidence from the Changing Main Bank Relations in Japan," *Journal of Finance*, **53**(2), 635–72.

Weisbach, Michael S. (1988) "Outside Directors and CEO Turnover," *Journal of Financial Economics*, **20**, 431–60.

von Weizsäcker, Carl C. (1971) "Notes on Endogenous Change of Tastes," *Journal of Economic Theory*, **3**, 345–72.

Wernerfelt, Birger and Cynthia A. Montgomery (1988) "Tobins q and the Importance of Focus in Firm Performance," *American Economic Review*, **78**(1), 246–50.

Weston, J. Fred. (1950) "A Generalized Uncertainty Theory of Profit," *American Economic Review*, **40**, 40–60.

Weston, J. Fred (1970) "The Nature and Significance of Conglomerate Firms," *St. John's Law Review*, **44**, 66–80.

Weston, J. Fred and S.K. Mansinghka (1971) "Tests of the Efficiency Performance of Conglomerate Firms," *Journal of Finance*, **26**, 919–36.

Weston, J. Fred and K.V. Smith and R.E. Shrieves (1972) "Conglomerate Performance Using the Capital Asset Pricing Model," *Review of Economics and Statistics*, **54**, 357–63.

Whittington, Geoffrey (1972) "The Profitability of Retained Earnings," *Review of Economics and Statistics*, **54**, 152–60.

Whittington, Geoffrey (1978) "The Profitability of Alternative Sources of Finance – Some Further Evidence," *Review of Economics and Statistics*, **60**, 632–34.

Williamson, John (1966) "Profit, Growth and Sales Maximization," *Economica*, **33**, 1–16.

Williamson, Oliver E. (1963) "Management Discretion and Business Behavior," *American Economic Review*, **53**, 1032–57.

Williamson, Oliver E. (1964) *The Economics of Discretionary Behavior: Managerial Objectives in a Theory of the Firm*, Englewood Cliffs, NJ: Prentice Hall.

Williamson, Oliver E. (1967) "Hierarchical Control and Optimum Firm Size," *Journal of Political Economy*, **75**, 123–38.

Williamson, Oliver E. (1970) *Corporate Control and Business Behavior: An Inquiry into the Effects of Organization Form on Enterprise Behavior*, Englewood Cliffs, NJ: Prentice-Hall.

Williamson, Oliver E. (1975) *Markets and Hierarchies: Analysis and Antitrust Implications*, New York: Free Press.

Williamson, Oliver E. (1985) *The Economic Institutions of Capitalism*, New York: Free Press.

Winter, Sidney G. (1984) "Schumpeterian Competition in Alternative Technological Regimes," *Journal of Economic Behavior and Organization*, **5**, 287–320.

Yermack, David (1996) "Higher Market Valuation of Companies with a Small Board of Directors," *Journal of Financial Economics*, **40**, 185–212.

You, Victor, Richard Caves, Michael Smith, and James Henry (1986)"Mergers and Bidders Wealth: Managerial and Strategic Factors," in Lacy Glenn Thomas, III (ed.), *The Economics of Strategic Planning: Essays in Honor of Joel Dean*, Lexington MA: D.C. Heath and Co., 201–19.

Yurtoglu, Burcin (2000) "Ownership, Control and Performance in Turkish Listed Companies," *Empirica*, **27**, 193–222.

Zingales, Luigi (1994) "The Value of a Voting Right: A Study of the Milan Stock Exchange Experience," *Review of Financial Studies*, **7**, 125–48.

Name index

Subject index

Printed in the United States
by Baker & Taylor Publisher Services